ECW'S BIOGRAPHICAL GUIDE
TO CANADIAN NOVELISTS

# ECW's Biographical Guide to Canadian Novelists

ECW PRESS

CANADIAN CATALOGUING IN PUBLICATION DATA

Main entry under title:

ECW's Biographical guide to Canadian novelists

Includes bibliographical references and index.

ISBN 1-55022-151-5

1. Novelists, Canadian (English) – Biography.* 2. Canadian fiction (English) – History and criticism.* I. Lecker, Robert, 1951– II. David, Jack, 1946– . III. Quigley, Ellen, 1955– . IV. Title: Biographical guide to Canadian novelists.

PS8081.E28 1993  C813'.009  C91-095032-6
PR9186.2.E28 1993

The illustrations are by Isaac Bickerstaff.

ECW's *Biographical Guide to Canadian Novelists* has been published with the assistance of grants from The Canada Council and the Ontario Arts Council.

Design and imaging by ECW Type & Art, Oakville, Ontario.
Printed and bound by Hignell Printing Limited, Winnipeg, Manitoba.

Distributed by General Publishing Co. Limited, 30 Lesmill Road, Toronto, Ontario M3B 2T6.

Published by ECW PRESS, 1980 Queen Street East, Toronto, Ontario M4L 1J2.

# CONTENTS

# Frances Brooke (1724–89)

### LORRAINE MCMULLEN

FRANCES MOORE, eldest of three daughters of the Reverend Thomas Moore and Mary Knowles, was baptized 24 January 1724 at Claypole, Lincolnshire, where her father was curate. The Moores were an old Lincolnshire family. On her father's death in 1727, his widow and three small daughters moved to Peterborough to live with Mrs. Moore's mother, Mrs. Sarah Knowles. On Mrs. Moore's death in 1737, her daughters went to live with a maternal aunt, Sarah, and her husband, the Reverend Roger Steevens, rector of Tydd Saint Mary.[1]

By 1748 Frances had left this family home; by the 1750s she was writing poetry and plays. She first attracted literary attention with her editorship, under the pseudonym "Mary Singleton, Spinster," of a weekly periodical, *The Old Maid*, which appeared from 15 November 1755 to 24 July 1756. In the vein of *The Spectator* of Addison and Steele, the journal included essays and letters written in a lively style commenting on theatre, politics, and religion. In 1756 Frances published a number of poems and a play, *Virginia*, written some years earlier, which she had given up all hope of having produced. During the next few years, Frances continued to write for the theatre, working on a farce and a pastoral, neither of which she succeeded in having produced. By the summer of 1756, she was married to the Reverend John Brooke, rector of Colney, Norfolk, and of several parishes in Norwich.

In 1757 John left for America as a military chaplain. That year their only son, John Moore, was born. The Brookes also had a daughter who did not survive to adulthood. Three years later, Frances published the *Letters from Juliet, Lady Catesby, to Her Friend, Lady Henrietta Campley*, a translation of Marie-Jeanne Riccoboni's popular novel of sensibility that had appeared only the previous year. Frances's own first novel, *The History of Lady Julia Mandeville*, which was, like Madame Riccoboni's novel, epistolary, appeared in 1763. It was immensely popular. By this time a writer of some note, Frances was included in the literary circle of Samuel Johnson. Because of her interest in theatre, she was, already, acquainted with many theatrical figures.

In July 1763 Frances sailed for Quebec with her son, John, and her sister, Sarah, to join her husband, who had been appointed chaplain to the British forces there. She made at least one trip back to England, in 1764, returning to Quebec late in 1765. At Quebec the Brookes participated in the social life around Governor James Murray and the ruling British circle, which included such members as the following: Adame Mabane, a member of the Council of Quebec; Henry Caldwell, Murray's land agent and later Receiver General for Lower Canada; surgeon Samuel Collier and his wife, Jane, who was to remain a close friend; George Allsopp and John Taylor Bondfield, British merchants; and, after 1766, Guy Carleton and his attorney general, Francis Maseres, who was to describe Frances as "a very sensible agreeable woman, of a very improved understanding and without any pedantry or affectation."[2]

Governor Murray, who had found John Brooke irascible, with a tendency to be politically and socially meddlesome, had hoped that the presence of Frances and her sister "would have wrought a change [in John Brooke], but on the contrary they meddle more than he does."[3] While in Canada, Frances wrote *The History of*

*Emily Montague*, which was published the year following her return to England. While Frances makes a point in her novel of indicating that politics is outside the realm of women, she was involved, as well as her husband, in the disputes at Quebec concerning political and religious affairs. The Brookes were adherents of the English party, composed largely of British merchants operating from Quebec and Montreal, who in the interests of their commerce sought to have Quebec assimilated politically, socially, and economically into the British Empire. Adam Mabane, who supported Murray in his attempt to retain for Canadians the rights they had always had, reported, writing to Murray after Carleton had been sent to replace Murray, that "particular Attention is paid to Mrs. Brookes [sic] either from fear of her bad Tongue, or from Gratitude for the good offices she rendered in retailing the Scandal of Quebec at the Tea Tables of London."[4]

In the fall of 1768, Frances was welcomed back into London's literary circle. In the twenty years following her return to England, she published two translations from the French and wrote one tragedy, two comic operas, and at least two novels. The first works to appear after *Emily Montague* were her translations. Her translation of Nicolas Framery's *Memoires de M. le Marquis de S. Forlaix*, a melodramatic and sentimental novel, was published in 1770, her translation of Abbé Millot's *Elémens de l'histoire d'Angleterre* in 1771. In 1773, with her close friend Mary Ann Yates, the great tragic actress, Frances became manager of the Haymarket Opera House, which had been bought by Mary Ann's husband, Richard, also a well-known actor, and Frances' brother-in-law, James Brooke. Here her knowledge of Italian, demonstrated in some early translations of poems, stood her in good stead. Besides directing productions, Frances took on negotiations with musicians. This venture lasted until 1778. Her tragedy, *The Siege of Sinope*, was produced by Thomas Harris at Covent Garden in 1782 with Mary Ann Yates in the title role of Thamyris. It had a run of ten nights. The following year, her comic opera *Rosina* was produced, also by Harris. It was an immediate success. Idyllically pastoral, with music by William Shield, *Rosina* continued to be one of the most popular productions of the century.

In the meantime a second novel of Canada, *All's Right at Last; or, The History of Miss West*, published anonymously in 1774, may have been written by Frances Brooke. Although there are several errors in fact, the novel has themes, attitudes, and elements of style that suggest her as author. The French translation ascribes the original to her. *The Excursion*, a novel similar in theme to Fanny Burney's *Evelina*, appeared in 1777, the year before *Evelina*.

Before the production of her second comic opera, *Marian*, in 1788, Frances Brooke had moved to Sleaford to live with her son, John, who had carried on family tradition by studying at Cambridge and entering the ministry. He was at this time vicar of Helpringham and rector of Folkingham, in Lincolnshire. *Marian* was well received, although it was never as popular as the earlier *Rosina*. On 23 January 1789 Frances Brooke died at Sleaford. She had been in failing health for some years. Her last novel, *The History of Charles Mandeville*, was published the year following her death. Intended as a sequel to *Julia Mandeville*, the novel's main interest is its description of the utopian world in which Charles finds himself as sole survivor of a shipwreck.

## NOTES

[1] See Lorraine McMullen, "Moore, Frances (Brooke)," *Dictionary of Canadian Biography*, IV (1979). Unless otherwise noted, biographical facts are from this source.

[2] [Francis Maseres], *The Maseres Letters 1766–1768*, ed. W. Stewart Wallace (Toronto: Univ. of Toronto Press, 1919), p. 46.

[3] Public Archives of Canada, Murray Papers, MG23, GII, Series 1, 2:184.

[4] Public Archives of Canada, Shelburne Mss. MG23, A4, 16:117.

# Thomas Chandler Haliburton (1796–1865)

## STANLEY E. MCMULLIN

IN THE NINETEENTH CENTURY, it was traditional to seek the source of genius in the lower branches of the family tree. In the case of the Haliburton family, a good deal of energy was spent tracing the family genealogy back to the maternal ancestors of Sir Walter Scott. Since this genetic link remains unproven, a more satisfactory explanation for Thomas Chandler Haliburton's remarkable career may be found in a consideration of the family's New World history.

Thomas Chandler Haliburton was born in Windsor, Nova Scotia, on 17 December 1796.[1] The family had moved to Windsor in 1760 or 1761, when his great grandmother and her second husband emigrated from Newport, Rhode Island. Thomas' grandfather, William Haliburton, began the study of medicine and surgery but left his studies to take part in an expedition against the Natives. Eventually, he became a justice of the peace, and later, a judge probate. Thomas' father, W.H.O. Haliburton, studied law and was a member of the provincial legislature and judge of the Inferior Courts of Common Pleas.

W.H.O. Haliburton married Lucy Chandler Grant, the daughter of Major Alexander Grant who fought with Wolfe at the seige of Quebec.[2] Thomas was the only child of this marriage. Upon the death of Lucy, W.H.O. Haliburton married a widow, Susanna Davis, the daughter of the one-time lieutenant-governor of Nova Scotia, Michael Francklin, who is also considered to be the founding father of Windsor, where the Haliburtons settled (Chittick, p. 15). Clearly, Thomas was born into a family that had linked itself with the leading Tory lights of the province.

His education was at the Anglican-controlled King's Grammar School, Windsor, from which he matriculated in 1810, and later at King's College, Windsor, from which he graduated in 1815. Haliburton's career as a student at King's College appears to have been unmarked by any unusual display of brilliance; however, his training there, coupled with the Tory attitudes of his father, secured for the boy a firm Tory perception of society. The Anglican Bishop, Charles Inglis, a moving spirit behind the college, saw it as providing protection against American influences; Inglis explained his views in a letter to a friend:

> . . . one of my principal motives for pushing it forward was to prevent the importation of American Divines and American policies into the province. Unless we have a seminary here, the youth of Nova Scotia will be sent for their education to the Revolted Colonies — the inevitable consequence would be a corruption of their religious and political principles.[3]

The statutes of the college were explicit in their directions that professors will not "teach or maintain any atheistical, deistical or democratical principles."[4]

Thoroughly indoctrinated in the values of Anglicanism and the monarchy, King's College graduates moved on to assume responsible positions within the colony's Tory élite. Of the twenty-five or so students who attended King's College with Haliburton, ". . . seven became clergymen of the Anglican Church, and counting twice those who held more than one office, one became a Chief Justice, five became Supreme Court Judges, one a Commissioner of Crown Lands, three Solicitor Generals, two Attorney Generals, and one a Master of the Rolls" (Chittick, p. 23).

By 1820 Haliburton had gone on to finish his law education in his father's office and had been called to the bar. His Tory education had been rounded off with two trips to the mother country. On his second visit, in 1816, he had met and married an English woman, Louisa Neville. The couple moved to Annapolis Royal in Nova Scotia, where Haliburton opened a law practice.

During his stay at Annapolis Royal, he befriended Judge Peleg Wiswall of Digby, who became a valued source of inspiration when Haliburton began his historical studies of the colony. Abbé Jean-Mandé Segogne, an Acadian priest in the district of Clare, also became a close friend at this time and no doubt helped Haliburton to establish a more humane view of Roman Catholicism. Another member of the legal profession who became a close friend was Judge Robert Parker of the Supreme Court of New Brunswick.[5]

In 1826 Haliburton began his career as a politician, successfully standing for election to the House of Assembly as the member for Annapolis Royal. His time in the assembly earned him a reputation as an orator. He was very much his own man in debate and supported such causes as permanent funding for Pictou Academy and the removal of restrictions on the province's Roman Catholic population. He held the seat until 1829, when, with the death of his father, he inherited an appointment as a judge of the Inferior Courts of Common Pleas.

The year 1841 was marked both by professional success and by personal tragedy. His legal career was capped when he was elevated to the Supreme Court, but that same year his wife died. This loss contributed to his decision to move permanently to England, which he did following his retirement from the Supreme Court in 1856. There he once again resumed a political career as the member of the House of Commons for Launceston.

While his political career in England was undistinguished, he appears to have settled into English life quite successfully. He married his second wife, Sarah Harriet Williams, and joined in the social life of Isleworth, Middlesex. He maintained an interest in British North America and became chairman of the Canadian Land and Immigration Company, travelling to Ontario to negotiate a deal for land that now lies in Haliburton County.

While his English friends included such people as R.H. Barham, Theodore Hook, Frances Trollope, W.B. Watkins, and Edmond Hopkinson, the British government paid little attention to Haliburton beyond offering him the presidency of Montserrat, "a wretched little West Indian Island," which he declined.[6] His literary achievement did attract the notice of Oxford University, which granted Haliburton a D.C.L. in 1858, making him the first colonial to be so honoured.

Upon his death on 5 August 1865, he was buried in Isleworth-on-Thames. His death went largely unnoticed in Nova Scotia even though he had by then established the most remarkable literary career of any British North American in the nineteenth century. A Nova Scotian who wrote about a Yankee clock-peddlar for an audience that was essentially British and American, he was left without an established literary culture to give his work its just critical response.

His first published work appeared in 1823, when he released anonymously a book entitled *A General Description of Nova Scotia*. It was reissued in 1825. This early work provided the basis for his next publication, *An Historical and Statistical Account of Nova Scotia*, published by Joseph Howe in two volumes in 1829. Neither of these first two ventures was commercially successful, although later historians have continually made use of the data contained in them.

Joseph Howe had acquired *The Novascotian* [Halifax] in 1828. He ran a regular column entitled "The Club," which grew out of political and literary talk conducted at Howe's home over cigars and whisky. Among those attending the sessions and contributing articles were Laurence O'Connor Doyle, Captain John Kincaid, S.G.W. Archibald, Beamish Murdoch, Jotham Blanchard, and Thomas Chandler Haliburton.[7] Haliburton's friendship with Howe was one of the most significant friendships of his early life. With subsequent problems over publication of *The Clockmaker*, and differing political views, the friendship turned to enmity.

In the brief sallies of satire in the writings of "The Club" can be found the first inspiration for Haliburton's interest in the genre. When he submitted a series a pieces entitled "Recollections of Nova Scotia" to Howe, they were immediately successful in *The Novascotian*. Twenty-one pieces were released before Howe and Haliburton decided to publish them as a separate volume to be augmented by the remaining unpublished numbers. *The Clockmaker; or, The Sayings and Doings of Samuel Slick, of Slickville* came off the presses in 1836. An English publisher, Richard Bentley, released a pirated English edition, and Sam Slick became an international celebrity. Haliburton's objections to the pirated edition were somewhat feeble. With the success of the English edition, he befriended Bentley, who continued to publish his works in England. A second series was published in 1838, and a third series followed in 1840. In 1843 Sam Slick reappeared, this time as a commentator on England, in *The Attaché; or, Sam Slick in England*. A second series followed in 1844. While he was writing the various Sam Slick books, he also wrote *The Bubbles of Canada* (1839), a condemnation of Lord Durham's report on the state of Upper Canada, and *The Letter-Bag of the Great Western; or, Life in a Steamer* (1840), which used an exchange of letters as its structure and depended upon puns for its humour.

During the 1850s, Haliburton edited two anthologies of work by American humorists and produced two more Sam Slick collections. Towards the end of the decade, he published the texts of two political speeches. Haliburton's final publication was *The Season-Ticket* (1860), a series of tales exchanged between travellers on the train between Southampton and London, which were first published in the *Dublin University Magazine*.

*The Old Judge; or, Life in a Colony* was released in 1849. This book contains a series of short narratives that provide a compendium on Nova Scotian life. Lacking the raw energy of *The Clockmaker* series, *The Old Judge* reflects a nostalgic and much more literary side of Haliburton.

*Rule and Misrule of the English in America*, a history of Massachusetts, appeared in 1851. This book provides a classic Tory examination of American republicanism.

NOTES

[1] Unless otherwise noted, biographical details are from V.L.O. Chittick, *Thomas Chandler Haliburton ("Sam Slick"): A Study in Provincial Toryism* (New York: Columbia Univ. Press, 1924). Further references to this work appear in the text.

[2] R.G. Haliburton, "A Sketch of the Life and Times of Judge Haliburton," in his *Haliburton: A Centenary Chaplet* (Toronto: Briggs, 1897), p. 14.

[3] Charles Inglis, letter to Richard Cumberland, 5 May 1790, quoted in F.W. Vroom, *King's College: A Chronicle, 1789–1939* (Halifax: Imperial, 1941), p. 21.

[4] *The Statutes, Rules and Ordinances of the University of King's College, at Windsor in the Province of Nova Scotia* (1807), quoted in Vroom, p. 40.

[5] See A. Wylie Mahon, "Sam Slick Letters," *The Canadian Magazine*, 44 (Nov. 1914), 75–79.

[6] R.G. Haliburton, p. 10.

[7] J.W. Longley, *Joseph Howe*, Vol. XII of *The Makers of Canada* (Toronto: Morang, 1906), pp. 9–10.

# John Richardson (1796–1852)

DENNIS DUFFY

BORN IN QUEENSTON, Upper Canada, in 1796, John Richardson died in 1852 in New York City, alone and poor.[1] Of United Empire Loyalist and Ottawa Native ancestry, Richardson fled from Canada to the United States, reversing the typical Loyalist pattern. His was an unusual literary career, and in this biographical sketch, I will try to display the unusual personality behind that career.

Educated in Detroit and Amherstburg, the son of a medical officer in the British army, Richardson fought beside Tecumseh in the War of 1812 as a gentleman volunteer. The ignominious disaster of Moraviantown in 1813 saw Tecumseh slain and Richardson taken eventually to a prisoner-of-war camp in Frankfort, Kentucky. The end of hostilities saw him released, given a commission in the British army, and stationed for a time in the West Indies. Placed on half pay in 1815, Richardson spent the next twenty years living the existence in London and Paris that produced his novel *Ecarté; or, The Salons of Paris* (1829). Gaming, sexual intrigue, and the efforts of the decently born hustler to live on nothing-a-year form the stuff of the novel, which Richardson notes came at least partly out of his personal experience.

His first published work had been *Tecumseh; or, The Warrior of the West* in 1828. This was a lurid, turgid epic in Byronic *ottava rima*, a verse form that the greater poet had employed for supremely comic purposes. Certainly Richardson's attempt to use it for tragic effect resulted in little beyond bathos. Yet the poem's pseudo-Miltonic horrifics, its dire prophecies, and bizarre combats presage the melodrama of *Wacousta*, Richardson's best-known work.

The unfinished *Kensington Gardens in 1830: A Satirical Trifle* was succeeded by *Wacousta; or, The Prophecy: A Tale of the Canadas* in 1832. With this remarkable work, Richardson made his mark on the English-Canadian imagination. It proved of sufficient popularity to be hacked into a touring-company melodrama soon after the author's death. It impressed itself sufficiently upon the consciousness of one of Canada's better twentieth-century poets to produce James Reaney's stage version of 1978.[2] For all its faults, *Wacousta* remains of interest still and seems virtually the sole reason for the survival of its author's name.

The Spanish civil war of 1936–39 was not the first occasion when British idealists and adventurers intervened in a Spanish internal conflict. While the twentieth-century British involvement consisted principally of figures on the left, the earlier one in which Richardson fought during 1834–37, the Carlist war, saw them on the Royalist side. The first literary evidence of the irascibility and quarrelsomeness that were to shadow Richardson's remaining years appears in a succession of Carlist war memoirs and polemics: *Journal of the Movements of the British Legion, with Strictures on the Course of Conduct Pursued by Lieutenant-General Evans* (1836) and, in 1837 and 1838, two further contentious self-vindications.

In 1838, *The Times* [London] dispatched Richardson to cover the 1837 rebellions in Upper and Lower Canada, a post from which he was dismissed when his support of Lord Durham contradicted editorial policy. Richardson remained in Upper Canada, founding a newspaper in Brockville, *The New Era*. The year 1842 saw the failure of that journal, though in the meantime he had written a sequel to *Wacousta* entitled *The Canadian Brothers; or, The Proph-*

*ecy Fulfilled* (1840). This latter incorporated his prisoner-of-war experience in Kentucky. During his time as an editor, Richardson also made a pet of a deer he had found. No finer index to this irascible man's complexity of character exists.

*War of 1812* appeared in 1842. This was the first of a projected series of volumes that the Legislative Assembly of Upper Canada had paid him to produce. Upon completion of that volume, Richardson decided that the grant had supported the opening of the project, but nothing more would be forthcoming unless the muse grew inspired by more cash. Inspiration ceased.

So did a second newspaper, *The Canadian Loyalist and Spirit of 1812*, which ran during 1843–44. In 1845, Richardson landed a pork-barrel appointment as superintendent of the Welland Canal police, a job he lost when the post was abolished in 1846 and after he had attempted to turn a group of local patrolmen into something like a crack hussar regiment. His wife of thirteen years had died in 1845.[3] Now the years darken.

*Eight Years in Canada* (1847) proves to the author's satisfaction that the claims to high public office to which his merits entitled him were disregarded through a dismal succession of stupidity and ill will on the part of his rulers. *The Guards in Canada; or, The Point of Honour* (1948) defends its author against rumours of card-sharping and personal cowardice in a manner certain to extend to those charges the widest publicity. In 1850 he set out to seek his fortune in the literary underworld of New York.[4]

The strictures against his erstwhile American enemies, who now formed his audience, were carefully excised from his novel of the War of 1812, *The Canadian Brothers*, reissued in a new edition entitled *Matilda Montgomerie* (1851). A number of brief, shoddy productions followed: *Hardscrabble; or, The Fall of Chicago* (1851), *Westbrook, the Outlaw; or, The Avenging Wolf* (1851), *Wau-Nan-Gee; or, The Massacre at Chicago* (1852). Only *The Monk Knight of St. John: A Tale of the Crusades* (1850) stands out from this period, and that on account of its wildly pornographic nature.

When in 1852 he died — of poverty more than any other cause — he was working on what we would now call an exploitive spin-off, a "quickie" account of the life of the internationally famous sex object Lola Montez, former mistress to the King of

Bavaria. John Richardson had come a long way from the youth who had shared the same battlefield with the noble Tecumseh.

## NOTES

[1] All biographical information is from the following sources: A.C. Casselman, Introd., *Richardson's War of 1812*, by John Richardson (1902; rpt. Toronto: Coles, 1974); pp. xi–lviii; William Renwick Riddell, *John Richardson* (Toronto: Ryerson, 1923); David Beasley, *The Canadian Don Quixote: The Life and Works of Major John Richardson, Canada's First Novelist* (Erin, Ont.: Porcupine's Quill, 1977); and Norah Story, "Richardson, John," in *The Oxford Companion to Canadian History and Literature*, 1967 ed.

[2] The text of the early melodrama, reproduced from the working script left behind by a touring actor in London, Ontario, during the 1850s, appears in R. Jones, ed., "Wacousta or, the Curse," *Black Moss*, 2nd ser., No. 1 (Spring 1976), pp. 41–74. For Reaney, see his *Wacousta: A Melodrama* (Erin, Ont.: Porcépic, 1979).

[3] Richardson had been married in 1825 to a Jane Marsh, who had died some time before 1832. The epitaph he composed for his second wife bears repeating:

> Here reposes, Maria Caroline, the Generous-Hearted, High-Souled, Talented and Deeply-Lamented Wife of Major Richardson, Knight of the Military Order of Saint Ferdinand, First Class, and Superintendent of Police on the Welland Canal during the Administration of Lord Metcalfe. This Matchless Wife and This (illegible) Exceeding Grief of Her Faithfully Attached Husband after a few days' illness at St. Catharines on the 16th August, 1845, at the age of 37 years. (Casselman, p. xxxviii)

[4] For a glimpse of the down-at-heel, Grub Street aspects of his final days, see *The Pick* [New York], 1, No. 14 (22 May 1852), quoted in Carl Ballstadt, ed., *Major John Richardson: A Selection of Reviews and Criticism* (Montreal: L.M. Lande Foundation, 1972), p. 53.

# Catharine Parr Traill (1802–99)

## CARL P.A. BALLSTADT

CATHARINE PARR STRICKLAND was a member of one of the remarkable literary families of nineteenth-century England. Her elder sister Agnes was famous for *Lives of the Queens of England* (1840–48), which she wrote jointly with another sister, Elizabeth. Immigration of three members of the family, Catharine, Susanna, and Samuel, to Canada extends the significance of the family to the development of Canadian literature, as well.

Catharine Parr was born 9 January 1802 in London, Kent, probably in Rotherhithe parish, the fifth daughter of Thomas and Elizabeth Strickland. Her father was manager of the Greenland Dock, and the family had resided on the south bank of the Thames for many years.[1] Shortly after Catharine's birth, Thomas Strickland retired, and the family moved to East Anglia, living first near Norwich and then at Stowe House on the Suffolk side of the River Waveney overlooking the river valley and the town of Bungay.

Catharine's earliest memories were of Stowe House, but in 1808 her father bought Reydon Hall, a large red-brick mansion near the coastal village of Southwold, Suffolk. Although Reydon was the principal residence of the family, Thomas also acquired a house in Norwich at Saint Giles Gates, with a coach manufactory on the premises.² He lived there for portions of each year, usually the winter months, with some members of the family accompanying him and some remaining at Reydon.

All these early environs were important in the education and the formation of the tastes of the Strickland children. In her auto-biographical writings, Catharine expresses vivid memories of the natural beauty of the Waveney valley, historical sites such as the ruins of Bungay castle, excursions in search of wild flowers, and details of life at Stowe House and the legends associated with it. Reydon, dating from Tudor times, and Southwold offered an even greater range of associations, historical, natural, and supernatural. The children heard stories of the Battle of Sole Bay during the reign of Charles II, of smugglers and adventures at sea, of Cardinal Wolsey and his bridge over Blythburgh Ford, of the ruined city of Dunwich, of ghosts and witches and other aspects of East Anglian folklore. Their rural location and proximity to the sea gave oppor-tunities to keep pets, to collect and to grow flowers, to wander the seashore in search of shells and other marine life, and to encounter gypsies, while time spent in Norwich afforded experience of a busy industrial and commercial centre.

The more formal education of the Strickland girls was chiefly parental, although, eventually, the elder sisters tutored the younger. It included the usual feminine accomplishments of sewing, embroi-dery, and handicrafts, but it was exceptional in that they had a wide range of literary and linguistic experience, as well. The relative isolation of Reydon allowed plenty of time for study, and Thomas Strickland's well-stocked library offered reading in the classics, in history and natural history, in books of travel, and in English literature, both early and modern. There is evidence that they also studied French and Italian and had available translations of Ger-man literature.³

According to Catharine, the availability of books and the isola-tion of their lives sparked the impulse to write in herself and Susanna, "to break the tedium of the dull winter." Their writing, in turn, "influenced . . . [their] elder and more gifted sisters, to take up the pen of authorship."[4] Catharine was fifteen at the time, and, by the date of her father's death in May 1818, she must have had a stock of manuscripts available. Within a few months, through the agency of one of the executors of her father's estate, Mr. Morgan, she was the first of the sisters to have a book published: *The Tell Tale: An Original Collection of Moral and Amusing Stories* (1818).[5] Following the publication of that book, five of the Strickland sisters found outlets for their work in the expanding literary markets of the pre-Victorian decades. They began shaping their knowledge of history, nature, Suffolk lore and legend, life in Norwich, and their own family life and travels into books of instruction and amusement for children, sketches and poems for the elegant annuals that flourished in England from 1823, and eventually their own collections of poetry and tales. Literary periodicals for women, especially *La Belle Assemblée* and *The Lady's Magazine*, became very important to them, Agnes and Eliza having editorial connections with the latter publication during the 1830s.[6]

It was common practice in the early decades of the nineteenth century for the authorship of books and periodical pieces to be indicated only by reference to other items the writer had produced. Catharine, in fact, maintained this policy even when her career was well established, many of her works being identified as by the authoress of *The Backwoods of Canada* (1836), her best-known work. She seemed to prefer anonymity, with the results that the extent of her contributions to annuals and periodicals is not yet known, although she certainly did submit items to particular editors,[7] and some of her early books have been attributed by bibliographers to her sisters, Agnes and Susanna. Fortunately, Traill produced a list of her early books in her old age to enable correct identification of authorship, and internal evidence supports her claims in several cases.[8]

According to her list, between the ages of fifteen and thirty she had published more than nine books, including the following: *The Tell Tale: An Original Collection of Moral and Amusing Stories* (1818); *Nursery Fables* (n.d.); *Little Downy; or, The History of a Field Mouse: A Moral Tale* (1822); *Prejudice Reproved; or, The History of the Negro Toy-Seller* (1826); *The Young Emigrants; or,*

*Pictures of Canada, Calculated to Amuse and Instruct the Minds of Youth* (1826); *The Keepsake Guineas; or, The Best Use of Money* (1828); *Sketches from Nature; or, Hints to Juvenile Naturalists* (1830); *Narratives of Nature, and History Book for Young Naturalists* (n.d.); and *The Step Brothers* (n.d.). To this list, we can add *Disobedience; or, Mind What Mama Says* (1819); *Reformation; or, The Cousins* (1819); *The Juvenile Forget-Me-Not; or, Cabinet of Entertainment and Instruction* (1827); *Amendment; or, Charles Grant and His Sister* (1828); *The Flower Basket; or, Botanical Blossoms* (n.d.); and some of the items in *Tales of the School-Room* (n.d.).

The list of works and Catharine's statement that she contributed many items to annuals and periodicals make it apparent that she was a very active writer in the dozen years preceding her immigration to Canada. Along with other members of the family, she also established friendships with other Suffolk literary figures, notably James Bird of Yoxford and Thomas Harral and his family. Bird was a poet who wrote frequently on Suffolk historical subjects, and Harral the editor of Suffolk newspapers and of *La Belle Assemblée* from 1821 to 1831. The Stricklands frequently visited the Birds and corresponded with them, and Catharine was affianced to Francis Harral, Thomas' son. She was much distressed when the engagement broke off in 1831. During that year, however, Catharine was also broadening her horizons. She followed Susanna to London and lived and travelled with her aunt, Mrs. Leverton of 13 Bedford Square, spending many months with her and visiting such places as Bath, Oxford, Cheltenham, and Waltham. The journey gave her opportunities to meet other relatives, visit historical sites and galleries, and to assist Mrs. Leverton in the conduct of a school for young girls.[9]

It was in London that she first met Thomas Traill, a friend of Dunbar Moodie and fellow officer in the Twenty-First Royal Scottish Fusiliers. She met him again at Susanna's house in Southwold the following year and married him on 13 May 1832. Two days later, the Traills left Southwold by steamer bound for Edinburgh, and after several weeks of visiting Thomas' friends and relatives in Edinburgh and the Orkneys, they sailed from Greenock bound for Upper Canada on 7 July 1832.

Catharine's life in Canada is much better known than her life in

England, largely because much of it is reflected in her many Canadian books. She and Thomas settled first near her brother, Samuel, on the shores of Lake Katchawanook north of Peterborough, and they lived subsequently at various locations: Ashburnham (now part of Peterborough), the Wolf Tower, Mount Ararat, and Oaklands on the shores of Rice Lake. They were burned out at Oaklands on 26 August 1857 and lived in a house provided by their friend Frances Stewart until Thomas' death on 21 June 1859, following which Catharine built a house at Lakefield, where she lived the rest of her life.

From her early days in Canada, Traill maintained an active literary career, keeping daily journals for long periods of time and transmitting the raw data of those journals into stories, essays, novels, and botanical studies. Following the publication of *The Backwoods of Canada* (1836), stories and sketches by her appeared in numerous British, American, and Canadian periodicals. In the 1850s, she began to produce books again: *The Canadian Crusoes: A Tale of the Rice Lake Plains* (1852); *The Female Emigrant's Guide, and Hints on Canadian Housekeeping* (1854) (reissued the following year and in several subsequent editions as *The Canadian Settler's Guide*); and *Lady Mary and Her Nurse; or, A Peep into the Canadian Forest* (1856). These were followed by botanical studies and natural-history essays: *Canadian Wild Flowers* (1868); *Studies of Plant Life in Canada; or, Gleanings from Forest, Lake and Plain* (1885); *Pearls and Pebbles; or, Notes of an Old Naturalist* (1894); and another book for children, *Cot and Cradle Stories* (1895).

Late in her life, she received a good deal of public recognition for her contributions to Canadian literature and nature study. Through the efforts of Lady Charlotte Greville, she received £100 from Britain, and in Canada she was the recipient of a testimonial organized by Sir Sandford Fleming and contributed to by many notable Canadians.[10] She also carried on lengthy correspondence with Canadian botanists. She died in 1899 at the age of ninety-seven.

NOTES

[1] Mary Agnes Fitzgibbon, "Biographical Sketch," in *Pearls and Pebbles; or, Notes of an Old Naturalist,* by Catharine Parr Traill (Toronto: Briggs, 1894),

p. iv. See also "Memorials of the Stricklands: A Family Chronicle," TS, in the Traill Family Papers (T.F.P.), VII, 10852; and "Family History," TS, T.F.P., V, 8262. These and all other unpublished papers cited in the Traill Family Papers are in the Public Archives of Canada, Ottawa.

2 Thomas Strickland's Will, Somerset House, London, England.

3 Catharine Parr Traill, *The Backwoods of Canada: Being Letters from the Wife of an Emigrant Officer, Illustrative of the Domestic Economy of British America* (London: Charles Knight, 1836), p. 15. See also T.F.P., VI, 8867. The Strickland's cousin Thomas Cheesman, an artist, was a student of Italian and interested his cousins in the language.

4 Catharine Parr Traill, "Some Reminiscences of the Life of Mrs. C.P. Traill," TS, T.F.P., VI, 8864–65.

5 Notebook, T.F.P., III, 4066. Mary Agnes Fitzgibbon calls this book *The Blind Highland Piper and Other Tales* (see Fitzgibbon, "Biographical Sketch," p. xiv), but I have found no evidence that the book was published with that title. "The Blind Highland Piper" is one of the stories in *The Tell Tale.*

6 Susanna Moodie, "To the Editor of *The Literary Garland*," *The Literary Garland*, 4 (June 1842), 319. Internal evidence also suggests that Agnes and Eliza were heavily involved in *The Lady's Magazine.*

7 Catharine Parr Strickland, letters to Susanna and to James Bird [1831], Glyde Papers, Public Record Office, Ipswich, England.

8 Notebook, T.F.P., III, 4066; see also the letter from Susanna to Mary Russell Mitford, in *The Friendships of Mary Russell Mitford as Recorded in Letters from Her Literary Correspondents*, ed. the Rev. A.G. L'Estrange (London: Hurst and Blackett, 1882), I, 212–13.

9 Letter to James Bird, 17 July [1831], Public Record Office, Ipswich, England.

10 "Auditor's Report" (Traill Testimonial), T.F.P., I, 1453. Some contributors were G.M Grant, John G. Bourinot, James Macoun, James Fletcher, and Hugh Fleming.

# Susanna Moodie (1803–85)

## MICHAEL A. PETERMAN

OF ALL the Canadian pioneering figures who found time to devote
to literary interest, Susanna Moodie is undoubtedly the best known
among contemporary readers. Indeed, one can postulate that over
the past decade Moodie has undergone a sort of literary and
cultural canonization; she has become a central foundation figure
in both critical and creative attempts to define the condition of the
imagination in Canada.

Given the interest that Moodie and her most famous work,
*Roughing It in the Bush; or, Life in Canada* (1852), have aroused,
it is surprising to note that so little attention has been paid to the
formative years of her life. She was nearly thirty when she left the
Suffolk countryside for the bush farms of Upper Canada. Hence,
as is the case with her older sister Catharine Parr Traill, hers is a
tale of two worlds. Any attempt to examine her work or to
understand her view of literature and sense of values must locate

itself firmly in the experiences of her English years.

The salient biographical details are as follows. Susanna Strickland was born in 1803 near Bungay, the sixth daughter of Thomas and Elizabeth Strickland, Thomas Strickland having recently retired from a London docks-management position and come to Suffolk in search of a gentler climate and a residence suitable to the rising status of his large family. That goal he realized in 1808 in buying Reydon Hall. A gloomy, deteriorating Elizabethan mansion on the outskirts of the village of Reydon near Southwold, it was to be Susanna's home until she married in 1831.

Reydon Hall seems to have been the summit of Thomas Strickland's ambitions and good fortune, a testament, on the one hand, to his independent, enlightened thinking and a symbol of his overreaching, on the other. It gave him status and visible proof of his achievement; moreover, it gave him a rural setting in which to continue his unusual and rigorous plan to educate his daughters in academic and outdoor skills. His watchwords were discipline, self-reliance, industry, and honesty. The fact of sex alone was for him no bar to individual capability or development. However, the twenty-mile move from Bungay to Reydon had its unforeseen consequences. It further isolated the Stricklands as Suffolk newcomers. More problematically, it removed Thomas Strickland farther from his business connections in Norwich. When illness and financial reverses forced him to spend longer periods in Norwich, the younger girls and his two sons were left increasingly on their own. His death in 1818, when Susanna was fourteen, deprived her of a guide and example she greatly depended upon. In the autobiographical story "Rachel Wilde; or, Trifles from the Burthen of a Life," she remembered him as a vigorous, independent, and conscientious thinker, an excellent father whose family "regarded him with a reverence only one degree less than that which they owed to their Creator." Thinking of her own adult life, she adds, "In afterlife they are proud to echo his words, and maintain his opinions."[1]

At Reydon, thereafter, the struggle under reduced circumstances to make do and keep face was a constant one. Led by the aggressive elder sisters, the businesslike Eliza and the romantic Agnes (who would later collaborate to write *Lives of the Queens of England* and other popular histories), the girls sought to find literary markets for the writing that, as children, they had found a pleasant, beguiling pastime. Initially, Agnes, Jane Margaret, Catharine, and Susanna sought outlets in the growing markets, centred in London, for writing addressed to children and adolescents.

Of the daughters, Susanna was most like Agnes in temperament. Impulsive and acutely sensitive, she was inclined to write enthusiastic poetry, tragic drama, and romantic tales of history. Like Rachel Wilde, "she fell in love with all the heroes of antiquity."[1] Catharine recalled that Susanna's first attempt at fiction, a tale of Gustavus Adolphus, was inspired by her reading of Coleridge's translations of Schiller. These tendencies Susanna modulated for the children's market in such early heroic or moralistic tales as *Spartacus: A Roman Story*, *The Little Quaker; or, The Triumph of Virtue*, *Rowland Massingham; or, I Will Be My Own Master*, and *Profession and Principle; or, The Vicar's Tales*, as well as in the stories and poems she submitted to the then-popular juvenile and gift-book annuals.[3]

Her great aim, however, was to become a famous literary figure and a recognized force in the London world. To this end, two paternal friends proved crucial. One was the poet James Bird of nearby Yoxford; the other Thomas Harral, whose daughter Susanna knew well. Bird encouraged her writing and helped her establish literary connections in remote London, while Harral, as editor of *La Belle Assemblée*, a court and fashion magazine, began publishing her poems and sketches in May 1827.[4] She was later to find outlets in other London magazines — *The Athenaeum* (through the fatherly influence of her most important literary friend, Thomas Pringle) and *The Lady's Magazine* (which her sister Eliza had a hand in editing) — and in many of the prestigious literary annuals.[5] In addition, she collaborated with Agnes on a small book entitled *Patriotic Songs* (1830) and produced her own book of poetry, *Enthusiasm, and Other Poems*, in 1831.[6] She was, then, making steady, if unspectacular, progress towards the realization of her goals.

It would be unfair, however, to see the young Susanna Strickland simply in terms of worldly aspiration. Coexistent with her eagerness for fame was a spiritual desire that led her not only to mistrust her literary aims but also, in the face of strong family resistance, to convert from the Anglican Church to the Nonconformist persuasion in 1830. Under the guidance of James Ritchie of nearby Wrentham (whose wife instructed Susanna in the art of painting), she risked the severe judgements of Agnes and Eliza in seeking a more personal, less complacent approach to her religious needs. As well, through Thomas Pringle, who was both an influential literary man and Secretary of the Anti-Slavery League, she became a strong critic of the injustices and tyranny of slavery and wrote two pamphlets for the League describing the respective sufferings of Mary Prince and Ashton Warner, both of whom she met in Pringle's London home.[7]

The man who was to change and dramatically uproot her life, she also met at Thomas Pringle's. This was J.W. Dunbar Moodie, an Orkney man who had returned to England from South Africa to have a book published and to find a wife. After considerable wavering (apparently because she resisted the possibility of immigrating to South Africa), Susanna married Lieutenant Moodie in the spring of 1831. A year later, after having exhausted any chance of securing the basis for an independent life in England, the Moodies and their young daughter immigrated to Upper Canada to take up land Dunbar had received for military services.

The major events of their Canadian life are generally well known. Their first two years were spent near Port Hope, where they decided to buy a farm "in the clearings." The unpleasant conditions of their life at "Melsetter" are amply described in the first half of Roughing It in the Bush. Misled by speculators, they sold that farm and moved to the shore of Lake Katchawanook near present-day Lakefield to take up Dunbar's land grant and be close to Thomas and Catharine Parr Traill and Susanna's brother Samuel, who had established himself as the area's most successful pioneer.[8] There they stayed nearly five years; during this time, upon the outbreak of the Rebellion of 1837, Dunbar served as a captain in a militia regiment, escaping from "the bush" only with his appointment as Sheriff of Hastings County late in 1839. From 1840 till his death in 1869, they lived in Belleville. Thereafter, Susanna spent her time with various of her grown children, often visiting her sister Catharine in Lakefield for extended periods. She died in Toronto in 1885, having written very little after the death of her husband. In her later years, she gave more of her time to painting.[9]

As in England, writing proved an important financial resource and personal outlet during Moodie's Canadian years. Still eager for fame and very sensitive to the opportunities she had abandoned, she was quick to seek markets for her work in North America and to encourage, as best she could, publication of her writing in England. Initially there were few solid opportunities. Though her poems began to appear in the early 1830s in *The Albion* [New York], *The Emigrant* [New York], *The Canadian Literary Magazine*, *The North American Quarterly Magazine*, and various provincial newspapers, it was not until she made contact with John Lovell, the editor of a newly established Montreal magazine, *The Literary Garland*, that she was regularly remunerated for her writing. From May 1839 to December 1851, she wrote prolifically for *The Literary Garland*, establishing herself as its steadiest and most versatile contributor. In *The Literary Garland* and *The Victoria Magazine*, which she and her husband edited during its short existence (1847–48), she produced virtually all the poems, sketches, and instalment fiction she would later rework into book form for the famous English publisher Richard Bentley. These later works included *Roughing It in the Bush; or, Life in Canada* (1852), *Mark Hurdlestone; or, The Gold Worshipper* (1853), *Life in the Clearings versus the Bush* (1853), *Flora Lyndsay; or, Passages in an Eventful Life* (1854), *Matrimonial Speculations* (1854), and *Geoffrey Moncton; or, The Faithless Guardian* (1855). Most were reprinted in New York and proved very successful there. Her last major effort, a three-volume novel for Bentley entitled *The World before Them* (1868), effectively closed out her writing career, though she did oversee a reprinting of *Roughing It in the Bush* in its first Canadian edition in 1871.

## NOTES

[1] Susanna Moodie, in *The Victoria Magazine, 1847–1848*, ed. Susanna Moodie and J.W.D. Moodie, introd. William H. New, facs. ed. (Vancouver: Univ. of British Columbia Press, 1968), p. 113.

[2] Moodie, in *The Victoria Magazine*, p. 114.

[3] Susanna Strickland's work appeared in several of these popular annuals, then in their heyday; for example, *Ackermann's Juvenile Forget Me Not* and *Marshall's Christmas Box*.

[4] *La Belle Assemblée; or, Court and Fashion Magazine* published her work intermittently from 1827 to 1830.

[5] Her work appeared in *Friendship's Offering, The Iris, The Amulet, Emmanuel,* and *The Forget Me Not,* among others.

[6] While no known copy of *Patriotic Songs* has survived, the evidence in letters and reviews indicates it was published.

[7] Carl Ballstadt, "Susanna Moodie: Early Humanitarian Works," *Canadian Notes and Queries,* No. 8 (Nov. 1971), pp. 9–10.

[8] Samuel Strickland, who buffered the arrival of the Traills, also produced a pioneering memoir, *Twenty-Seven Years in Canada West; or, The Experience of an Early Settler* (London: Bentley, 1853).

[9] This skill Susanna passed on to her daughter Agnes, who distinguished herself in illustrating such books as *Canadian Wild Flowers,* the text of which was written by Catharine Parr Traill.

# William Kirby (1817–1906)

## MARGOT NORTHEY

THE BARE FACTS of his biography may suggest that William Kirby led a dull life.[1] He came to Canada in 1839, after the Mackenzie-Papineau rebellion had been put down, and he died in 1906, a few years before the disasters of World War I. Having settled in what is now Niagara-on-the-Lake, he remained there for over sixty years, working first as a journeyman tanner, then as a newspaper editor, government customs official, magistrate, and reeve. He married, brought up a family, and became a leading citizen of the community, all the while writing about life as he saw it or wished it to be. Following a path of deliberate routine, he was untouched by scandal or even impropriety.

But if Kirby's life was unexciting, it does not follow that he was a dull man. On the contrary, he was a man of considerable learning and strong opinions. Widely read, he was well versed in the classics and in contemporary literature. He was also an accomplished linguist, who early learned to read Greek, Latin, French, and German, and later mastered Hebrew, Italian, and Swedish, as well as the dialects of some of the North American Native tribes. Most important of all, he was endlessly curious, taking an active part in the life of his region and country and writing editorials and letters about the controversies and policies of his time. His historical romance *The Golden Dog* was one of the most popular works of early Canadian literature.

Yet the view persists, reinforced by his chief biographer, Lorne Pierce, that Kirby was a narrow man. Probably the main reason is that he was not caught up in the progressive ideas and movements of his age. He was a man who deplored, and sought ways to avoid, revolution or radicalism, seeking stability and order rather than change or excitement. He was a conservative — a Tory Loyalist — at a time when liberal ideas were increasingly popular. From the perspective of twentieth-century democracy, his attitudes may seem caught in a stagnant backwater. But he was neither stuffy nor a handwringer. Rather, he was a fighter for his ideas, caught up in the fray of conflicting political and social directions in a land that was largely unsettled and thus easily changed.

Like so many others of his day, Kirby was an immigrant. He was born in England on 13 October 1817, in Kingston-upon-Hull in the county of York. On his paternal side, the Kirbys had long lived in the area; his father and grandfather were journeymen tanners. The family was unshakeably loyal to king and country and to the established Church of England. Yet in 1832 the deteriorating economy forced John Kirby, William's father, to emigrate with his wife and sons. The United States seemed the land of opportunity, and the Kirbys settled in Cincinnati, a rough-and-ready city, rapidly growing with new immigrants, but with as yet few cultural assets. Fortunately, William acquired a remarkable tutor, Alexander Kinmont, a native Scot who deeply influenced his charge.

Working in a tannery by day and studying under Kinmont in his off hours, young Kirby acquired a sound education and an interest in literature and language. Through Kinmont, he also became interested in the philosophy of Emanuel Swedenborg; together, in 1837, Kirby and his tutor signed the documents of the Second New Jerusalem Society of Cincinnati, a society based on Swedenborg's philosophic and religious principles. Swedenborg had a mystical side, but he also wanted to unite the two worlds of religion and science. Although Kirby never swerved from his Anglican faith, his admiration for Swedenborg was enduring — as indicated in the distillation of Swedenborg's views in a chapter of *The Golden Dog*.

The increasing noise of extreme jingoists in the United States and their attempts to stir up anti-British feeling prompted Kirby's decision to move to Canada in the summer of 1839. He took a week to sail to Niagara Falls via the Ohio River. As Pierce reports, he arrived with a meagre wardrobe and a rifle, his trunks being filled with books. Kirby felt that he had come home. He was later to recall seeing the Union Jack waving in the breeze off Lake Erie: "I recognised my own country's symbol, and hailed it as the true flag of Freedom, Justice and Christian Civilization."[2]

Although Kirby had arrived in Canada many years after those immigrants who fled the effects of the American Revolution, he considered himself a United Empire Loyalist. In the year he came, the fear of American invasion was no idle one: "Hunter's Lodges" in the western and northern states had supplied themselves with arms and had made incursions across the border. But Kirby was to spend the rest of his years defending his adopted land not so much against the possibility of military attack and takeover from the south as against the republican and annexationist ideas that were creeping into the country and endangering it from within. Ironically, Kirby fought to preserve the traditions of élitist government, by which he thought the population as a whole would best be served, at a time when England was adopting sweeping reforms that ensured a greater political role for its masses. Like so many other colonials, he sought to maintain the ideals and way of life he associated with the motherland at a time when the motherland was herself changing.

When he set foot in Canada, Kirby did not stay put, but travelled to Quebec by boat, stopping *en route* to see the sights of Toronto and Montreal. During his travels, he saw reminders of violent American raids across the border and of the more recent acts of rebellion within the colonies. Not sure whether he wanted to settle in Quebec or in Upper Canada, he tossed a coin in the air and headed back to Niagara-on-the-Lake, at that time simply called Niagara, a town of about fifteen hundred inhabitants.

After working a few months in a tannery outside the town, he leased his own tannery and took in a partner who, six years later, absconded with the company funds. Kirby found himself in jail for debtors as a result, but he was helped out by some friends who settled the company debts. Kirby worked hard at the tannery, but his soul was in his books. He also immersed himself in the history of the area, gathering stories from old settlers and gradually building up a store of information that he later used in his writing.

Despite his own position as a labourer, he never mixed much with the ordinary people of the town, although he was considered modest and courteous. Tall and handsome, he had the air and manners of a gentleman, and he soon became a familiar part of the gatherings in the leading homes of the area. He liked music and dancing and good-looking women, although he was apparently not a high liver but retiring by nature. In 1847, the year following his bankruptcy, Kirby married Eliza Whitmore, from a prominent old Loyalist family he much admired. They had three sons, the first of whom died in infancy. Kirby used some of his wife's dowry to buy a house, a fine frame building that remains to this day. He also used some of her money in 1853 to buy himself a newspaper, *The Niagara Mail* (later called simply *The Mail*), of which he had been editor since 1850. For many years he was to write editorials and articles, marked usually by their vehemence and sometimes splashed with vitriol.

Kirby's political involvement started with his writing in the paper. On 31 October 1849, he published in *The Niagara Mail*, under the assumed "Britannicus," a long letter, "Counter Manifesto to the Annexationists of Montreal," in which he denounced the British North America League's proposal for peaceful annexation with the United States. The Canadian government ordered eight thousand copies of the letter, which Kirby reprinted in pamphlet form, although it was only years later that he disclosed his authorship. Kirby continued to use his editorial influence through the years on the side of the Tories and was consistently opposed to most of the ideas of the Grits, especially their call for free trade with the United States. But while *The Mail* was the chief vehicle for his views, he also kept a journal and established a wide-ranging network of correspondence with political and literary figures of the time. In 1846 Kirby finished a long poem he had been working on for ten years, *The U.E.: A Tale of Upper Canada*. It was not until 1859, however, that he published it, setting and printing it himself in the office of *The Mail*.

The two great political events of Kirby's life were the American Civil War and Confederation. Although proud of the abolition of slavery in Canada and sympathetic to the Black Americans who made their way to Canada via the underground railroad, Kirby supported the Southern cause, as did others in Canada. During the war years, several prominent Southern families came to live in the Niagara area; Kirby saw the Southerners as closest to his own Tory ideals, by contrast with the Northerners, whom he saw more as unscrupulous demagogues. Like many others, he thought the North had gone to war for mercantile reasons.

Kirby supported Confederation and the policies of John A. Macdonald because he saw the union of the provinces as the best way to preserve independence. The Fenian raids of 1866, tacitly if not openly supported by many American politicians, had emphasized the precariousness of the Canadian position. Kirby viewed Confederation as a way of strengthening the imperial tie, rather than loosening it.

Although he resigned from *The Mail* in 1863, Kirby continued to write for it when he felt strongly, and he increased his involvement in the affairs of the region and of the country. In 1861 he had been appointed reeve of the town, and he worked hard at his duties. At the same time, he had become something of an advisor on national matters to Macdonald, who later saw to it that Kirby became a police magistrate and customs collector at the port of Niagara. He was thus able to maintain a comfortable, if not luxurious, standard of living; since his retirement from the paper, his only income had come from his low-paying job as curator for the Niagara military reserve.

From 1865 to 1873, Kirby spent much of his spare time working on a historical romance about Quebec when it was still a colony of France. *The Chien d'Or (The Golden Dog): A Legend of Quebec* was published in February 1877 by Lovell, Adam, Wesson, and Company of New York and Montreal, but the firm soon went bankrupt without giving Kirby adequate copyright protection. Consequently, other publishers soon put out editions for which Kirby was to receive little or no money. *The Chien d'Or*, or *The Golden Dog* as it was alternatively called, was well received critically and was soon translated into French by Pamphile LeMay and published in two volumes in 1884. As a result of his new prominence as an author, Kirby was elected to the Royal Society of Canada in 1882, and he took an active part in it.

For years Kirby had been writing poetry and having it published in his paper or in local magazines. Between 1879 and 1883, several of his poems were printed individually or in small groups in pamphlet form. These were collected, together with various other poems, a number of translations, and an address, in *Canadian Idylls*, published in a limited edition in 1884 and a second edition in 1894. In 1891 Kirby became the founding president of the Niagara Historical Society and was largely responsible for the growth of its archives. His last work, *Annals of Niagara*, which traces the history of the region, was published in 1896, after which he confined his literary effort to letters to his friends and acquaintances. His final years were spent quietly in seclusion at his old house. He died on 23 June 1906, having survived his wife by fifteen years.

## NOTES

[1] Much of the biographical information in this essay is based on Lorne Pierce's comprehensive biography *William Kirby: The Portrait of a Tory Loyalist* (Toronto: Macmillan, 1929). Janet Carnochan's "Reminiscences of William Kirby, F.R.S.C.," *United Empire Loyalist Transactions, 1904–1913* (Toronto: 1914), VI, 49–53, was also useful for its contemporary character sketch.

[2] Kirby, quoted in Pierce, p. 35.

# Rosanna Leprohon (1829–79)

### CAROLE GERSON

ROSANNA ELEANOR LEPROHON, née Mullins, was born in Montreal on 12 January 1829 and died in the same city on 20 September 1879. Her father, Francis Mullins, had emigrated from Ireland in 1819 and prospered in Canada as a ship chandler. He later expanded his business to include importing and real estate, eventually becoming a substantial Montreal landowner. Her mother, Rosanna Conelly, the daughter of a schoolmaster, presumably set a high value on education. Young Rosanna attended the Convent of the Congregation, at the time the best school for young ladies in the city. In November 1846, at the age of seventeen, she published her first poems in *The Literary Garland* . During the following four and a half years, she produced a steady stream of *Garland* contributions: fifteen poems, one story, and five serialized novels, all set in England. Rosanna's marriage to Dr. Jean-Lukin Leprohon in June 1851, coupled with the demise of *The Literary Garland* the following December, ended the first phase of her career.

Seven years his wife's senior, Dr. Leprohon was himself remarkably active in both professional and cultural circles. He founded *La Lancette Canadienne*, the country's first medical journal; was professor of hygiene at Bishop's College in Lennoxville; helped to establish the Women's Hospital in Montreal; served on the Catholic section of the provincial Council of Public Instruction and on the Montreal city council; helped to institute the National League; was vice-president of the College of Physicians and Surgeons; founded and belonged to various local and international medical societies; and from 1871 was Vice-Consul for Spain.[1]

After her marriage, Rosanna moved to Saint Charles on the Richelieu River, where her husband was then practising. For about eight years, her literary output declined to a trickle of poems published in Montreal newspapers, as she turned her attention to maternal and domestic concerns. Indeed, one wonders how she managed to write at all, considering that between 1852 and 1872 she bore thirteen children, five of whom (including her first) died in infancy. In 1855 the Leprohons returned to Montreal, which was to be Rosanna's home for the rest of her life. She resumed her production of fiction in 1859 with "Eveleen O'Donnell" (reputedly a prize-winning story),[2] published in *The Pilot* [Boston], and "The Manor House of de Villerai," serialized in the Montreal *Family Herald*. These were followed by her best-known work, *Antoinette de Mirecourt; or, Secret Marrying and Secret Sorrowing* (1864), her only novel in print today. Four years later, *Armand Durand; or, A Promise Fulfilled* was serialized in *The Daily News* [Montreal], then appeared in book form as her last separately published work. During the remainder of her life, her literary activity waned due to ill health and family cares, but she continued to write poems and produced five more tales: "Clive Weston's Wedding Anniversary" for *The Canadian Monthly and National Review* (1872) and four others for the *Canadian Illustrated News*: "Ada Dunmore; or, A Memorable Christmas Eve: An Autobiography" (1869–70); "My Visit to Fairview Villa" (1870); "Who Stole the Diamonds?" (1875); and "A School-Girl Friendship" (1877). Her posthumously collected *Poetical Works* were published in 1881, with an introduction attributed to John Reade,[3] fellow poet and literary editor of *The Gazette* [Montreal].

## NOTES

[1] Henry Morgan, *Canadian Men and Women of the Time* (Toronto: Briggs, 1898), II, 577–78.

[2] Henry Morgan, "Leprohon, Mrs.," in *The Dominion Annual Register and Review for 1879* (Ottawa: MacLean, Roger, 1880), p. 409.

[3] Archibald MacMurchy, *Handbook of Canadian Literature* (Toronto: Briggs, 1906), p. 89.

# James De Mille (1833–80)

CAROLE GERSON

JAMES DE MILL (he added the final "e" after 1865) was born in Saint John, New Brunswick, on 23 August 1833, the third child in a large family of Loyalist descent. At the time of his death in Halifax, on 28 January 1880, he was "the widest read and most productive of Canadian writers,"[1] although there is little in his early childhood to predict his later career. When James was nine, his father, Nathan Smith Demill, a prosperous merchant and shipowner, left the Church of England for the Baptists, his views on alcohol earning him the cognomen "Coldwater Demill." A colourful, rather eccentric figure, the elder Demill is reputed to have "burned a package of novels that had found their way into a cargo" and to have "rather disparaged book-learning." He put James and his elder brother, Elisha Budd, "at an early age into his counting-house" (MacMechan, p. 405), yet he was also a governor of Acadia College — founded as a Baptist school — to which he sent his sons. At the age of fifteen, James attended Horton Academy, the congenial Grand Pré School of his boys' adventure stories, then spent eighteen months at Acadia before moving on to Brown University (Providence, Rhode Island), which granted him his M.A. in 1854.

Before entering Brown, however, James and Budd set out on a year and a half of travels that deeply impressed the future novelist. In August 1850, the youths sailed from Quebec City for Liverpool. The two brothers toured Scotland and England, crossed the channel, then "followed the old diligence line, the route of the *Sentimental Journey*, through central France to Marseilles" (Mac-Mechan, p. 406). Italy proved the most memorable country on their itinerary, providing James with scenes and incidents that were to enhance more than half his novels.

De Mille returned to North America to enter Brown in February 1852. His academic work was undistinguished — not from lack of ability, but from boredom, as Archibald MacMechan infers from the sketches and caricatures in the margins of De Mille's notebooks (MacMechan, p. 410). According to MacMechan, while at Brown De Mille began to toss off fictions for "story papers" like the *Waverly Magazine*, more for fun than for profit. Upon graduation, he spent a year and a half in Cincinnati helping friends investigate the affairs of a mining company in which Maritime Baptists (including Acadia College) had invested heavily. One of De Mille's biographers has suggested that his "lost" serial novel, "The Minnehaha Mines" (1870), may shed light on this period of its author's life.[2] The novel has since been found,[3] but in common with the rest of De Mille's light fiction, it simply transforms incidents drawn from his experiences into amusing fantasy. The Cincinnati episode ended tragically when one of De Mille's companions was murdered; the novel ends comically with the hero (with a good deal of aid from the heroine) trounces the villains, recovers the capital of the gullible investors (mostly clergymen), and turns the mine into a profitable enterprise.

For De Mille, however, success in business occurred more frequently in fiction than in fact. In 1855 he returned to Saint John to help with the family's failing lumber company. With a partner he opened a bookstore, but his partner proved "negligent, or dishonest, or both" (MacMechan, p. 412) and De Mille was left with a burden of debt that he may not have paid off until shortly before his death. In 1859 he married Elizabeth Ann Pryor, daughter of Dr. John Pryor, first president of Acadia College. The following year he embarked on his academic career, first as professor of classics at Acadia, then as professor of history and rhetoric at Dalhousie College. During this time, he returned to the Church of England and published a pamphlet on its early history. In Halifax, De Mille was well known as an exciting teacher and a fine scholar, in 1878 producing *The Elements of Rhetoric*. According to one source, "Harvard had been for some years anxious to secure him for her services, and at the time of his death was making a special effort."[4] The immediate cause of De Mille's sudden death, at the age of forty-six, was pneumonia; many felt overwork to be a contributing factor.

De Mille's frenzied literary career may have begun during his student days, but most of his more than twenty-five novels were published after 1868, at least three appearing posthumously. Most are utterly negligible adventure stories, dependent upon impossible coincidences and predictable characters and padded to suit serial publication. Even these, however, are often composed in a rather tongue-in-cheek manner; as MacMechan put it, they are "literary practical jokes on the public" (MacMechan, p. 414). De Mille's first commercial success was *The Dodge Club; or, Italy in MDCCCLIX* (1869), which pokes gentle fun at Americans abroad. He himself set great store by his major historical novel, *Helena's Household* (1867), a turgid reconstruction of first-century Roman life. More readable is his series of boys' novels, published between 1869 and 1873. To modern readers, however, he is known almost solely for *A Strange Manuscript Found in a Copper Cylinder*, not published until 1888 and possibly left unfinished.

## NOTES

[1] Archibald MacMechan, "De Mille, the Man and the Writer," *The Canadian Magazine*, 27 (1906), 404. Further references to this work appear in the text.

[2] Douglas MacLeod, "A Critical Biography of James De Mille," M.A. Thesis Dalhousie 1968, p. 70.

[3] James De Mille, "The Minnehaha Mines," *The New Dominion and True Humorist*, 4 (8 Jan.–25 June 1870). A complete run of *The New Dominion and True Humorist* for 1870 is held by the University of British Columbia library.

[4] A.J. Crockett and George Geddie Patterson, "Concerning James De Mille," in *More Studies in Nova Scotian History*, by George Geddie Patterson (Halifax: Imperial, 1941), p. 146.

# Agnes Maule Machar (1837–1927)

### CAROLE GERSON

AGNES MAULE MACHAR was born on 23 January 1837 in Kingston, where she died ninety years and one day later on 24 January 1927. Her parents had immigrated to Canada in 1827; her mother, Margaret Machar (1798–1883), had been raised in a Scottish manse, and her father, Dr. John Machar (1796–1863), had studied theology in Edinburgh and was licensed to preach in the Church of Scotland. From 1827 until his death in 1863, John Machar served as minister of Saint Andrew's Church in Kingston and was principal of Queen's University from 1846 to 1854. Agnes and her younger brother, John (1841–99), grew up in an environment that was both religious and intellectual. With her father and private teachers, she "studied Greek and Latin before she was ten, and by the time she was fifteen she had made good progress in French, Italian, and German, besides mathematics, drawing and music."[1]

Machar's first poem, written at the tender age of seven, recounted "the painful deaths of two young emigrants"; shortly afterwards, "a few verses, descriptive of a mother preparing tea for her family, appeared in one of the Kingston papers."[2] One source claims that her first three books were "written before she was within sight of her twenties" (MacCallum, p. 355). However, two of these were not published until 1870 and 1871; more widely accepted is the story that her first novel, *Katie Johnstone's Cross: A Canadian Tale* (1870), was "written in six weeks" (Wetherald, p. 301) and garnered a prize offered by a Toronto publishing house, Messrs. Campbell and Son, "for the book best suited to the needs of the Sunday School library" (MacCallum, p. 355). Machar carried off Campbell's prize the following year, as well, with *Lucy Raymond; or, The Children's Watchword*. Three years later, she captured another literary honour when *For King and Country* won a competition sponsored by *The Canadian Monthly and National Review*, and in 1887 she won *The Week*'s prize for the best native poem on the Queen's Jubilee.

Despite these successes, Machar always avoided publicity, usually writing anonymously or under the pseudonyms "A.M.M.," "Canadensis," and possibly "A.M." and "F."[3] Her favourite and most familiar pen name was "Fidelis," because, as she is reported to have said, "Faithfulness is the quality I most value and care most to possess" (Wetherald, p. 300). Throughout her long and prolific career, she remained faithful to the social and religious principles inherited from her parents, who had cooperated with the Abolitionists in aiding escaped slaves. She advocated the application of Christian ideals to everyday life, her causes including better working conditions for labourers, charity towards the poor and unfortunate, improved education for women, love of country and Empire, and, of course, temperance. In 1926, near the end of her life, she appeared to be a relic from the past, "a true Victorian optimist" who viewed the world "from her parlour window [with] a naïve simplicity."[4]

Today, it is easy enough to dismiss Agnes Maule Machar as a second-rate, didactic writer whose imaginative work displays the inevitable shortcomings of morally earnest fiction and Maple-Leaf poetry. During the nineteenth century, however, she was at the centre of Canadian intellectual life and, sometimes, considerably to the left of centre. She was a major contributor of poetry, fiction, book reviews, and articles to the country's most important periodicals, publishing over sixty-five items in *The Canadian Monthly and National Review* (1872–78) and its successor, *Rose-Belford's Canadian Monthly and National Review* (1878–82);[5] more than one hundred pieces in *The Week*;[6] countless items in unindexed Canadian periodicals like *The Canadian Magazine* and the *Canada Presbyterian*; and various pieces in important British and American periodicals for both adults and children, including *Scribner's*, *The Century*, *The Westminster Review*, *St. Nicholas Magazine*, and *Wide Awake*.

Only a small proportion of Machar's total output appeared in book form, all of it now out of print. In addition to her prize-winning Sunday-school novels, she appealed to young readers with *Marjorie's Canadian Winter: A Story of the Northern Lights* (1892), in which she intertwined stories about old Quebec with discussions of proper Christian behaviour. She sought to reach an adult audience with *Roland Graeme, Knight: A Novel of Our Time* (1892), which proposes Christian brotherhood and understanding as a solution to labour problems. Her other novels include *Down the River to the Sea* (1894), essentially a travelogue extolling the beauties of the Saint Lawrence Valley, and *The Heir of Fairmount Grange* (1895), a romance that ends with the heroine choosing a life of service over the comforts of an English estate. As well, she published several chapbooks of poetry and one major collection, *Lays of the "True North" and Other Canadian Poems* (1899), which was popular enough to require an enlarged edition in 1902. In addition, she wrote a number of biographies, including one of her father, and translated several others from French. She also produced, or contributed to, eight volumes of historical writing, three of them about Kingston, and three others for young readers. Unfortunately, all her writings on social issues remain buried in the periodicals where they first appeared. She was a competent artist, as well, but never exhibited her sketches and watercolours.

Machar never married, and her personal life seems to have been uneventful and healthy. (In 1888 she claimed to have "never spent a sick day in bed in her life" [Wetherald, p. 300].) Her life in Kingston was punctuated by several trips abroad, but she usually spent her winters at her house in town and her summers at Ferncliffe, her cottage near the Thousand Islands, which figure so prominently in her poetry. Although almost unknown today, she was an acknowledged figure during her lifetime: her poetry was anthologized in Canadian school texts and read at the Royal Society of Canada's 1895 "Evening with Canadian Poets," and in 1903 she was elected vice-president of the Canadian Society of Authors.

## NOTES

[1] Ethelwyn Wetherald, "Some Canadian Literary Women — II. 'Fidelis,' " *The Week*, 5 April 1888, p. 300. Further references to this work appear in the text.

[2] F.L. MacCallum, "Agnes Maule Machar," *The Canadian Magazine*, 62 (1924), 354. Further references to this work appear in the text.

[3] Nancy Miller Chenier, "Agnes Maule Machar: Her Life, Her Social Concerns, and a Preliminary Bibliography of Her Writing," M.A. Thesis Carleton 1977, p. 2.

[4] R.W. Cumberland, "Agnes Maule Machar," *Queen's Quarterly*, 34 (Jan. 1927), 331, 335.

[5] Marilyn Flitton, *An Index to* The Canadian Monthly and National Review *and* Rose-Belford's Canadian Monthly (Toronto: Bibliographical Society of Canada, 1976), pp. 87–88.

[6] D.M.R. Bentley and Mary Lynn Wickens, *A Checklist of Literary Materials in* The Week (Ottawa: Golden Dog, 1978), pp. 14–16, 55, 81, 114, 150.

# Charles W. Gordon
# ["Ralph Connor"]
# (1860–1937)

## JOHN LENNOX

CHARLES WILLIAM GORDON was born on 13 September 1860 at Indian Lands, Glengarry County, Canada West, the fourth son of Daniel Gordon, a Highlander and missionary of the Free Church of Scotland who had immigrated to Canada in 1853. Charles Gordon's mother was Mary Robertson, who had also emigrated from Scotland to Sherbrooke, Quebec. A woman of acknowledged intellectual accomplishments, she was invited at the age of twenty-two to become principal of Mount Holyoke Ladies' Seminary, where she had attended school. She declined and within a year had married Daniel Gordon. Charles Gordon's first ten years were spent in Glengarry County, where he received his early education. Then, in 1870, his father moved to Zorra in Oxford County. Gordon graduated from high school in St. Mary's in 1879, from the university of Toronto in 1883, where he had studied classics and English and was active in sports and music, and from theological studies at Knox College in 1887. He then spent a year at the University of Edinburgh during 1887–88.

In 1885 Gordon had heard and admired James Robertson, Superintendent of Presbyterian Missions in the North West. Upset and at loose ends after his mother's sudden death in 1890, Gordon met personally with Robertson, who offered him a mission at Banff, a small tourist settlement in the new national park on the recently completed CPR line. Gordon accepted and was ordained in Calgary in June 1890. His mission lasted from 1890 to 1893 and included mining and lumber camps, two or three railway stations, and pioneering districts on the prairie around Calgary. Out of these years came the material for his first books.

In 1893, prior to taking up duties at St. Stephen's Church in Winnipeg, Gordon returned to Scotland for a year and personally raised fifty thousand dollars for the Western Mission. He then came to Winnipeg in August 1894 and stayed at St. Stephen's, which flourished under his leadership until his death.

In 1896 Gordon complained to James MacDonald, editor of the Presbyterian church publication *The Westminster Magazine*, of the church's failure to sustain its Western missions adequately. MacDonald challenged Gordon to win support for them by writing about his experiences in the West. The first story, subsequently divided into three chapters, described Christmas Eve in a Selkirk lumber camp and so impressed MacDonald that he not only published it in *The Westminster Magazine* but suggested that it be the core of a book. Thus, in 1898, *Black Rock* was published by the Westminster Publishing Company, and "Ralph Connor" was born, the pseudonym being formed from Gordon's abbreviation of British Canadian North West Mission — "Can Nor" — misread by a telegraph operator as "Connor" and MacDonald's choice of a suitably Irish first name. Gordon's first three novels — *Black Rock: A Tale of the Selkirks* (1898), *The Sky Pilot: A Tale of the Foothills* (1899), and *The Man from Glengarry: A Tale of the Ottawa* (1901) — became international best sellers that sold in the millions of copies and brought Gordon great fame for their didactic evangelism and their mythical evocation of the Canadian West. George H. Doran, a Canadian beginning his publishing career with the Fleming H. Revell Company of Chicago, had read the Black Rock stories in *The Westminster Magazine* and arranged to publish that novel and most of Gordon's subsequent twenty-three works of fiction, which appeared over the next forty years.

St. Stephen's prospered — increasing from fourteen to one thousand members between 1895 and 1915 — and Gordon was busy in a rapidly expanding and changing Winnipeg with its great influx of immigrants, its growing industries, and its labour unrest. As a temperance advocate and president of the Social Service Council of Manitoba, Gordon unsuccessfully fought the liquor interests and engaged in the summer of 1914 in a bitter confrontation with Solicitor General Arthur Meighen. With all these added responsibilities, he continued to serve his very large parish and, with his wife, Helen King, daughter of the principal of Manitoba College (whom he had married in 1899), to raise a large family that eventually included one son and six daughters.

Although fifty-four when World War I began, Gordon went to France as Chaplain to the 79th Cameron Highlanders and was mentioned in dispatches. One of the officers with whom he served was a partner in the law firm that handled his affairs. After the officer's death at Regina Trench in October 1916, Gordon learned that the lawyer had mismanaged his estate — estimated at between $750,000 and $1,000,000 — and had further indebted him to the sum of $100,000. Gordon was obliged to return home to arrange his affairs and then, early in 1917, was asked to speak in Canada and the United States on behalf of the war effort, advocating conscription and urging the Americans to enter the war. Always active, he was not without financial resources. Continuing royalties from both his earlier books and those published in the post-war period, along with whatever he could spare from his clerical salary, helped him in his struggle to discharge his debts, which he succeeded in doing a few years before his death.

After the Armistice, Gordon ostensibly took up duties at St. Stephen's but was, in fact, busier elsewhere. Following the Winnipeg General Strike of 1919, he served as chairman of the Manitoba Joint Council of Industry for three years until its dissolution. He was moderator of the Presbyterian Church of Canada during 1921–22 and spoke in favour of the church union between Methodists and Presbyterians, which took place in 1925. He represented the church as a delegate in 1927 at the World Conference of Faith and Order at Lausanne and delivered the sermon at the inception of the League of Nations' 1932 assembly. He was an early supporter of the Canadian Authors Association and was its national president from 1933 to 1935. In the 1930s, he spoke out against fascism and criticized the silence of Christian churches in international affairs. He also spoke in favour of public ownership of certain industries, nationalization of banks, and a system of public services including unemployment insurance and government pensions for the elderly.

Public recognition was constant, even though Gordon's literary reputation declined after World War I. He was elected a Fellow of the Royal Society of Canada in 1904, and he received honorary degrees from Toronto's Knox College, Queen's University, and the universities of Glasgow and Manitoba. In 1935 he became a companion of the prestigious Order of St. Michael and St. George. He was admired as a writer and personality by world leaders like Theodore Roosevelt, Woodrow Wilson, Herbert Asquith, and Ramsay MacDonald. At his death on 31 October 1937, he was, as Ralph Connor and the Reverend Charles William Gordon, the most famous Canadian of his generation.

# Gilbert Parker (1860–1932)

### ELIZABETH WATERSTON

GILBERT PARKER'S LIFE was ultimately a triumphant progression from Canadian small-town teacher to London socialite, knight, and baronet; from Anglican deacon to British member of Parliament and privy councillor; from colonial newspaper columnist to worldwide best-selling novelist.[1] Early days in provincial Canada and later years of global success produced tensions that Parker learned to release in fictional forms acceptable to hundreds of thousands.

Horatio Gilbert Parker was the son of a British officer sent to Quebec with troops reinforcing the garrison just before the Rebellion of 1837.[2] Joseph Parker later moved to Ontario, became a storekeeper, attorney, and justice of the peace, and married (as his second wife) Samantha Jane Simmon, a woman of American Loyalist stock. Gilbert was the fourth child, second son, in a family of seven surviving children;[3] he was born on 23 November 1860 in Camden East, about thirty kilometres from Kingston.

At sixteen, Gilbert Parker capped an education at village schools in Seaforth, Frankford, and Belleville by taking a six-week teacher-training course; he taught school from 1877 to 1882, including one year's work at the Ontario Institute for the Deaf and Dumb at Belleville. He performed locally as an elocutionist, wrote for the Belleville paper, and embarked on training for the Anglican ministry by serving as a summer curate in Trenton, where the rector's daughter, Florence Bleasdell, became a lifelong friend.

In January 1883 Parker entered divinity courses at Trinity College, Toronto, enroling as a mature student. This bypassing of the normal undergraduate path to theological studies led to some college antipathy towards Parker as an "outsider," but college days also brought friendships with several sympathetic people, including Charles G.D. Roberts. Toronto fostered Parker's flair for the theatrical: he attended plays, saw Henry Irving and Lillie Langtry on stage, and heard Oscar Wilde lecture; he became noted among fellow students as a tutor in elocution. The following year he moved to Queen's University, Kingston, as lecturer in oratory. There he formed a friendship with George Frederick Cameron, a prize-winning poet, and tried his own hand at patriotic poems, under the impact of news of the Riel Rebellion of 1884–85. Parker's younger brother, Reginald, had joined the Canadian forces in the West; his letters home stirred Gilbert's interest in Métis and Native life.

Tragically, Reginald died by drowning in the summer following his safe return from war. By September, Cameron had also died suddenly of a heart attack. Parker's health broke; he gave up his work in the church and at the university and set out on a recuperative voyage to the South Seas. *En route* he met Frank Tarboe, a professional gambler, and Alice Rahlo, a strong-willed young American. The paths of these three intense young people would cross again many times. Parker arrived in Australia in May 1886, via Arizona, Los Angeles, Honolulu, and New Zealand. During a four-year stay as a reporter on *The Morning Herald* [Sydney], he covered floods and royal visits, political contests and massacres. He also worked in Sydney theatres as recitalist, entrepreneur for visiting troupes, and dramatist (author or coauthor of four plays). Yet he maintained his interest in Canada, reviewing Archibald Lampman's poetry, welcoming distinguished visitors such as Principal George Monro Grant of Queen's University, Kingston, and including in his stories written in Australia some sketches set in Madawaska, in Ontario lumber camps. When he left for England in 1889, he took with him a sizeable bankroll and a bundle of short stories.

In London a friendly journalist ironically commented that Parker had an excellent collection — of titles.[4] Parker grimly burned the collection. Then the sight of a Hudson's Bay trapper's outfit, glimpsed in a London store window, brought a surge of new ideas: the Canadian North West through which Reginald Parker had travelled could become the setting for adventure stories featuring a Métis and his frontier world. Gilbert Parker settled in Bloomsbury into an absorbing stint of writing, interrupted in spring by a trip home, a transcontinental train ride across Canada, and a visit to New York and Boston to interview potential editors and publishers for the stories he was concocting. By December 1890 he had completed several Canadian and Australian short stories and also a longer work entitled *The Chief Factor: A Tale of the Hudson's Bay Company* (1892).

British editors, including W.E. Henley, discoverer of Rudyard Kipling, were enthusiastic. The Canadian stories, collected as *Pierre and His People: Tales of the Far North* (1892), were favourably reviewed. Back in Canada to gather new material, Parker visited Ottawa, met Archibald Lampman and Duncan Campbell Scott and also the historian J.G. Bourinot, who suggested he consult James MacPherson LeMoine in Quebec about possible subjects for a novel. LeMoine had been a friend of Francis Parkman and of William Kirby; he took a fancy to the earnest, square-bearded young man, introduced him to other Quebec antiquarians, and read to him the memoirs of adventures in 1763 that would become the germ of Parker's most successful novel, *The Seats of the Mighty* (1896). Parker also dropped in to Montreal with an introduction to William Van Horne, president of the Canadian Pacific Railway Company, who told him tales of the Canadian West. Then he dashed to New York to arrange American publication of *The Chief Factor*, forestalling pirated editions, and there made friends with several innovative young American writers. His publications in this hectic year also included *Round the Compass in Australia* (1892), a book of travel sketches.

In 1893 Parker moved in three literary directions. His first modern novel, *Mrs. Falchion*, appeared; his first historical romance, *The Trail of the Sword* (1894) was accepted for publication; and his play *The Wedding Day* was staged in London. On a crest of success, he summered in Brittany, where he wrote *The Trespasser* (1893). Aboard the train going back to London, the romantic young writer met the contemporary equivalent of a fairy-tale princess: Amy Van Tine, a very wealthy, very beautiful young American.

That autumn, back in London, he made the acquaintance of Pauline Johnson, who was charming fashionable audiences with her dramatic presentations of Native poems. Parker's next novel, *The Translation of a Savage* (1893), was a modern romance about the marriage of a Canadian Native into a socially prominent British family. By 1894 the novelist himself became engaged to Amy Van Tine. As a tribute to Amy, he published a sequence of love sonnets, written earlier (*A Lover's Diary: Songs in Sequence* [1894]). Parker spent most of the winter in the United States — in Hot Springs, Virginia, where he lived and wrote in the luxurious Hot Springs Hotel, and in New York, where he dined with Charles G.D. Roberts and Bliss Carman and read his work to an American writers' workshop frequented by novelists ranging from Stephen Crane to Frances Hodgson Burnett. He wrote and revised *When Valmond Came to Pontiac: The Story of a Lost Napolean* (1895) in a five-week surge, writing in Virginia and New York. In the summer of 1894 he returned to England and in a remote part of Lincolnshire began work on *The Seats of the Mighty*.

*The Seats of the Mighty* began to run in *The Atlantic Monthly* in March 1895. A successful adaptation of the "Pretty Pierre" stories went on stage as *Pierre of the Plains*. In December 1895, at his New York wedding to Amy, guests included Andrew Carnegie, William van Horne, Henry Irving, William Dean Howells, Kate Douglas Wiggin, and Bram Stoker. In the new year the handsome young couple joined the Bourinots in arranging an Ottawa pageant for Governor General and Lady Aberdeen. Wilfrid Laurier became a personal friend, and the mighty of Toronto who fêted the best-selling author included Edmund B. Osler and Dr. George Parkin. Returning to London, Parker was invited to collaborate with Herbert Beerbohm Tree on a stage production of *The Seats of the*

*Mighty* and to tour with this production in the United States. President Grover Cleveland attended the Washington performance.[5] The play was not successful, but Parker's writing had surged again.

Parker used Quebec scenes in *The Pomp of the Lavilettes* (1896), and, after he and his wife holidayed on Jersey Island, he used that setting for *The Battle of the Strong: A Romance of Two Kingdoms* (1898), which he later adapted, at the urging of Lillie Langtry, into a play starring Maurice Barrymore. On their next visit to Canada, in 1898, the Parkers stayed at the Governor General's residence, Rideau Hall. They travelled to Egypt and Italy in 1899, the year Parker entered British politics; the next year, 1900, he was elected Conservative-Unionist candidate for Gravesend.

Over the next few years, in spite of parliamentary business, he found time to publish a collection of stories set in rural Quebec, *Born with a Golden Spoon* (1899; reprinted as *The Lane That Had No Turning* [1900]), to write one novel set in modern Quebec, *The Right of Way: Being the Story of Charley Steele, and Another* (1901), another set in the Near East, *Donovan Pasha, and Some People of Egypt* (1902), to collaborate with Claude G. Bryan on a work of nonfiction, *Old Quebec, the Fortress of New France* (1903), and to collect his early Australian tales as *Cumner's Son and Other South Sea Folk* (1904). As a member of the Conservative group surrounding young Winston Churchill, he represented Dominion interests in the mother country. As a parliamentarian, he worked on Free Trade policies, on the Marriage with a Deceased Wife's Sister Bill, and on the first Colonial Universities Conference. When the Boer War moved into its gravest stage, he spoke for imperial loyalties and against colonial import duties. He was knighted as a world-famous Canadian writer and politician in 1902. On his next trip to Canada, in 1904, Parker travelled as a celebrity, accompanying Wilfrid Laurier to the North West for ceremonies celebrating the entry of Saskatchewan and Alberta into Confederation.

*The Right of Way* had sold almost 750,000 copies in the United States and over 20,000 copies in Canada. Parker returned to historical romance set in Jersey Island in *A Ladder of Swords: A Tale of Love, Laughter, and Tears* (1904) and to Egypt in *The Weavers: A Tale of England and Egypt of Fifty Years Ago* (1907).

Not everyone loved him. He spoke against the suffragettes and led a movement to facilitate Chinese labour in South Africa. But when his party was defeated in 1906, Parker was reelected, though as a member of the opposition. He was disappointed not to receive the major political plum of appointment as Canadian high commissioner, to succeed Lord Strathcona. Nevertheless, 1907 found him hosting parties in connection with the Colonial Conference, entertaining Mark Twain, socializing with Arthur Conan Doyle, J.M. Barrie, and others, watching the dramatization of *The Right of Way* and of *Pierre and His People*, battling Lloyd George in parliament, and writing a minority report on the Royal Commission on the Poor Law. He collected a volume of his lyrics, many of which had been set to music by prominent composers such as Sir Edward Elgar, and published them privately as *Embers: Being a Book of Verses* (1908); a further collection of stories appeared as *Northern Lights* (1909). Parker's health was not good, but in spite of flu, malaria, and nervous exhaustion, he stood again and was reelected in 1910. He clarified his conservative stance in a book written in collaboration with Richard Dawson, *The Land, the People, and the State: A Case for Small Ownership, and a Handbook* (1910). On Canadian politics, he had quarrelled with Wilfrid Laurier over the question of reciprocity with the United States.

But if politics and health posed problems, Parker's literary career was at its apparent apex. In 1912 his publishers in England and in America began bringing out an Imperial Edition of his works — treatment allotted only to Rudyard Kipling, Robert Louis Stevenson, and George Meredith among British authors. Other honours had been accorded: he was invited to Ireland for a three-week visit to study attitudes to home rule, made president of the Sir Walter Scott Society in Edinburgh, and given honorary degrees by McGill University and by Université Laval. *The Judgment House* (1913) reflects his interests as chairman of the Imperial South African Association.

At the outbreak of World War I, Parker was made director of British publicity in the United States. He used his unique social and political connections in order to keep American sympathy for Britain strong during the years before the United States entered the war on the Allied side. He wrote pamphlets and press releases, published *The World in the Crucible: An Account of the Origins and Conduct of the Great War* (1915), and also made less formal representations on Britain's behalf. Early in the war he went with Herbert Hoover on a joint commission to establish food relief in Belgium and to document conditions in refugee camps. For his efforts he was raised in 1915 to a baronetcy and was made a member of the British Privy Council in 1916. Under the burden of work in England and America, his health broke. He returned to the United States to hear President Woodrow Wilson announce the breaking of American diplomatic relations with Germany, then he resigned his position as unofficial ambassador and headed for Arizona, his health refuge since 1911. Before the war ended in 1918, he also resigned his seat in Parliament, concluding eighteen years as member for Gravesend.

During the war years, a film version of *The Seats of the Mighty*, starring Lionel Barrymore, kept Parker's fame as novelist before the public, as did the publication of *You Never Know Your Luck: Being the Story of a Matrimonial Deserter* (1914), *The Money Master* (1915), and *The World for Sale* (1916) — all written before the war broke out. After the war came *Wild Youth, and Another* (1919) and *No Defence* (1920). Then, after a grand tour of Canada organized in conjunction with the Imperial Press Conference in 1920, Sir Gilbert and Lady Parker went to Hollywood to join a group of writers in the burgeoning movie business. *The Translation of a Savage* was revamped as *Behold My Wife!*; "She of the Triple Chevron" from *Pierre and His People* became *Over the Border*; *The Money Master* he rewrote as *The Wise Fool*; and *The Lane That Had No Turning* was also adapted. During this year's American sojourn, Parker accepted an honorary degree from the University of Toronto and was installed as a member of the Royal Society of Canada.

On his return to England, where his friend and fellow Canadian Bonar Law had now become prime minister, Parker published his political novel *Carnac* (1922). He was offered an earldom, but declined, feeling the honour had come too late in his career to mean much, especially since he had no children to inherit the title. He and his wife now lived quietly, entertaining old friends in London and wintering in Arizona. Amy Parker was facing imminent death from cancer. Parker's family ties with Canada were lessening: his sister and her family were still in Belleville, but he had quarrelled with one brother, another had died in 1916, and the two youngest brothers had moved to the southwestern United States. But Parker still visited Canada regularly; he spoke imperially at the Empire Club, and around 1924 he opened a correspondence about his life-story with Lorne Pierce, since a biography (never completed) was planned for the Makers of Canadian Literature series. His historical novel *The Power and the Glory: A Romance of the Great La Salle* was published in 1925. Amy Parker died that same year.

A visit to a Canadian writers' conference in Muskoka, Ontario, in the summer of 1926 went some way towards lifting Parker's depression. He turned in memory to his early days and reconsidered youthful friendships in *Tarboe: The Story of a Life* (1927). His last travels were to Palestine, which he then used as the scene of *The Promised Land: A Story of David in Israel* (1928) — dedicated to the Prince of Wales — and in 1930 to California for a long visit with his brothers. At this time he was still corresponding with such old friends as Winston Churchill and with members of the royal family. He spent the last year of his life in London, where, frail and lonely, he died on 6 September 1932.

## NOTES

[1] References to sales of Parker's works are based on Alice Hackett, *Seventy Years of Best Sellers* (New York: Bowker, 1967); Frank Luther Mott, *Golden Multitudes: The Story of Best Sellers in the United States* (New York: Macmillan, 1947); Claud Cockburn, *Bestseller: The Books That Everyone Read, 1900–1939* (London: Sidgwick & Jackson, 1972); Mary Vipond, "Best Sellers in English Canada, 1899–1918: An Overview," *Journal of Canadian Fiction*, No. 24 (1979), pp. 96–119; and Mary Vipond, "Best-Sellers in English-Canada: 1919–1928," *Journal of Canadian Fiction*, Nos. 35–36 (1986), pp. 73–105.

[2] Biographical details are based on Parker's introductions in *The Works of Gilbert Parker*, Imperial ed., 24 vols. (New York: Scribner, 1912–23), and on John Coldwell Adams, *Seated with the Mighty: A Biography of Sir Gilbert Parker* (Ottawa: Borealis, 1979). Adams' biography corrects errors in earlier accounts, even the birthdate having been erroneously reported in standard references.

[3] The siblings were Frederick, Cynthia (died just before Gilbert was born), Gilbert, Albert (died in infancy), Reginald, Lionel, Henry, George (another infant death), and Arthur.

4 See Gilbert Parker, Introd., *Pierre and his People: Tales of the Far North*, Vol. 1 of *The Works of Gilbert Parker*, p. ix.

5 *Gilbert Parker and Herbert Beerbohm Tree Stage* The Seats of the Mighty, ed. John Ripley (Toronto: Simon and Pierre, 1981) offers an illuminating picture of the contemporary theatre. See also W.J. Thorold, "Gilbert Parker: An Interview," *Massey's Magazine*, Feb. 1897, pp. 117–23.

# Charles G.D. Roberts (1860–1943)

TERRY WHALEN

CHARLES G.D. ROBERTS was born in Douglas, near Fredericton, New Brunswick, on 10 January 1860. He was the child of Reverend George Goodridge Roberts and Emma (Bliss) Roberts.[1] Cousin to Bliss Carman on his mother's side of the family, he was therefore a distant relative of Ralph Waldo Emerson. His background was an Anglican and a United Empire Loyalist one, and, again like Carman, he would later move to the United States and earn for himself a reputation as a popular writer, one who would produce nearly six dozen titles of prose and poetry during his eighty-four dynamic years of what Desmond Pacey has termed a life of spiritual "restlessness."[2]

The Roberts family moved to Westcock, New Brunswick, in August 1861, and, for the first fourteen years of his life, Roberts was tutored by his father and enwisened by the nature visible to him around the Tantramar River district of New Brunswick. The

Tantramar is one of the two rivers that some commentators see as highly formative of Roberts' imaginative life.[3] The other river he grew to know intimately was the Saint John, after the Roberts family moved to Fredericton in 1874 when his father was appointed rector of St. Ann's Church and canon of Christ Church Cathedral. Charles was enrolled in Fredericton Collegiate School and was taught an appreciation of classical, Romantic, and Victorian poetry by the school's energetic headmaster, George Parkin, a man who was part of what Roberts later named a "strange aesthetic ferment"[4] in the New Brunswick capital during Carman's and Roberts' undergraduate years. Roberts was an athletic, intelligent, and accomplished youth, and he composed his first verses ("Sonnet: On the Dying Year" and "Spring") during 1874–75, items that were later published in the *Canadian Illustrated News* (30 March 1878) when he was eighteen years of age. He graduated from Fredericton Collegiate School with highest honours in 1876 and enrolled in the University of New Brunswick in the fall of that year.

Roberts graduated from university in 1879 with honours in philosophy and political economy, scholarships in Latin and Greek, and a medal in Latin prose competition. In September of that year, he was appointed headmaster at the Chatham Grammar and High School in Chatham, New Brunswick. In December 1879 he became engaged to Mary Isobel Fenety, daughter of the King's Printer, and he married her in December of 1880. With the help of his father-in-law, he published his first book, *Orion and Other Poems* (1880); at the age of twenty, he was now the author of an acclaimed book, a seminal one that helped earn him the title "The Father of Canadian Poetry."[5] Precociousness marks and disturbs much of Roberts' life, and it is obvious that his talent had already begun, by this time in his life, to interfere with his peace of mind and with the stability of his household: his writerly concerns constantly involved him in choices which upended his attempts at achieving a domestic stability.

An uncomfortable quality of vocational haste and confusion can be detected in Roberts' life after his marriage to Mary Fenety, and an overview of the period from 1881 to 1885 provides us with a short version of the difficult choices he had to make in the midst of his busy day-to-day existence: He received a master's degree from the University of New Brunswick in 1881, while still teaching.

He resigned from the Chatham School in January 1882 to be appointed headmaster of York Street School in Fredericton, only to resign from that post in the summer of 1883 to take up an appointment as editor of Goldwin Smith's *The Week* in Toronto in November of the same year. Because of his disagreements with Smith's political views — Smith was an annexationist, Roberts a nationalist (he was later an imperialist) — he resigned the editorship in February 1884, in a gesture of moral authenticity. He spent just over a year in Fredericton, trying to survive on freelance work, and he travelled to New York for a brief visit to forage for more work.

By the time of Roberts' appointment as a professor of English and French at King's College, Windsor, Nova Scotia, in September 1885, he was the father of two sons, Athelstan (b. 1882) and Lloyd (b. 1884). Edith Roberts was born in 1886, and Douglas Roberts was born in 1888. At the age of twenty-eight, Roberts now had what Pelham Edgar terms a "bevy of young children"[6] and had begun a ten-year term at King's College, where he was very popular as a teacher and was active in the community. In this period he managed to author three books of poetry (*In Divers Tones* [1886], *Autochthon* [1889], and *Songs of the Common Day, and Ave: An Ode for the Shelley Centenary* [1893]), two guidebooks (*The Canadian Guide-Book* [1891] and *The Land of Evangeline and the Gateways Thither* [1895]), and three novellas (*The Raid from Beauséjour, and How the Carter Boys Lifted the Mortgage: Two Stories of Acadie* [1894] and *Reube Dare's Shad Boat: A Tale of the Tide Country* [1895]). He also translated Phillipe Aubert de Gaspé's *Les Anciens Canadiens* (1863) as *Canadians of Old* (1890) and largely completed his *A History of Canada* (1897), in which he demonstrated his political bias as a Canadian imperialist.

If there was a "strange aesthetic ferment" in Fredericton during the last two decades of the nineteenth century, the presence of Roberts in Windsor from 1885 to 1895 also made possible a miniature, somewhat mixed bohemian and civilized life of letters at King's College. As Lloyd Roberts reports in his *The Book of Roberts* (1923) — and as visible in other related memoirs[7] — the Roberts household was at the centre of an aesthetic ferment of its own. During these years, Carman would often visit Roberts with his friend the American Vagabondia poet Richard Hovey in tow.

Roberts had many other literary visitors as well. The most significant literary event during the Windsor decade, for our purposes, is
the publication of Roberts' first animal story, "Do Seek Their Meat
from God," in 1892.

Roberts resigned his professorship at King's College in 1895 and
once again tried to survive on freelance work in Fredericton until
February of 1897.[8] His first historical romance novel, *The Forge
in the Forest*, and his first collection of nature stories, *Earth's
Enigmas*, were published in 1896. He was also having some
continued success with his nonfiction prose. Roberts always
viewed himself as primarily a writer of poetry, but the success he
was having with his novels and short stories persuaded him that
he could best provide for himself on his earnings from fiction. The
vogue for romance fiction and the sudden new market for animal
stories provoked by the sales success of Ernest Thompson Seton's
*Wild Animals I Have Known* (1898) were eventually to convince
Roberts that he had better live for poetry, by prose — that even
though his heart was primarily in his verse, he had better be sensible
about where his imaginative energies should flow.[9]

In February 1897 Roberts departed on his own for New York,
where he took up a position as an assistant editor for *The Illustrated American*. From this point onward he was to visit his family
in Fredericton only intermittently, and, with the death of his son
Athelstan in October 1897, he seems to have decided fully to
commit himself to a relatively genteel bohemian life of freelance
work, making his intellectual life amidst the literati, travelling, and
writing less poetry and more fiction — the romance and wilderness
fiction that would earn for him a literary reputation on both sides
of the Atlantic.[10] Roberts resigned his position at *The Illustrated
American* in January 1898.

He was a success in New York, for all of his initial unease as a
writer from the northern wilds.[11] He was elected a member of the
Author's Club of America in 1897 and was elected as the only
non-American charter member of the National Institute of Arts and
Letters in 1898. The close to ten years he lived in New York were
punctuated with trips to England, France, Holland, and Cuba —
where he twice visited the poet Francis Sherman, a Fredericton
native, who often made return visits to Roberts in New York.
Roberts published eight books of fiction during his time in New

York, including the novels *The Heart of the Ancient Wood* (1900), *Barbara Ladd* (1902), *The Prisoner of Mademoiselle* (1904), and *The Heart That Knows* (1906). The major collection of animal stories he published in this period was *The Kindred of the Wild* (1902).

Personally, however, Roberts again became restless, and he moved to Europe in November of 1907; during the next seven years he lived in Italy, France, Germany, and England. He published more collections of animal stories, including *Kings in Exile* (1909) and *More Kindred of the Wild* (1911). In spite of his being fifty-four years of age at the outbreak of World War 1 in 1914, he enlisted in the British army. He was promoted to captain in late 1915, was transferred to the Canadian War Records Office in London in 1916 with a promotion to major, and was sent to France in December of the same year as a press correspondent, where he remained until the spring of 1918.

Roberts was demobilized from the army in 1919 and resided in London until February 1925. During this time he made visits to North Africa, Switzerland, and Italy and published several collections of stories, including *Wisdom of the Wilderness* (1922) and *More Animal Stories* (1922). His still fascinating novel about prehistoric people, *In the Morning of Time*, appeared in 1919. When he returned to Canada in 1925, he was immediately greeted with honours and with a great deal of work.

Roberts resided in Toronto from 1925 until his death on 26 November 1943. He crossed the country on a reading tour in 1925 and again the following year. In 1926 he was awarded the Lorne Pierce Gold Medal of the Royal Society of Canada and accepted the presidency of the Toronto branch of the Canadian Authors Association. In 1927 he was elected national president of the same association. Bliss Carman died in June 1929, and Roberts' wife, Mary, died in May 1930. Roberts' own autumn years went on for much longer, and he remained busy. During the 1930s he acted on the editorial boards of the *Standard Dictionary of Canadian Biography* and the *Canadian Who's Who*. He was knighted in 1935, and a year later his *Selected Poems* appeared as evidence of his continuous interest in writing poetry.

During the last three years of his life he continued to receive honours. He had received an honorary LL.D. from the University of New Brunswick in 1906, and Mount Allison University, Sackville, New Brunswick, presented him with a Litt.D. in 1942. He married Joan Montgomery in October 1943, and in his last years he encouraged and scrutinized Elsie M. Pomeroy's *Sir Charles G.D. Roberts: A Biography* (1943). In addition to his other works, he published during his lifetime nine novels and romances, five volumes of stories for young adults, nineteen volumes of original short stories, and five selections of stories. His restlessness was a highly creative one, to say the least. *The Vagrants of the Barren and Other Stories*, a new collection edited by Martin Ware, is scheduled to be published by Tecumseh in 1992.

Roberts had copious success as a fiction writer, in both market and critical terms. *Barbara Ladd*, to cite but one sales example, sold over eighty thousand copies in the United States alone, and, according to Pomeroy, *The Heart of the Ancient Wood*, in addition to seeing many editions in the United States and England, was "translated into French, German, Dutch, Czecho-Slovakian, Danish and Swedish" and "sold well in all these countries."[12] He had written stories for *Harper's Monthly*, *Cosmopolitan*, *Lippincott's Monthly Magazine*, *The New York Times*, *The Atlantic Monthly*, *Saturday Evening Post*, *The Metropolitan*, and *The Fortnightly Review*, to mention only a few of many.[13] He had earned the encouragement of Matthew Arnold, Oliver Wendell Holmes, Hamlin Garland, and George Meredith — among others — and, by the time of his death in 1943, he had a durable reputation in Canada as one of its finest writers, a reputation that has never since been in radical doubt.[14]

## NOTES

[1] Elsie M. Pomeroy's *Sir Charles G.D. Roberts: A Biography* (Toronto: Ryerson, 1943) is usually considered a work of hagiography, but it is commonly used as a source for other studies primarily because, as Michael J. MacDonald says, Pomeroy was Roberts' "secretary and companion for almost twenty-five years" (Introd., *The Heart That Knows*, by Charles G.D. Roberts [Sackville, N.B.: Ralph Pickard Bell Library, Mount Allison Univ., 1984], p. viii) and thus had the advantage of gathering firsthand the many details offered in her book. Pomeroy tells us a great deal about her bias when, in "Sir Charles G.D. Roberts: Final Chapter," she says: "When, as a child at public school, I was thrilled by

the patriotic poem, 'O Child of Nations, giant-limbed,' Charles G.D. Roberts became the subject of my hero-worship" (*The Canadian Author and Bookman*, 20, No. 20 [June 1944], 6).

John Coldwell Adams' *Sir Charles God Damn: The Life of Sir Charles G.D. Roberts* (Toronto: Univ. of Toronto Press, 1986) appeared after the present essay was written, but I have attempted to incorporate Adams' corrections of fact. Other biographical sources of note now include the letters of Roberts that are available at the archives of the University of New Brunswick and profiles of the author from newspaper clippings, collected in the Hathaway Vertical File, Rufus Hathaway Collection, Harriet Irving Library, Univ. of New Brunswick. In 1985 the Harriet Irving Library received from Lady Joan Roberts a gift of 207 books and pamphlets (with many items inserted in their pages) which came from her husband's personal library, and the National Library announced in 1986 that it was the recipient of a small collection of books and other memorabilia donated by relatives of Roberts.

For a relatively extensive list of important dates in Roberts' life, see "Chronology," in *The Collected Poems of Sir Charles G.D. Roberts* , ed. Desmond Pacey, introd. Fred Cogswell (Wolfville, N.S.: Wombat, 1985), pp. 349–55. In instances where this chronology is in conflict with Adams' biography, I have used Adams as the final authority. Finally, I have found particularly useful "Lorne Pierce's 1927 Interview with Charles G.D. Roberts (as Reported by Margaret Lawrence)," ed. and introd. Terry Whalen, *Canadian Poetry*, No. 21 (Fall–Winter 1987], pp. 59–76.

[2] Desmond Pacey, "Sir Charles G.D. Roberts," in *Ten Canadian Poets: A Group of Biographical and Critical Essays* (1958; rpt. Toronto: Ryerson, 1969): "Restlessness — this is the clue to Roberts' career" (p. 57).

[3] See Fred Cogswell, "Charles G.D. Roberts (1860–1943)," in *Canadian Writers and Their Works*, ed. Robert Lecker, Jack David, and Ellen Quigley, Poetry Series, II (Downsview, Ont.: ECW, 1983), 187–88; and Laurel Boone, "Organizing Bohemia: The Letters of Charles G.D. Roberts," in *The Sir Charles G.D. Roberts Symposium*, ed. and introd. Glenn Clever, Reappraisals: Canadian Writers, No. 10 (Ottawa: Univ. of Ottawa Press, 1984), pp. 15–25. See also the transcript of John Fisher's radio broadcast "The Bard of Tantramar," *John Fisher Reports*, CBC Radio, 12 Jan. 1947, which is available in the Hathaway Vertical Files. Roberts acknowledged these formative influences from his youth in the poem "Two Rivers" (*The Collected Poems*, p. 336).

[4] Charles G.D. Roberts, "Bliss Carman," *The Dalhousie Review*, 9 (Jan. 1930), 416. For additional commentary on the Fredericton cultural context, see: Alfred G. Bailey, "Creative Moments in the Culture of the Maritime

Provinces," *The Dalhousie Review*, 29 (Oct. 1949), 231–44; Wilfrid Eggleston, *The Frontier and Canadian Letters* (Toronto: Ryerson, 1957), pp. 101–17; and Malcolm Ross, " 'A Strange Aesthetic Ferment,' " *Canadian Literature*, Nos. 68–69 (Spring–Summer 1976), pp. 13–25.

5 See, for example, Arthur Stringer, "Eminent Canadians in New York, II: The Father of Canadian Poetry," *The National Monthly of Canada*, Feb. 1904, pp. 61–64. For a post-structuralist reaction to this kind of image, see Ed Jewinski, "Michel Foucault, the AuthorS [sic] Charles G.D. Roberts, and Some Post-Structuralist Implications for Canadian Criticism," in Clever, ed., pp. 191–206. For a contemporary author's discussion of his struggle with Roberts' fatherly literary influence, see Irving Massey, "Influence without Anxiety: Sir Charles G.D. Roberts — and Me," *The Kenyon Review*, NS 9, No. 1 (Winter 1987), 114–28.

6 Pelham Edgar, "Sir Charles G.D. Roberts and His Time," rev. of *Sir Charles G.D. Roberts: A Biography*, by Elsie M. Pomeroy, *University of Toronto Quarterly*, 13 (Oct. 1943), 122.

7 See Pomeroy, *Sir Charles G.D. Roberts: A Biography*; and Bernard Muddiman, "A Vignette in Canadian Literature," *The Canadian Magazine*, 40 (March 1913), 451–58.

8 The move was partly a result of Roberts' restlessness. Pelham Edgar tells us that Roberts was ready for a move as early as 1891 and that, by 1892, Roberts felt thoroughly trapped:

> In 1892 his restlessness is more marked, and letters to Carman show how strongly the urgency for wider horizons seized his imagination. "Get away we must. Have change we must. Readjust the focus of life we must. We must soar out of our present fetters . . . . I hunger and thirst fiercely for escape." (Edgar, p. 122)

9 This remark is based on Pomeroy's comment in *Sir Charles G.D. Roberts: A Biography* that "in later years Roberts had been heard to remark, half-humourously, of course, that he had lived *for* poetry but that he had lived *by* prose" (p. 110). See also Pierce's 1927 interview with Roberts, where Roberts says, "I regard my poetry as my most vital work, though I do believe that my novels will attract more attention later when the present vogue for intimate characterization is past" (p. 75).

10 For an interesting biographical piece on Roberts' Canadian literary connections in New York, see John Coldwell Adams, "Roberts, Lampman, and Edmund Collins," in Clever, ed., pp. 5–13.

11 In the Pierce interview, Roberts consents to Pierce's suggestion that the

New York years were some of the best of his life (pp. 74–75).

[12] Elsie M. Pomeroy, "The Novels of Sir Charles G.D. Roberts," *The Maritime Advocate*, April 1950; rpt. privately in pamphlet form, p. 3. This item is also the source of the sales figures for *Barbara Ladd*.

[13] For a thorough list of the dozens of magazines to which Roberts contributed, see John Coldwell Adams, "A Preliminary Bibliography," in Clever, ed., pp. 221–49.

[14] With the availability of Roberts' letters, and as more details of his biography are made visible, there is much data now just coming into view that shows us the more unconventional side of Roberts' life — his love affairs, for instance, and his sexual drives. Humorously, he once remarked on the momentary embarrassment of a speaker who introduced him as one who would be talking that evening about his "wild life" (see C.B. Robertson, "Have Audiences Souls?" *The Toronto Star Weekly*, 3 July 1926, p. 34). For reasons that seem to be a combination of reaction by critics against Pomeroy's genteel view of the man, an odd love of zesty matter wherever it can be found, and perhaps a literary-critical Oedipal reaction to Roberts' title "The Father of Canadian Poetry," it seems inevitable that Roberts will end up quite visible, in the near future, as a figure with feet of clay. Yet, in the midst of all this, it is worth anyone's while to read the interview with Lorne Pierce (see above note 1) for the sake of noticing the forthrightness of the man; and it is worth sifting through the many newspaper clippings in the Hathaway Vertical File for a visage of a man who was seen by many as, above all else, generous in his bearing. Finally, for a concise portrait of the artist, there is the following summary comment made by Roderick Kennedy:

> My own admiration for Sir Charles is based on three fine characteristics, not always combined in one man, one is his loyalty to his friends, the second is his loyalty to literature, his invincible determination to make every line he writes the finest which the genius of Charles Roberts can produce, — to keep his work purged of slovenly thinking and slipshod writing. The third is his loyalty to himself, — his courage under the discouragements which face very serious author, particularly a poet, and most particularly of all a Canadian poet, — his firmness in living, as he wishes to live, and writing as he chooses to write with little regard to convention, fashion or favour. ("Dean of Canadian Authors," *Family Herald and Weekly Star* [Montreal], 10 Feb. 1937, p. 36)

# Ernest Thompson Seton (1860–1946)

## LORRAINE MCMULLEN

ERNEST EVAN THOMPSON was born on 14 August 1860 in the town of South Shields at the mouth of the Tyne River near Newcastle, England. He was the son of Joseph Logan Thompson and Alice Snowdon. His father, like both his grandfathers, was a shipowner. A series of shipping disasters led Joseph Thompson to immigrate to Canada in 1866. By this time the family consisted of ten sons, of which Ernest was eighth, and an adopted cousin, Polly, then eighteen.

The Thompson family claimed to be connected with George Seton, Fifth Earl of Winton, a Highland Scot who had fled to Italy after the Jacobite rising of 1715. For this reason, Ernest legally changed his surname to Seton in 1883, although in deference to his mother's wishes he reverted to the name Thompson in 1887 until her death in 1897. During this ten-year period, while he used the name Thompson, he signed his works Seton-Thompson.[1]

The family settled on a backwoods farm near Lindsay, Ontario.

71

Here Ernest's interest in nature and in the denizens of the wilderness developed. Joseph Thompson proved an unsuccessful farmer, and four years later he moved his family to Toronto, where he worked as an accountant. Ernest's interest in nature continued to flourish. He spent most of his spare time in the nearby Don Valley or in the marshes of Toronto Island. At fifteen, run down from overwork — he was a studious boy — Ernest returned for the summer to the family's former farm, now being successfully run by William Blackwell, in whom he found a more sympathetic father-figure than his own extremely severe father. Ernest passed several summers with the Blackwells, helping with the chores and rambling in the woods. He was now making careful notes and sketches of his observations of nature. *Two Little Savages: Being the Adventures of Two Boys Who Lived as Indians and What They Learned* (1903) is based on Ernest's adventures at this time.

Ernest grew up with the desire to become a naturalist. His father had other ideas. Noting the artistic ability in his son's nature sketches, he decided the boy should be an artist. As this would have been his second choice, Ernest agreed. He apprenticed for two years with a portrait painter and at the same time took night classes at the Ontario School of Art, where he became the protégé of Charlotte Schreiber, whose friendship and encouragement were significant to his development as an artist. He won the Ontario School of Art Gold Medal for 1878–79. That summer he sailed for England to continue his studies, and the following year he won a seven-year scholarship to the Royal Academy, one of six students chosen from several hundred applicants. He took advantage of the free entry to the London Zoo granted to Royal Academy students to spend much time there sketching the animals, and, after considerable struggle, he gained access to the British Museum, where he studied books on natural history. It was in London that Seton first read Darwin's *On the Origin of Species* and *The Descent of Man*. Because of poor health, Seton returned to Canada in the fall of 1881. He was not home long before his father stunned him with the announcement that, having reached the age of twenty-one, Ernest was on his own. Thompson presented his son with an itemized account of the expenses of his upbringing, on which the father would henceforth charge the son interest. Ernest set to work immediately. He obtained an assignment for Christmas-card sketches of birds, and with the money he made went west to join his brother Arthur, homesteading near Carberry, Manitoba. Here he began his serious study of wildlife.

In November 1883 Ernest left his brother's farm for New York. For several years he alternated, spending summer and fall in Manitoba and winter in New York, where he studied art, renewed acquaintances with fellow art students, made more friends among the students, and met naturalists, editors, and publishers. Among those he met at this time were the artist Dan Beard, then a fellow student; Frank M. Chapman, later curator of birds at the American Museum; the naturalist C. Hart Merriam; W. Lewis Fraser, art manager of *The Century Magazine*; and Henry M. Steele, later art director of *Scribner's Magazine*. He made a living illustrating books, including one thousand drawings for *The Century Dictionary* (1889–91). (When the distinguished ornithologist Elliott Coues was asked to edit the biological material for *The Century Dictionary*, he agreed to do so provided Seton made the drawings to illustrate the text.) In the evenings he wrote animal sketches. In 1884 he was invited to become a member of the American Ornithologists' Union. When in Manitoba, Seton worked on his brother's farm and made long expeditions into the bush. He learned woodcraft and deerstalking from the Cree (in particular, from Chaska, of whom he speaks with admiration in his autobiography) and made copious notes of his findings. He tells us that at one time he travelled three hundred miles in nineteen days stalking a moose. His experiences provided the basis for animal stories and for sketches and notes for his *The Birds of Manitoba*, published in 1891 by the Smithsonian Institution.

In the spring of 1887 Seton made another change in his pattern of activities. He moved to a large tract of land that another brother, Joseph, had bought on Lake Ontario at Port Credit. Here, too, in the surrounding woods and hills, he encountered animals that became the heroes of his stories. A few years later, when Joseph was forced to sell his land, Ernest was again on the move. Seton was always to live a life of contrasts, spending part of his time in the city, where he mixed increasingly with the élite of the artistic, literary, and scientific world, and part in the wilderness, where his companions were hunters, trappers, and ranch hands.

In 1890 Seton travelled to Paris, via London, to continue his study of painting. In England he became acquainted with the animal painter Joseph Wolf. In Paris he studied at Julian's Academy. For six years Seton alternated between Paris and North America. During these years he studied animal anatomy, publishing in 1896 *Studies in the Art Anatomy of Animals: Being a Brief Analysis of the More Familiar Mammals and Birds*. In Paris, as in New York, Seton made many friends. Through one of them, a young American woman studying art, he was invited to hunt wolves on her father's New Mexico ranch. His adventures here became the basis for several stories, of which "Lobo, King of Currumpaw" is possibly the best known. On his trip to France in July 1894 he met Grace Gallatin, whom he married on 1 June 1896. They bought a country house near New York City, and Seton more or less settled down, his long apprenticeship over.

By this time, Seton knew many of the important New York artists, illustrators, editors, and writers. His first assignment was making drawings of well-known American birds as illustrations for Frank M. Chapman's *Bird Life* (1897). On 14 November 1896, at a small dinner party for the Scottish novelist James Barrie, Seton met Theodore Roosevelt. Roosevelt, whom he impressed with the entertaining wolf stories he was called upon to relate, was to be a lifelong friend.

Seton's animal stories had appeared in a variety of periodicals. In 1898 he collected eight of these stories, together with their illustrations, and published them in October of that year as *Wild Animals I Have Known*. The book was an immediate success. The first printing sold out within weeks, and three more large printings sold out by Christmas. Seton was now established as a public figure. To his activities as artist, writer, and naturalist, he added lecturing, and he continued to make regular trips into the wilderness, gathering material for his scientific and literary writing.

In 1900 Seton bought a large tract of land not far from New York. When he found that the neighbourhood boys resented his presence on what used to be considered public land, Seton invited them to camp on his grounds. He taught them woodcraft, organized them into a community with a constitution and a code of laws, and had them elect a chief and a council, modelled on Native government. This was the beginning of Seton's Woodcraft Indians and led to his involvement with the formation a few years later of the Boy Scouts of America, of which he was from 1910 to 1915 honorary Chief Scout.[2]

In 1911 Seton published *Rolf in the Woods*, a novel dedicated to the Boy Scouts of America. It is a very pro-American book, in which the fifteen-year-old protagonist is befriended by a Native, learns woodcraft from him, and becomes a scout for the American forces in the War of 1812. In this novel the Native is clearly the noblest figure.

Seton continued as a successful writer, illustrator, and naturalist. In 1907 he made a seven-month trip to the Arctic, which he describes in *The Arctic Prairies* (1911). He made an international reputation lecturing in England, France, and Germany. The animal stories collected in *Lives of the Hunted* (1901) and *Animal Heroes* (1905) were, like his first collection, immensely popular. He published many more volumes; some were individual animal biographies, others selections from previous volumes. Seton's scientific works were also successful. His four-volume *Lives of Game Animals* (1925–28) won the John Burroughs Medal and the Elliott Gold Medal of the National Institute of Sciences.

In 1930, at the age of seventy, Seton bought 2,500 acres near Santa Fe, New Mexico, and built a large adobe house, that became known as Seton Castle. He developed the area into a preserve for Native lore and established a library, a museum, and a school. For some years he and his wife had been drifting apart, and, after their daughter Ann — later the well-known author Anya Seton — was married, they divorced. At Santa Fe, Seton married his secretary and assistant, Julia Buttree. They had one adopted daughter, Beulah. Seton continued his life of writing, painting, and lecturing, remaining active until the last week of his life. He died at Seton Castle on 23 October 1946.

### NOTES

[1] See Ernest Thompson Seton, *Trail of an Artist-Naturalist: The Autobiography of Ernest Thompson Seton* (1940; rpt. New York: Scribner, 1946), pp. 392–93. See also Betty Keller, *Black Wolf: The Life of Ernest Thompson Seton* (Vancouver: Douglas & McIntyre, 1984), pp. 70–76.

[2] See John Henry Wadland, *Ernest Thompson Seton: Man in Nature and the Progressive Era, 1880–1915* (New York: Arno, 1978), pp. 380–445, for a detailed explanation of Seton's role in the development of the Boy Scout movement in North America.

# Sara Jeannette Duncan (1861–1922)

## THOMAS E. TAUSKY

IN AN EARLY, autobiographical essay, Sara Jeannette Duncan proclaimed that "in this golden age for girls, . . . we all . . . want to do something . . . ."[1] Her tombstone carries the inscription "This leaf was blown far."[2] Together, the energy and self-confidence of the first quotation, combined with the cosmopolitan world-weariness of the second, contain the clues to an extraordinary literary life.

Duncan was born in Brantford, Ontario (the "Elgin" of her best-known novel, *The Imperialist*), on 22 December 1861, the eldest to survive infancy in a family of eleven children.[3] Her father, Charles Duncan, was an immigrant from Scotland; her mother, Jane Bell, was a New Brunswick native of Ulster stock whom Charles had met while working in Saint John. Brantford was Charles Duncan's final stop; after arriving in 1855, he operated a prominent dry-goods and furniture store for decades.

Sara Duncan received her primary education at Central School in Brantford. Her high-school years were divided between Brantford Collegiate Institute and Brantford Ladies' College, a private school. She later remarked breezily that in adolescence her "Secret Purpose was to distinguish herself in literature . . . . Naturally, our aspirant wrote poems, and stories, and articles upon the seasons of the year."[4] She subsequently attended a brief teacher-training course in Brantford and then improved her qualifications by spending six months at the Toronto Normal School. Like her contemporary Stephen Leacock, Duncan had little enthusiasm for teaching as a permanent vocation.

In the 1880s, journalism would have appeared infinitely more alluring than teaching for a young woman of Duncan's adventurous spirit. After a few months of apprenticeship on a Brantford newspaper, she made the kind of dash into the spotlight that she must have dreamed about in her teenage years. Some lithographs she saw advertising the New Orleans Cotton Centennial of 1884 inspired her to obtain commissions from *The Globe* [Toronto] and *The London Advertiser* [London, Ont.] to write about the World's Fair as a special correspondent. Duncan was utterly captivated by the languid hedonism of New Orleans; the experience created a taste that never left her for seeking out and analyzing diverse cultures. Soon she was whisked away on a whirlwind trip to Florida led by Joaquin Miller, the bohemian "poet of the Sierras," and given a tour of British Honduras as the guest of the governor.

Her progress in the world of journalism during the next few years was no less breathtaking. During the fall and winter of 1885–86, she worked as a book reviewer and editorial writer for *The Post* [Washington]. Though she complained that ". . . the Canadian newspaper world . . . is a very conservative world indeed, and we know what conservatism means in relation to the scope of women's work,"[5] by July 1886 she overcame that barrier too, becoming the first woman to be employed full-time on the staff of *The Globe* [Toronto]. Her restless energy took her to *The Montreal Daily Star* in November 1887, and, the following March, she moved to Ottawa as one of the *Star*'s parliamentary correspondents. From early 1886 until 1888, she also wrote very extensively for *The Week*, the leading literary journal.

In the fall of 1888, Duncan's taste for travel inspired a grander adventure. With a fellow journalist, Lily Lewis, she went around the world in eight months, perched on the cowcatcher of a train thundering down the Rockies, living in delirious forgetfulness of the West in Japan, and feeling the dignity of being a memsahib in India. Her impressions were first chronicled for the *Star*; then, with a fictionalized framework added, they were made into her first book, *A Social Departure: How Orthodocia and I Went round the World by Ourselves* (1890). Accorded extremely enthusiastic reviews, this book triumphantly launched Duncan's prolific literary career. During the next three decades, she was to write twenty-one more books employing a wide variety of forms and subjects: several social comedies exposing national characteristics and foibles; novels dealing with the struggles of women and artists (and women artists) for self-realization; novels exploring political issues in Canada, Britain, and India; two autobiographies; a collection of short stories; and a story for children about the Indian Mutiny.

At a viceregal reception in Calcutta, Duncan met her future husband, Everard Cotes, then a museum official and subsequently a journalist. They were married on 6 December 1890. Duncan lived in India from 1890 to 1915, with extended periods of residence in London and frequent visits to Canada. Nearly half of her books, beginning with the excellent *The Simple Adventures of a Memsahib* (1893), have India as their settings, and from 1895 to early 1897, Duncan wrote editorials and book reviews for *The Indian Daily News* [Calcutta], a newspaper edited by her husband. While in India, Duncan had a comfortable income and, according to her niece's testimony, was a person of considerable influence in government circles. She was apparently on friendly terms with a famous vicereine, Mary Curzon. Yet the evidence of her books, and of some newly discovered letters, suggests that she gradually became dissatisfied with life in the philistine world of British India, a world in which temperamentally she was a perpetual outside. E.M. Forster, who visited the Cotes's in India, described her as "difficult, and I fancy unhappy."[6] She longed to return to Canada: she wrote in a 1905 letter, "I want to come back and work at it [the 'individuality of the Canadian type'] from closer range, and soon I think this will be possible .... The Empire is a big place and interesting everywhere, but ours [Canada] is by far the best part of it."[7] Sara and Everard had sharply opposed temperaments, as well as only partly overlapping interests, and there is some reason to believe that there was tension, as well as affection, in their relationship. The marriage was childless.

The critical response to Duncan's work may have added to her discontent. Throughout the 1890s, the reviews of her books were usually very favourable. In the next decade, however, when, on the whole, she attempted more ambitious themes, some books fared better than others. Sadly, *The Imperialist* (1904), her best book, was given the most hostile reception; the critics were opposed in principle to the use of a Canadian setting to dramatize the issue of imperialism. Duncan published three substantial and interesting novels between 1906 and 1909, including *Cousin Cinderella* (1908), a penetrating study of the Canadian character as it reveals itself abroad. After 1909, for whatever reason, a disturbing decline in the quality of Duncan's output is evident. She remained in India for six more years, yet wrote no more fiction set in India. She did write four more novels before her death, but none is of any value. A determined attempt to become a playwright, during World War I and afterwards, did not yield any commercial or artistic success.

Conceivably, ill health was a factor in the declining curve of a career that began brilliantly and remained at a high level of achievement for nearly two decades. By the turn of the century, Duncan was already suffering from bronchitis (a common malady among Anglo-Indians) and had to endure a nasty encounter with tuberculosis. Her final attack of bronchitis occurred while she was in the midst of moving into the last of her many homes, in Ashtead, Surrey. She died on 22 July 1922; in the moving words of her niece, ". . . she . . . opened her wonderful blue eyes, so live and clear, as if she would impress something on my mind, and then closed them for ever."[8]

## NOTES

[1] Sara Jeannette Duncan, "How an American Girl Became a Journalist," in *Sara Jeannette Duncan: Selected Journalism*, ed. Thomas E. Tausky (Ottawa: Tecumseh, 1978), p. 6.

[2] Marian Fowler, *Redney: A Life of Sara Jeannette Duncan* (Toronto: House of Anansi, 1983), p. 304.

[3] Biographical information has been taken from the following sources: G.B.

Burgin, "A Chat with Sara Jeannette Duncan," *The Idler*, Sept. 1895, pp. 113–18; Florence Donaldson, "Mrs. Everard Cotes (Sara Jeannette Duncan)," *The Bookman*, June 1898, pp. 65–67; Duncan, "How," pp. 6–13; Fowler (see above, note 2); Rae Goodwin, "The Early Journalism of Sara Jeannette Duncan, with a Chapter of Biography," M.A. Thesis Toronto 1964; Marjory Mac-Murchy, "Mrs. Everard Cotes," *The Bookman*, May 1915, pp. 39–40; M.E.R. [Mrs. Sandford Ross], "Sara Jeannette Duncan: Personal Glimpses," *Canadian Literature*, No. 27 (Winter 1966), pp. 15–19.

4 Duncan, "How," pp. 6–7.

5 Sara Jeannette Duncan, in *The Montreal Daily Star*, 25 Jan. 1888, p. 2; rpt. "Women in Journalism," in *Sara Jeannette Duncan: Selected Journalism*, p. 49.

6 E.M. Forster, Indian Diary 1912–13, entry for 18 Nov. 1912, Forster Papers, King's College Library, Cambridge; quoted in Fowler, p. 290.

7 Sara Jeannette Duncan, letter to Archibald MacMechan, 4 May [1905], MacMechan Papers, Dalhousie Univ. Archives, quoted in Fowler, p. 270.

8 M.E.R., p. 19.

# Stephen Leacock (1869–1944)

RALPH CURRY

BORN in "exactly the middle year of Queen Victoria's reign,"[1] Stephen Butler Leacock was both a nineteenth- and a twentieth-century author.

Stephen's father, Walter Peter Leacock, tried farming at three different places before he finally gave up and turned to his natural calling — remittance man. In succession, he tried farming in Maritzburgh, South Africa, in Kansas, and in Ontario. Between the first two abortive attempts, he returned to England to study farming by "drinking beer under the tutelage of Hampshire farmers — who, of course, could drink more than he could" (*BILB*, p. 19). Here, in Swanmore, Stephen Leacock was born on 30 December 1869.

Stephen Leacock first saw Canada in the spring of 1876, when he came with the rest of his family to join his father, who was already settled on a hundred-acre farm near Sutton, Ontario. In later years, Leacock regarded the life on the farm with great dislike, but the Leacock farm was as comfortable as any other Upper Canada farm. The roomy house was big enough for all eleven children, though cutting wood for the nine stoves was a time-consuming chore. The older children attended a "little red school-house" (*BILB*, p. 64) near the farm until Agnes, Leacock's mother, decided the children were losing their Hampshire accents and installed a tutor in a classroom at the farm.

Young Stephen learned to fit into Upper Canada life. He did his work on the farm, but he swam in, and sailed on, Lake Simcoe. He played cricket at Sibbald's Point; he saw construction of the lovely little Church of Saint George the Martyr finished. He watched the lake steamers handle the commerce of the region, and he saw the railroad come to Sutton and Jackson's Point, ultimately to replace those same steamers. And when he had learned all his tutor had to teach him, he enrolled, with two brothers, in Upper Canada College, his first real connection with the formal education that would occupy him the rest of his life.

At Upper Canada College, young Leacock met a more sophisticated life than he had known before. Here was the life of the city. Here was the world of popular journalism, including the comic magazines that were to play such a role in his career. Here was algebra. Here was a school paper, *The College Times*, for which he could and did write. Stephen quickly outdistanced his brothers, who shortly left Upper Canada College; and he presently outdistanced the rest of the students, being "head boy" in 1887, the year of his graduation.

In the same year, Stephen saw his father for the last time. At the age of seventeen, he was the oldest son still at home. Walter Peter had been in and out since 1878, siring children and leaving them to the care of Agnes. In 1887 Stephen could no longer accept his father's treatment of his mother. He drove his father to the train station in Sutton, put him on the train, and, brandishing the buggy whip, told him, "If you come back, I'll kill you!" From that day, Stephen clearly had to take a responsibility for his mother that the other children did not feel.

In the autumn, he entered the University of Toronto, where he had a very successful year. With his superior training from Upper Canada College, Leacock was granted third-year status after one year at university. But the impoverished state of his mother and younger brothers and sisters weighed on him. Deciding that he had to support himself and help support his family, he applied for teacher training and was assigned to Strathroy Collegiate Institute. He taught at Uxbridge and then went to Upper Canada College as a junior master, where he could also enter university again. Teaching at the college and attending classes at the University of Toronto, he took his B.A. in 1891 in modern languages.

For the next eight years, he doggedly taught languages, and he was finally appointed senior housemaster at the age of twenty-five. Unchallenged by the job, he began to write short pieces for the comic magazines of the time and to study political economy on his own. Thorstein Veblen's *The Theory of the Leisure Class* (1899) increased his interest. And he met Beatrix Hamilton, whom he wanted to marry. He left Upper Canada College in 1899 to study for his Ph.D. in political economy at the University of Chicago.

By the time Leacock received his degree *magna cum laude* in 1903, he had moved far toward establishing his life pattern. He had married Beatrix in 1900, and he had started teaching at McGill University as a special lecturer in 1901. His career at the University of Chicago had been distinguished. His students at McGill had been impressed enough to report to the principal their admiration. And his marriage to Trix, as he usually called her, had been singularly happy. When McGill offered him a full-time position, the Leacocks made a permanent move to Montreal.

In 1908, after a world tour for the Rhodes foundation, Leacock was made head of the Department of Political Science and Economics; he helped found the University Club of Montreal, and he bought Old Brewery Bay, thirty-three acres on Lake Couchiching. Developing these enterprises took a large part of Leacock's energy and time the rest of his life.

He published a text in political science and other serious articles intended to enhance his professional reputation during the first part of his career. And while *Elements of Political Science* (1906) sold well, Leacock began to need more money to live the way he desired. He could not ignore that he had earlier started a small reputation as a humour writer, so he collected the fugitive pieces and submitted them. The publisher of his textbook turned the project down. With courage but no little trepidation, Leacock published his first book of humour himself. John Lane immediately picked it up, published an enlarged edition, and introduced Leacock to his audience with *Literary Lapses* in 1910.

In quick annual succession, Leacock turned out some of his most lasting works for that voracious audience: *Nonsense Novels* (1911), *Sunshine Sketches of a Little Town* (1912), *Behind the Beyond, and Other Contributions to Human Knowledge* (1913), and *Arcadian Adventures with the Idle Rich* (1914). But in this last year, 1914, as if to remind himself of his scholarly stance, he wrote three volumes of history.[2] The birth of his only son the next year perhaps strengthened a resolve to do "serious" writing. After *Moonbeams from the Larger Lunacy* (1915), Leacock collected some earlier popular essays into *Essays and Literary Studies* (1916). This mixed call to make the public laugh and make them listen continued through Leacock's life, but the lure of humour was stronger: in only two of the years from 1910 until his death did he not produce a humorous volume for his waiting readers.

The birth of Stephen Lushington Leacock, on 19 August 1915, was a long-delayed happiness for Stephen and Beatrix and began the most fulfilling part of Leacock's private life. They went to England on a very successful lecture tour. The book sales soared. *The Unsolved Riddle of Social Justice* (1920), perhaps his most significant serious work, was well received. World War 1 ended, and the enrolment in his department began to grow. His books during this time were generally respectable in quality, and at least one, *My Discovery of England* (1922), ranks with his best. However, it was increasingly apparent that young Stephen, because of hormonal problems, was not growing as he should, and early in 1925, Beatrix was diagnosed as suffering from advanced breast cancer. She died before the end of the year.

For the next ten years, Leacock gave himself more to McGill and his scholarly profession than to his comedic one, though he turned out his funny book in nearly every year. During this decade, he wrote most of his biographies, much of his literary criticism and economics, and a number of internal contributions for McGill University. He worked more closely with the Political Economy Club, and he pushed his graduate students harder — starting a published series for their M.A. theses. With the help of his niece Barbara Nimmo, he reestablished his life and routine.

Leacock, however, was shocked by notification of his forced retirement in 1935. He had turned more and more to McGill for the centre of his life, and the abrupt termination might have devastated him. Instead, it made him angry, and evidently the anger stirred the creative juices in him again. A study of humour, a book about a lecture tour through the West, more funny books — now mixed with a quieter, serious intent — and more serious books — now relieved by gentle humour — poured from his prolific pen. This period produced such different books as *My Remarkable Uncle and Other Sketches* (1942), *Montreal, Seaport and City* (1942), and *How To Write* (1943).

With the outbreak of World War II, Leacock frequently turned his talents to patriotic causes, supporting the war effort wherever possible. He wrote for the Victory Loan drives; he wrote to encourage the United States to join with Britain and Canada and, when they did, wrote in appreciation; he wrote of the noble cause of the Allies; and he wrote on the prospects for Canada after the war. He put his automobile up on blocks, determined to use no more gasoline until after the war.

Late in 1943, he began having trouble with hoarseness and difficulty of swallowing. The ailment seemed to respond to treatment at first but then grew steadily worse. When it became clear that he was suffering from cancer of the throat, the necessary operation was scheduled. Meanwhile, he went on with his work, though slowly. He finished a manuscript he had underway. He sorted through his papers and on 22 February 1944 wrote a memorandum, which he laid on top of a stack of odd papers:

Sorted
*All Ready*
None Needed for —
Barbara's Book.[3]

"Barbara's Book" was a reference to his agreement with his niece to gather his unpublished materials into a posthumous volume that she would edit. She would not need to look through this stack. On March 16 the operation was performed, but at the age of seventy-four, his stamina depleted, he had not the strength to recover. Twelve days later Stephen Leacock was dead.

His had been a distinguished career. He had been awarded seven honorary degrees and three medals for literary excellence. He had written sixty-one volumes in more than a half-dozen fields, more than half in humour, of course. He had produced over ninety articles of a serious and scholarly nature. He had advised prime ministers. But mostly, he had made the world laugh. As *The Christian Science Monitor* said at his passing: "It is all that a man can ask that his fellows should be unable to remember him without a smile, that laughter should be the ultimate expression of their love."[4]

## NOTES

[1] Stephen Leacock, "The Boy I Left behind Me" (Toronto: McClelland and Stewart, 1946), p. 9. Further references to this work (*BILB*) appear in the text. Unless otherwise noted, biographical information is taken from the following sources: Leacock, *BILB*; Ralph L. Curry, *Stephen Leacock: Humorist and Humanist* (Garden City, N.Y.: Doubleday, 1959); and David M. Legate, *Stephen Leacock: A Biography* (Toronto: Doubleday, 1970).

[2] Stephen Leacock, *The Dawn of Canadian History: A Chronicle of Aboriginal Canada and the Coming of the White Man, The Mariner of St. Malo: A Chronicle of the Voyages of Jacques Cartier*, and *Adventurers of the Far North: A Chronicle of the Frozen Seas*, nos. 1, 2, and 20 of the Chronicles of Canada series (Toronto: Glasgow, Brook, 1914).

[3] Holograph memorandum, Stephen Butler Leacock Archives, Leacock Memorial Home, Orillia, Ontario.

[4] "Perfect Tribute," *The Christian Science Monitor*, 30 March 1944, p. 20.

# Frederick Philip Grove (1879–1948)

## W.J. KEITH

IN OCTOBER 1971 Douglas O. Spettigue made a discovery in the British Museum Library in London that rendered out of date all that we thought we knew about the life of the Canadian novelist Frederick Philip Grove. After subsequent research, which confirmed the original revelation, he was able to announce that "Frederick Philip Grove" was in fact an *alias*: that his real name was Felix Paul Greve; that his numerous autobiographical statements were either fabrications or at best rearrangements of actual experience; and that he had made a separate literary reputation in Germany (and led a dramatic, even notorious life there) before coming to North America in the early part of this century. This new information is fascinating in itself, but it also casts light (some might say, shadow) on his Canadian writings which, we now see more clearly, are invariably concerned with the relation between fact and truth, between what seems and what is, between the mask that an individual assumes in public and his real self.

Felix Paul Greve, as I shall call him while he used the name, was born on 14 February 1879 at Radomno in what was then East Prussia and is now Poland. His parents, both German, were from Mecklenburg, his father — at that time an estate-manager — coming from traditional farming stock, while his mother (*née* Reichentrog) was descended from a family of millers. By the time Felix was two, the Greves (there was an elder daughter, who apparently died young) had moved to Hamburg where the father worked first as a tram-conductor and later as a minor clerk in the city transportation system. This was far from the early life of wealth and comfort to which Grove laid claim in his supposed autobiography *In Search of Myself* and by implication in the opening chapter of *A Search for America*, where Phil Branden is described as "the young Croesus."[1] The parents' marriage broke up while Felix was in his early teens. Graduating from a Hamburg technical school in 1896 and from a classical grammar school two years later, he enrolled in philology at Friedrich-Wilhelms University in Bonn in April 1898. Within a few weeks of his entering university, his mother died.

We know infuriatingly little about Greve's financial position from the time of his parents' separation, but it would always have been precarious. He must have got increasingly into debt as a university student since he had expensive tastes and attempted to move in literary and artistic circles that were far beyond his means. Intent upon pursuing a literary career, he aspired towards entering the neo-Romantic circle gathered around the poet Stefan George and came under the influence of *fin-de-siècle* writing in general, especially that of Oscar Wilde and, a little later, André Gide. In 1902 he published a slim volume of poems entitled *Wanderungen*, and this was soon followed by a verse-drama and articles and pamphlets of literary criticism (notably on Wilde). But his attempt to live by his pen depended for the most part on a battery of translations over the next seven years, mainly from English, French, and Spanish authors but also including the *Arabian Nights* adapted from the English version. Yet Greve's surviving correspondence makes it clear that his literary earnings fell pitifully short of his financial needs.

Moreover, Greve was involved at this time in a liaison with Elsa, the wife of August Endell, an architect whom Greve mentioned as a friend in his correspondence. After Elsa eloped with Greve in 1902, the couple travelled in Italy and Sicily, growing even deeper in debt. For some years Greve had been borrowing considerable sums of money from a wealthy university friend, Herman Kilian, apparently with the assurance that he had means that could eventually be tapped. But Kilian ultimately lost patience and discovered that Greve was in no position to repay what he had borrowed. On his return to Bonn in 1903, Greve was arrested and sentenced to a year's imprisonment for fraud.

While in prison he continued to translate at a furious pace, often using pseudonyms in an endeavour to evade enforced terms of repayment (he claims, indeed, to have translated forty volumes at this time). Immediately on his release from prison, he obtained an interview with André Gide, from whose account we derive Greve's first concerted attempt to construct a fictional autobiography. Within the next few years, moreover, he attempted to make a name for himself as a writer of naturalistic fiction, two novels subsequently being published, *Fanny Essler* (1905) and *Maurermeister Ihles Haus* (1906). Meanwhile Elsa's marriage had been annulled in 1904, while Greve was still in prison. He announced to Gide their intention to marry, though whether they legally did so is not known.

The pressure soon became unbearable. Translations continued to roll from Greve's pen, but their declining quality led to criticism, and he could hardly have paid off all his debts, much less maintained or improved his hopeless financial position. At last, Greve and Elsa agreed to a separation, at least temporarily. After gaining some quick cash by selling the same translation to two different publishers, Greve boarded a ship to Sweden in September 1909 — and disappeared. The scanty evidence available suggests that he faked a suicide with Elsa's co-operation. Little definite is known of his life in the United States, though recently discovered evidence reveals that Elsa followed him there. In December 1912, after a final separation from her, he emerges as "Fred Grove" in Manitoba.[2]

When Frederick Philip Grove published *A Search for America* in 1927, it was generally regarded as veiled autobiography. Devious as ever, Grove described it later as "to a certain extent, fiction."[3] Whether the book is based even in part on the author's personal experience remains uncertain. Many of the North American scenes contain a vividness of detail that appears genuine; on the other hand, close examination reveals it as a decidedly artful book, highly structured and full of covert allusions to literary models. From evidence of his mode of life during the years 1909–12 he is virtually non-existent. All we have are vague rumours about another marriage in the United States and the possibility that he may have had prior experience as a teacher before coming to Canada. Since he probably travelled under another *alias* in the United States, the difficulties of tracing his movements at this time are considerable. What can be said is that *A Search for America* ends with Branden embarking on a teaching career in the Canadian west, and at this point fiction and biography merge.

In a 1944 letter to Desmond Pacey, in answer to biographical queries, Grove wrote: "From then on (i.e., after 1914) the years are as it were certified."[4] He means, of course, that an account of his life in Canada is readily open to verification or challenge from external sources. Certainly *In Search of Myself* becomes more accurate (and, be it said, less interesting) when Grove comes to his Canadian years. Exaggerations and anomalous details remain, but its broad lines can be accepted. Grove's teaching career lasted from January 1913 until June 1924. He married Catherine Wiens, a fellow-teacher from a Mennonite background, in 1914, and they taught in a variety of schools, sometimes together, sometimes separately. Grove began by putting enormous energy and enthusiasm into his teaching, but his overbearing manner tended to lead to conflicts with the local school boards, and in consequence the Groves rarely spent more than one year in the same place. The impression derived from these years is that of a talented, restless man who has not yet found his proper vocation.

Grove began writing seriously in English in October 1919 and, from that time, was determined to devote his main energies to literary work. The order of composition of his novels is still in dispute, but it is clear that he wrote fast and furiously during the 1920s. Both *Over Prairie Trails* (1922) and *The Turn of the Year* (1923) are nonfiction in form, but the attraction of fiction had been latent ever since his German years (he apparently began *Settlers of the Marsh* in German some time during World War I[5]), and he finds his true medium with *Settlers of the Marsh* (1925) and *A Search for America* (1927). For a brief period at the end of the 1920s, the latter book made him a celebrity, and he embarked on a number of lecture-tours across Canada. His main address, along with other articles, was published in *It Needs to Be Said* (1929).

A combination of circumstances frustrated Grove's burgeoning ambitions. First, a daughter born in 1915 died with tragic suddenness in 1927; this was a crushing blow to the Groves, only partly redeemed by the birth of a son in 1930. Then the Wall Street crash and the economic depression of the 1930s affected sales and opportunities, and an attempt to find more congenial employment in the publishing industry failed in 1931. The same year, the Groves moved to Simcoe, Ontario, close to the shores of Lake Erie, where Grove dabbled with indifferent success in farming, and his wife provided a modest degree of financial security through teaching. Grove continued to write and publish, but his work failed to attract the attention that it deserved. In 1942 he even made a brief foray into politics, standing unsuccessfully as CCF candidate at a provincial election.[6]

In these later years, however, literary honours began to come his way. In 1934 he had been awarded the Lorne Pierce Gold Medal by the Royal Society of Canada, and he was elected Fellow of the Society in 1941. An honorary degree was conferred upon him by the University of Manitoba in 1946, and in the same year *In Search of Myself* was published and won the Governor General's Award for Nonfiction in English. (Given the fictional nature of much of the book, and the official neglect of his novels, Grove must have relished the multiple ironies in the situation.) But he was by then a sick man. He had suffered a stroke in 1944 and was an invalid thereafter. He died on 19 August 1948 and was buried in Rapid City, Manitoba, where his daughter had been laid to rest twenty-one years before.[7]

NOTES

[1] Frederick Philip Grove, *A Search for America* (Ottawa: Graphic, [1927]), p. 2.

[2] The biographical information about Felix Paul Greve is derived from Douglas O. Spettigue's *FPG: The European Years* (Ottawa: Oberon, 1973), supplemented by information on Elsa Endell in Desmond Pacey, ed., *The Letters*

of *Frederick Philip Grove* (Toronto: Univ. of Toronto Press, 1976), pp. 524, 554. For information on Greve and Elsa in the United States, see Paul Hjartarson, "Of Greve, Grove, and Other Strangers: The Autobiography of the Baroness Elsa von Freytag-Loringhoven," in *A Stranger to My Time: Essays by and about Frederick Philip Grove*, ed. Paul Hjartarson (Edmonton: NeWest, 1986), pp. 269–84.

[3] Frederick Philip Grove, *In Search of Myself* (Toronto: Macmillan, 1946), p. 181.

[4] Pacey, ed., p. 437.

[5] See Henry Makow, ed., "Letters from Eden: Grove's Creative Rebirth," *University of Toronto Quarterly*, 49 (Fall 1979), 59, 60.

[6] For a brief memoir of Grove at this time, see Bernard Webber, "Grove in Politics," *Canadian Literature*, No. 63 (Winter 1975), pp. 126–27.

[7] For biographical information on Grove's Canadian years I am indebted to Margaret R. Stobie, *Frederick Philip Grove* (New York: Twayne, 1973).

# Robert Stead (1880–1959)

## ERIC THOMPSON

ROBERT JAMES CAMPBELL STEAD was born on 4 September 1880 at Middleville, in Lanark County, Ontario.[1] He was the only son (he had four older sisters) of Richard Thomas Stead, a farmer, and of his wife, the former Mary Campbell. His parents had spent some thirty years scrabbling to make a living in the rocky soil of the district, but, in the spring of 1882, they caught the "Manitoba fever" and decided to join the westward trek. Journeying by immigrant train and horse-drawn sleigh, the family reached their destination, the rolling landscape of the Pembina Valley, and settled near the present town of Cartwright.

Growing up on the new farm, the young Stead received the usual smattering of irregular schooling available in a pioneer community; however, being good Presbyterians, his parents saw to it that his religious education was not neglected.[2] Among the earliest influences on him was the student missionary Charles W. Gordon —

later to become known by his pseudonym as the celebrated Western novelist "Ralph Connor" — who boarded with the family in the summer of 1885. Stead attended school in Cartwright for two years (1892–94) before quitting to go to work for several small businesses in the town. In 1897 he studied for a term at the Winnipeg Business College, and then, at eighteen, he decided to begin his career in journalism. Returning to Cartwright, he founded its first newspaper, *The Rock Lake Review* (later called the *Southern Manitoba Review*).

During the next decade, Stead carved out a local but respected reputation as the weekly's editor and publisher. By 1908, indeed, he was also proprietor of *The Courier* in the nearby town of Crystal City. But, by the end of 1909, attracted by opportunities in the "farther West," Stead sold his newspapers and moved with his brother-in-law to High River, Alberta, to open an automobile sales agency. Eventually, on the strength of his experience as a journalist and his growing repute as a poet, he was hired as a columnist for the local paper, *The High River Times* (founded and operated by Charles Clark, grandfather of future Conservative Prime Minister Joe Clark). After a stint as a staff member on *The Calgary Albertan*, he joined the Canadian Pacific Railway as a general publicity agent in 1913 — a rather ironic decision for him since he had not infrequently attacked the company's western development policies in his editorials and columns. Then, in 1919, he accepted an appointment as publicity director for the federal Department of Immigration and Colonization and moved permanently to Ottawa. Subsequently, in 1936, he became superintendent of publicity for the Department of National Parks and Resources, the post in which he served until his retirement in 1946.

Stead's last years were taken up for a time by his work as a lecturer in creative writing at Carleton College, as well as by his active memberships in several civic clubs and organizations. Among his important memberships over the years was the Canadian Authors Association, of which he had been president (1923–24) and for whom he worked effectively in the struggle to improve Canadian copyright legislation.[3] Named to the editorial board of the *Canadian Geographical Journal* in 1933, he wrote occasionally for that publication until 1955. Stead was twice married, first in 1901 to Nettie May Wallace, who bore him three sons and who died in

1952, and again in 1953 to Mrs. Nancy Rankin, the widow of a colleague. One of Stead's sons, Robert, himself a civil servant, remembered his father as being of serious temperament, of medium height, and of stout constitution. His favourite authors, as noted by his close friend and fellow Prairie writer Wilfrid Eggleston, included Alfred Lord Tennyson and Rudyard Kipling among poets and Sir Walter Scott and Oliver Wendell Holmes among novelists. Stead died in Ottawa on 26 June 1959.

Stead's career as a journalist and publicist was invaluable to him as a creative writer. Through his work, he gained added knowledge of farming and rural life generally; equally important, he became a sharp observer of small-town customs and attitudes. Moreover, his assignments and travels in these professions broadened his understanding of Western Canada in its larger political and economic framework.

His career as an author began early. According to Prem Varma, one of Stead's first published poems, "The Price of Wheat," appeared in *The Winnipeg Tribune* "some time between January and June of 1894."[4] Ten years later, his first published short story, "Driver Dick's Last Run: A Railway Story," appeared in *The Canadian Magazine*.[5] His first volume of verse, *The Empire Builders and Other Poems* (1908), was enthusiastically read throughout the West, and *Prairie Born and Other Poems* (1911) solidified his achievement as a spokesperson for that part of the country. (One waggish reviewer of the latter book even dubbed him the region's "poet lariat"!)[6] In 1917 he published one of his most popular collections, *Kitchener and Other Poems*.[7]

In 1914 Stead made his debut as a novelist with *The Bail Jumper*. It was followed by *The Homesteaders: A Novel of the Canadian West* (1916) and *The Cow Puncher* (1918).[8] As the 1920s began, Stead published *Dennison Grant: A Novel of To-Day* (1920), his most ambitious work in terms of ideas. The nostalgic romance *Neighbours* appeared two years later, and then came *The Smoking Flax* (1924). Interest today in the latter tale lies largely in the fact that it introduced Gander Stake as a minor character. Two years later, Gander emerged as the hero of Stead's most accomplished novel, *Grain*. Finally, *The Copper Disc* (1931) appeared as part of Doubleday-Doran's Crime Club of America series; it is of no interest, being a conventional whodunit and lacking wholly in any

of his themes as a Prairie writer. Between 1932 and 1947, Stead
wrote several drafts of a new novel about the West, "Dry Water"
(as he usually entitled it in manuscript), but he was unable to get
it published before his death. In 1983 *Dry Water: A Novel of
Western Canada* was printed in an edition prepared by Prem
Varma.

Throughout his writing career, Stead published a variety of
miscellaneous prose — short-shorts (in the parlance of the pulp
industry of the day), short stories, novelettes, sketches, publicity
pamphlets, and other nonfiction. None of this prose has literary
merit, but some of the shorter fiction, articles, and addresses he
gave on numerous occasions are enlightening about aspects of his
life, opinions, and practices as a novelist.

## NOTES

[1] The indispensable source for biographical information and for other
materials related to Stead is the Stead Papers, presented to the Public Archives
of Canada by his son, Robert A. Stead, in 1963. The thirteen volumes consist
of correspondence, diaries, manuscripts and printed copies of works, newspaper clippings, and miscellanea.

[2] In an interview with R.E. Knowles, Stead paid tribute to his mother as "the
most capable woman I ever knew" (" 'Great Canadian Novel' Not Yet Written
— Stead," *Toronto Daily Star*, 6 April 1936, p. 3).

[3] William Arthur Deacon, reporting on the Canadian Authors Association
annual meeting in 1923, saluted the qualities of the incoming president:
"Robert J.C. Stead has proven his abilities as an executive; he is staunch without
being impulsive; he knows thoroughly the problems to be solved during his
term of office; and there is every reason to look forward hopefully to his
leadership" ("Canadian Authors Association Annual Convention, 1923," *The
Canadian Bookman*, 5 [May 1923], 123). But Deacon, who as Candide
reviewed Stead's *Neighbours* (*Saturday Night*, 28 Oct. 1922, p. 10), could be
waspish in private; in a letter written about the same time to Emily Murphy,
who felt dispirited because of comparisons of her work to Stead's, Deacon
wrote: "I can understand an author committing suicide because on comparison
his or her work appeared to resemble that of Robert Stead (i.e. without
imagination or emotion — perfectly *wooden* . . . . Bob is a decent fellow but
he can't write" (quoted in Clara Thomas and John Lennox, *William Arthur
Deacon: A Canadian Literary Life* [Toronto: Univ. of Toronto Press, 1982],

p. 61). For further information about Stead's tenure as president of the association, see Lyn Harrington, *Syllables of Recorded Time: The Story of the Canadian Authors Association 1921–1981* (Toronto: Simon & Pierre, 1981), pp. 75, 88–90.

[4] Prem Varma, "Robert Stead: An Annotated Bibliography," *Essays on Canadian Writing*, No. 17 (Spring 1980), pp. 164, 177.

[5] Robert Stead, "Driver Dick's Last Run: A Railway Story," *The Canadian Magazine*, Aug. 1904, pp. 359–62.

[6] Tom Folio, rev. of *Prairie Born and Other Poems*, *Saturday Night*, 15 July 1911, p. 12.

[7] The title poem, "Kitchener," was inspired by the death by drowning of the war leader Horatio Herbert Kitchener on 5 June 1916 and was widely reprinted in Canada and throughout the British Empire. Many of Stead's works became known first in publications serviced by the Winnipeg Newspaper Union and, in the United States, by the Western Newspaper Union (which serialized his first five novels).

[8] *The Cow Puncher* was in the top ten in sales in Canada in 1918 and sold some 70,000 copies by the mid-1920s. See Mary Vipond, "Best Sellers in English Canada, 1899–1918: An Overview," *Journal of Canadian Fiction*, No. 24 (1979), pp. 106, 119.

# Ethel Wilson (1888–1980)

## BEVERLEY MITCHELL

ETHEL DAVIS WILSON, née Bryant, was the only child of the former Eliza (Lila) Davis Malkin, and Robert William Bryant, an English Wesleyan minister. She was born on 20 January 1888 in Port Elizabeth, South Africa, where her parents were missionaries. Following her mother's death two years later, she returned with her father to England, where she lived until his death in 1898. Describing this period, she wrote, "In the few years in which I remember my Father, life was luminous and merry and beloved . . . ."[1]

Orphaned by her father's death, she came to Vancouver, British Columbia, to live with her maternal grandmother, Mrs. James Malkin, in the Victorian Methodist household described in *The Innocent Traveller*.[2] While in Vancouver, she attended Miss Gordon's School (now Crofton House School for Girls) until 1902, when she returned to England to become a boarder at Trinity Hall, Southport, a Wesleyan girls' school noted for its high academic standards. During the four years she attended Trinity Hall, she specialized in English and French and wrote the junior Cambridge examinations.[3] "From this school," Constance MacKay notes, ". . . she carried with her a passionate interest in history, an admiration for Greek life and thought and a fine taste in English prose."[4] Having passed the London Matriculation,[5] she returned to Vancouver, where she attended the Vancouver Normal School. She received her second-class teacher's certificate in 1907 (Pacey, p. 13) and taught in various city schools until her marriage to Dr. Wallace Wilson, a Vancouver physician, in 1921.

As the wife of a prominent physician, Ethel Wilson's life was changed dramatically from the sheltered "Methodist ostrich egg"[6] of her childhood and youth. She once remarked, "It was not until I married that I learned it was possible to enjoy life without first passing a moral judgment on it" (MacKay, p. 67). During the forty-five years of their "long happy marriage" (Pacey, p. 13) (Dr. Wilson died in 1966), she was engaged in various social and professional activities and travelled extensively with her husband in the course of his distinguished career. The last years of her life were spent in a Vancouver nursing home, where she died on 22 December 1980 in her ninety-third year.

Her career as a writer began officially with the publication of her short story "I Just Love Dogs" in *The New Statesman and Nation* of 4 December 1937. Unofficially, it had begun some years before with stories that she made up for the benefit of the family:

> For many years Mrs. Wilson had been making up stories for her numerous young cousins; stories based on the characters of elderly members of the family. Her relatives always urged her to write down these little inventions. It was no surprise to them, therefore, when her writing met with such instant success. (MacKay, p. 101)

While these family sketches eventually became part of *The Innocent Traveller*, published in 1949, a series of newspaper clippings among her papers (now in the Special Collections Division of the University of British Columbia library) suggests that she had written a children's story before her marriage to Wallace Wilson. These clippings of episodes entitled "The Surprising Adventures of

Peter" served as the "Malkin's Best" advertisement and are initialled "E.D.B.," apparently for Ethel Davis Bryant.[7]

During the early years of her marriage, Ethel Wilson accompanied her husband as he made his evening house calls, and, as he visited his patients, she sat in the car and wrote. In the Preface to the Alcuin edition of *Hetty Dorval*, she describes the beginning of her career as a writer:

> I do not know why I had no ambition or thought of "writing," as we use that word. Or publishing. Simply, I wrote. In 1937, to my own surprise and in silent daring, I sent three short stories to *The New Statesman and Nation* in London, in the Kingsley Martin and Raymond Mortimer days. I knew of nowhere in Canada to send them. In those immediately pre-war days, *The Statesman* published an occasional story. I had truly no ambition to be published and was equally content to receive "No" (is that believable? it is true) and was stunned yet pleased when *The Statesman* took all three, and then two or three more, and still more stunned when O'Brien published the first of these in his current volume of *Best British Short Stories*.[8]

Because she felt that ". . . it was impossible in that terrible time to be trivial,"[9] she did not write any fiction during the war, although she edited and wrote the local Red Cross bulletin, *The Handbook of Red Cross*, and the bimonthly bulletin *Vancouver Calling* (MacKay, p. 67). She also had three short stories — "On Nimpish Lake," "We Have to Sit Opposite," and "The Cigar and the Poor Young Girl" — published in Canadian magazines during this time.[10] However, it was only when she resumed writing in 1947 that her reputation in Canada was established with the publication of *Hetty Dorval*.

This highly complex yet deceptively simple short novel, which earned Ethel Wilson immediate recognition as a "writer's writer,"[11] was followed in 1949 by *The Innocent Traveller* and in 1952 by *The Equations of Love*, a collection of two novellas, "Tuesday and Wednesday" and "Lilly's Story." In 1954 *Swamp Angel* was published, followed in 1956 by *Love and Salt Water*. Her last novel, "The Vat and the Brew," was not published,[12] although the short story "Fog," which is taken from it, was included in the collection *Mrs. Golightly and Other Stories* (1961). Her career as a published writer apparently ended when the short story "A Visit to the Frontier" appeared in the Autumn 1964 issue of the *Tamarack Review*. In addition to these works of fiction, she wrote a number of articles and essays, many of which have been published. Ethel Wilson's novels, novellas, and short stories were reissued in six paperbacks in 1990 by McClelland and Stewart as part of their New Canadian Library series, each with an afterword (by Alice Munro, Northrop Frye, P.K. Page, Anne Marriott, George Bowering, and David Stouck).

Although her work has not yet received all the serious critical attention that it deserves, it has not gone unrewarded. In 1955 Ethel Wilson was given the honorary degree of Doctor of Letters by the University of British Columbia, followed in 1961 by the Canada Council Medal in recognition of her contributions to Canadian literature. (She was among the first recipients of this award.) In 1964 she was awarded the Lorne Pierce Medal by the Royal Society of Canada and, in 1970, was given the Order of Canada Medal of Service.

## NOTES

[1] Ethel Wilson, "Reflections in a Pool," *Canadian Literature*, No. 22 (Autumn 1964), p. 30.

[2] In a talk entitled "Somewhere Near the Truth," which Wilson gave at the University of British Columbia in 1957, she described *The Innocent Traveller* as a "family chronicle," stating that "the persons and incidents are true, or, when I made some up (as I did), they are so truly characteristic of certain persons that they approximate to truth." (Ethel Wilson, "Somewhere Near the Truth," 9–18, p. 10. This and all other unpublished works cited are in the Ethel Wilson Papers, Special Collections Division, Main Library, Univ. of British Columbia, Vancouver.)

The "Edgeworth" family is the Edge family. "Great-Grandfather Edgeworth" was Joseph Edge, Ethel Wilson's maternal great-grandfather. The "Hastings" family is the Malkin family, for "Mrs. Hastings" was Wilson's maternal grandmother, Mrs. James Malkin. "Great-Aunt Topaz" was Miss Eliza Edge; "Aunt Rachel" was Miss Belle Malkin. "Rose" is Ethel Wilson herself (then Ethel Bryant), who came to live with her maternal grandmother, great-aunt, and aunt when she was ten. For a more detailed account of both her maternal and paternal forbears, see Wilson, "Reflections in a Pool," pp. 29–33.

[3] Dorothy Livesay, "Ethel Wilson: West Coast Novelist," *Saturday Night*, 26 July 1952, p. 20.

[4] Constance MacKay, "Vancouver's New Novelist," *Mayfair*, Nov. 1947, p. 101. Further references to this work appear in the text.

[5] Desmond Pacey, *Ethel Wilson*, Twayne's World Authors Series, No. 33 (New York: Twayne, 1967), p. 13. Further references to this work appear in the text.

[6] Ethel Wilson, "A Frail and Powerful Word" [unpublished essay], ms. 7–15.

[7] Taken from *The Province* [Vancouver] and dated 3 March 1919 to 13 June 1919. There are eighty-seven episodes.

[8] Ethel Wilson, Preface, *Hetty Dorval* (Vancouver: Alcuin Society, 1967), pp. 8–9. The Alcuin Society of Vancouver printed 375 copies with lino-block engravings by Gus Rueter as its Centennial project in 1967. Since Wilson suffered a stroke in 1966, this must be the last of her published writing.

[9] Wilson, Preface, p. 9.

[10] "On Nimpish Lake," *The Canadian Forum*, July 1942, pp. 119–20; "We Have to Sit Opposite," *Chatelaine*, May 1945, pp. 15, 46–47; "The Cigar and the Poor Young Girl," *Echoes: The Official Publication of the Imperial Order of the Daughters of the Empire*, Autumn 1945, pp. 11, 46. The first two of these stories are included in *Mrs. Golightly and Other Stories*.

[11] In a conversation with John Gray, Wilson's literary executor and retired chairman of Macmillan (Canada), in January 1975, he told me that when *Hetty Dorval* was published he received letters and calls from writers wanting to know who "Ethel Wilson" was.

[12] This is a purposely didactic novel that condemns parental irresponsibility (the "vat") because it results in juvenile delinquency (the "brew"). It is not up to Wilson's "usual standards."

# Raymond Knister (1899–1932)

## JOY KUROPATWA

JOHN RAYMOND KNISTER was born in Ruscom,[1] near Stoney Point on Lake St. Clair, in Essex County, Ontario, on 27 May 1899. His mother was a teacher, his father a farmer "extremely active in the social and political life of Ontario farmers."[2] What is probably a fictionalized account of this activity is found in Knister's still unpublished novel "Turning Loam." Reading and writing appealed to Knister from the first; he kept a record of his reading between late 1914 and mid-1924 in which over a thousand works are listed,[3] and he started writing as a teenager. There is evidence that much of his poetry was written in the early 1920s,[4] and his first published story, "The One Thing," appeared in the January 1922 issue of the American publication *The Midland*,[5] a magazine that H.L. Mencken described as "perhaps the most important magazine ever founded in America."[6]

In 1919 Knister attended the University of Toronto, until he was hospitalized for pneumonia (Waddington, p. 176). While at the university, he contributed to his college's publication *Acta Victoriana*[7] and was the student of Pelham Edgar, author of *Henry James, Man and Author* (1927).

From 1920 to 1923 he wrote while working on his father's farm near Blenheim, Ontario. It was during this time that "Mist-Green Oats," probably his best-known short story, appeared.[8] By the autumn of 1922, Knister turned his attention to novel writing; he also began reviewing books for a Windsor newspaper, *The Border Cities Star*, and "within a year earned for the *Star* the reputation of printing one of Canada's outstanding Literary Pages" (Waddington, p. 179).

In the autumn of 1923 Knister moved to Iowa City:

> Knister began his work with *The Midland* in October, 1923 as the Associate Editor. This was a special new position representing a kind of scholarship Frederick [the editor] had created for young writers of exceptional promise. Ruth Suckow had been the first appointed to the position a year before. Knister's duties ranged through almost every aspect of *Midland* work, and included reading and judging manuscripts, proofreading them and participating in editorial decisions. He was entitled to choose his own hours, perhaps two or three a day, so as to have substantial leisure for his own creative work. (Waddington, p. 179)

Knister attended courses at Iowa University and completed two still-unpublished novels, "Group Portrait" and "Turning Loam," while working on *The Midland*.[9] After his term as associate editor ended in June 1924, he went to Chicago, where he wrote during the day and drove taxi by night. Chicago would become the setting for more than one work: the short story "Hackman's Night," the published novella "Innocent Man," and the unpublished novella "Cab Driver" (which surfaced only in January 1984). In October 1924 Knister left Chicago to return to Canada; this homecoming is considered to be the background to the poem "After Exile" (Waddington, p. 181).

By 1925 his work appeared in *This Quarter*, an American expatriate magazine published in Paris, in which the work of Djuna Barnes, e.e. cummings, Ernest Hemingway, James Joyce, and Carl

Sandburg also appeared (Waddington, p. 182). In a letter from Ernest Walsh, editor of *This Quarter*, Knister was told, "Your stuff is real."[10]

Knister wrote many reviews, articles, and sketches for popular magazines and newspapers, but a 1925 letter suggests that he tolerated rather than rejoiced in bread-and-butter composition:

> You will be interested to know that I have taken on the job of turning out a story a week . . . . a series of rural character sketches — *Toronto Star Weekly*'s request . . . . Loth to have anything to do with Can. (or any other kind of) journalism, I says, How much? 2 c. per word, quoth 'e. Aweel, says I, you've brought it on yourself.[11]

In 1926 Knister moved to Toronto, where he wrote full-time. It was during his years in Toronto that he met Morley Callaghan, Dorothy Livesay, Wilson MacDonald, Charles G.D. Roberts, Mazo de la Roche, and Duncan Campbell Scott. It was also during the Toronto years that Knister became the mentor of Thomas Murtha, whose short stories were not published in book form until 1980.[12]

Knister married Myrtle Gamble in 1927, and the couple spent the summer at the "Poplars," a cottage at Hanlan's Point, Toronto Island. Here Knister completed the final draft of *White Narcissus*, his only novel to be published during his lifetime. In September 1927, Macmillan accepted the novel for publication and in October commissioned him to edit an anthology of Canadian short stories (Waddington, p. 186). *Canadian Short Stories*, dedicated to Duncan Campbell Scott, was published in 1928 and is thought to be the first anthology of its kind. Knister's Introduction to the collection is still considered a helpful discussion of the Canadian short story. In 1929 *White Narcissus* was published in Canada, England, and the United States.

In the spring of 1929 Knister and his wife moved to a farmhouse on the lake road near Port Dover, Ontario; here he wrote *My Star Predominant*, a well-researched novel based on the life of John Keats. A daughter, Imogen, was born in Port Dover in 1930. *Show Me Death*, a World War I novel, appeared in 1930 under the name of W. Redvers Dent, but was actually, to a currently unknown extent, ghost-written by Knister. Frederick Philip Grove encour-

aged Knister to submit *My Star Predominant* to the Graphic
Publishers' Canadian Novel Contest; Grove was chairman of the
committee adjudicating the award, the other committee members
being W.T. Allison, who taught English at the University of Mani-
toba, and Barker Fairley, who taught German at the University of
Toronto.[13] The novel won the $2,500 first prize in 1931, but
Graphic went bankrupt and the novel did not appear until 1934,
when it was published in Canada and England. Knister had written
*My Star Predominant* between 1929 and 1931; the dates of com-
position of other works overlap with the time of writing the novel:
"Innocent Man" was written between 1927 and 1931, while "Cab
Driver" was written between 1927 and 1930.[14] The novella,
"There Was a Mr. Cristi," became available in February 1986; the
typescript ends with the notation, "May–June, 1928, Toronto —
December, 1930, Port Dover."[15]

In 1931 and 1932 Knister lived in Quebec, first in Montreal and
then in Ste. Anne de Bellevue; it was while in Quebec that his
friendship with Leo Kennedy was established.[16] Knister's last novel,
"Soil in Smoke," was written between 1931 and 1932; it is a revised
version of his first novel, "Group Portrait."[17] Both remain unpublished. During the same period, Knister wrote a number of short
stories and the novella "Peaches, Peaches" (O'Halloran, p. 198).
He returned to Ontario in 1932 and was offered a job on the
editorial staff of Ryerson Press that would allow him time for his
own writing.

Raymond Knister drowned while swimming off Stoney Point,
Lake St. Clair, on 29 August 1932. An account of this last day has
been published.[18] He was thirty-three at the time of his death.

Knister was a writer of short stories, poems, novels, and novellas,
and a playwright, as well as being a critic and editor. Much of his
writing remains unpublished, and therefore unknown. Moreover,
during the 1970s some works were published for the first time, and
some reprinted, and with this revival of interest emerged a reevaluation of his role in Canadian letters as being that of an
interesting but minor author. An important contribution to this
reevaluation is the Knister issue of the *Journal of Canadian Fiction*
(1975), also published in book form as *Raymond Knister: Poems,
Stories and Essays*, edited and introduced by David Arnason, in
which work by and about Knister appears.

A selection of Knister's poetry, edited by Dorothy Livesay, was published as *Collected Poems of Raymond Knister* (1949). Further poems, many previously unpublished, appear in *Raymond Knister: Poems, Stories and Essays* and *Windfalls for Cider: The Poems of Raymond Knister* (1983). There is no collected edition of Knister's short stories, but a few appear in *Selected Stories of Raymond Knister* (1972), and many can be found in *Raymond Knister: Poems, Stories and Essays* and *The First Day of Spring: Stories and Other Prose* (1976). Of Knister's nine currently known works of longer prose fiction, five remain unpublished. A 1990 reprint of *White Narcissus* includes an Afterword by Morley Callaghan (in McClelland and Stewart's New Canadian Library series).

## NOTES

[1] For this and subsequent information, I am indebted to Imogen Knister Givens.

[2] Marcus Waddington, "Raymond Knister: A Biographical Note," *Journal of Canadian Fiction*, No. 14 (1975) [Raymond Knister issue], p. 175. Further references to this work appear in the text.

[3] Imogen Givens courteously provided a copy of this list.

[4] "Raymond Knister," an unpublished essay, kindly made available by Imogen Givens. It may have been written by Knister and seems to form the basis for Leo Kennedy's "Raymond Knister," *The Canadian Forum*, Sept. 1932, pp. 459–61.

[5] Anne Burke, "Raymond Knister: An Annotated Bibliography," in *The Annotated Bibliography of Canada's Major Authors*, ed. Robert Lecker and Jack David, III (Downsview, Ont.: ECW, 1981), 292.

[6] David Arnason, "Canadian Poetry: The Interregnum," *CV/II*, 1, No. 1 (Spring 1975), 31.

[7] Bonita O'Halloran, "Chronological History of Raymond Knister," *Journal of Canadian Fiction*, No. 14 (1975) [Raymond Knister issue], p. 194.

[8] O'Halloran, p. 195.

[9] Raymond Knister, letter to Elizabeth Frankfurth [copy], 11 April 1924, Raymond Knister Papers, Queen's Univ. Archives, Kingston, Ont.

[10] Ernest Walsh, letter to Raymond Knister, 23 April 1925, Raymond Knister Papers, Queen's Univ. Archives, Kingston, Ont.

[11] Raymond Knister, letter to Elizabeth Frankfurth [copy], 19 Nov. 1925, Raymond Knister Papers, Queen's Univ. Archives, Kingston, Ont.

[12] William Murtha, ed. and introd., *Short Stories of Thomas Murtha* (Ottawa: Univ. of Ottawa Press, 1980). The Introduction discusses the friendship of Murtha and Knister.

[13] Desmond Pacey, ed. and introd., *The Letters of Frederick Philip Grove* (Toronto: Univ. of Toronto Press, 1976), pp. 283–84.

[14] Joy Kuropatwa, "A Handbook to Raymond Knister's Longer Prose Fiction," Diss. Western Ontario 1985, pp. 135, 162.

[15] Raymond Knister, "There Was a Mr. Cristi," p. 129. Knister Family Papers. Imogen Knister Givens kindly provided a copy of the typescript, and permitted quotation from the work in this essay.

[16] Leo Kennedy, "A Poet's Memoirs," rev. of *Journal of Canadian Fiction*, No. 14 (1975) [Raymond Knister issue], CV/II, 2, No. 2 (May 1976), 23–24.

[17] Marcus Waddington, "Raymond Knister and the Canadian Short Story," M.A. Thesis Carleton 1977, p. 223.

[18] Imogen Givens, "Raymond Knister — Man or Myth?" *Essays on Canadian Writing*, No. 16 (Fall–Winter 1979–80), pp. 5–19.

# Martha Ostenso (1900–63)

## STANLEY S. ATHERTON

MARTHA OSTENSO (pronounced Austin-so), the eldest of three children of Sigurd Brigt and Olina (née Tungeland) Ostenso, was born 17 September 1900 on a small farm near the village of Haukeland, not far from Bergen, Norway. Haukeland was the home of her mother's parents. The Ostensos came from the township that bears their name, situated beside the hardangerfjord near the coast, where according to family tradition they had lived since the time of the Vikings. Sigurd Ostenso, as a younger son, was not in line to inherit family land, so in 1902 he indulged an adventurous nature and emigrated to North America. He spent two years in Winnipeg, where he was joined by his wife and daughter, and the family then moved to the United States.[1] Settling first in South Dakota, the family soon began a series of moves that would take them from one small town to another in the Dakotas and Minnesota over the next thirteen years while Sigurd sought work as a stationary steam engineer or as a butter maker in one of the many local dairies then flourishing in the area. In the meantime the family continued to grow with the birth of Bjarne (Barney) in 1903 and Oivind (nicknamed Spot) two years later.

In 1915 Sigurd Ostenso's restlessness drove him back to Canada. He had not prospered, and to save money the family travelled from Benson, Minnesota, to Brandon, Manitoba, in a railway boxcar. Fifteen-year-old Martha was soon enrolled at Brandon Collegiate, where attendance records show her as a diligent student from September 1915 through June 1917, when the family moved yet again. When she arrived in Brandon, Martha Ostenso was already a published writer.[2] By the age of eleven she was being paid (at the rate of eighty cents a column) for regular contributions to the Junior Page of the Minneapolis *Journal*.[3] And her only surviving notebook has an entry dated 12 January 1915 indicating that one of her poems, entitled "The Price of War," had won a prize in a contest sponsored by the *Winnipeg Telegram*.[4] The notebook also reveals that even as a schoolgirl she enjoyed casting herself in the role of creative writer: it is entitled "runaway Rhymes: A Book of Spasmodic outbursts from the cranium of ye youthfull poet Laureate of ye Goldenn Schoole Days."

In 1917 the family moved to Winnipeg, where Sigurd had taken employment as a butter maker with the Dominion Produce Company. Martha continued her education at Kelvin Technical High School, where in the winter of 1917–18 it seems likely she earned the credentials for a temporary teaching certificate. In the late summer of 1918 she took a teaching position in the Hayland School District, about a hundred and sixty kilometres northwest of Winnipeg.[5] While living in Hayland, she boarded with the family of Alexander Hay, his wife and four children (two boys and two girls), and it seems likely that she modelled some of the characters in her first novel, *Wild Geese*, on the Hays and half a dozen other families living in the area at the time, including the Sandmoens, Eggertsons, Gudmundsons, and Gislassons. She enrolled for a single course in literature at the University of Manitoba for the spring term of 1919, and began full-time studies there in September, when she took a number of traditional arts courses. Among them were "English Prose" and "English Verse," both taught by an assistant professor named Douglas Durkin, a married man sixteen years her senior who was to become her inseparable companion and the most important influence on her literary career. In the spring and summer of 1920 she worked as a reporter for the *Winnipeg Free Press*, but left in the fall to enrol for her second, and last, year of university studies.[6] In the meantime Durkin had moved to New York, leaving his wife and children in Winnipeg, and was teaching extension courses for Columbia University. In the fall of 1921 Ostenso joined him there. It was the beginning of a remarkably successful personal and professional relationship that was to last until Ostenso's death more than forty years later. Durkin had already published two novels, *The Heart of Cherry McBain* (1919) and *The Lobstick Trail: A Romance of Northern Manitoba* (1921), when he was hired by Columbia to teach an evening course in Techniques of the Novel. According to the prescription, it was designed primarily as a creative-writing course in which "exercises and class discussions will bear more particularly upon specific technical problems arising out of work submitted by students."[7] In the winter of 1921–22 Ostenso was a student in the course and may have begun work on *Wild Geese* then, submitting parts of it for assessment under its working title, "The Passionate Flight." For the next two years she earned her living as a social worker on New York's Lower East Side and continued to write in her spare time. Late in 1923 she returned to Winnipeg, where she spent most of the winter finishing the first full draft of *Wild Geese* (Buckley, p. 11).[8] In the spring of 1924 she returned to the United States for good, and later that year her first book was published, a collection of poems entitled *A Far Land*.[9] In the meantime Durkin had published *The Magpie* (1923), a powerful novel set in Winnipeg in the years just after the First World War.

It was not for poetry, however, that the name Martha Ostenso was to become well known. Within a year the manuscript of "The Passionate Flight" was revised, retitled, and submitted in a competition sponsored jointly by the publishing firm of Dodd Mead, *The Pictorial Review*, and the Famous Players Lasky Corporation to find the best first novel by an American author. There were 1389 entries, and *Wild Geese* was chosen to win the $13,500 first prize. It was a remarkable *coup*, and it launched a long and financially rewarding career for Ostenso and for Durkin, her companion and collaborator. The extent to which Durkin had a hand in the composition of *Wild Geese* is unclear, but more than three decades later both writers were willing to sign a legal document admitting him to a collaboration on the novel.[10] What is clear is that after 1925 the name Martha Ostenso became a pseudonym representing the combined and complementary efforts of the two writers. *Wild Geese* quickly became the source of a financial bonanza. The novel went into multiple print runs (twelve within the first year alone), was translated into seven languages and serialized in Norwegian in *Skandinaven*, a Chicago paper, and was turned into a film starring Belle Bennett.[11] It was followed in 1926 by *The Dark Dawn* and a year later by *The Mad Carews*, both set in rural Minnesota. In 1928 Ostenso was awarded an honorary M.A. from Wittenberg University in Springfield, Ohio, in recognition of her literary achievement.[12] The next novel, *The Young May Moon* (1929), returned to a southern Manitoba setting. Within two months a second printing of the novel was required, and before the year was out it had been translated into a number of languages, including Norwegian. By now the Ostenso name on a novel was a guarantee of commercial success, and the titles proliferated: *The Waters under the Earth* (1930), *Prologue to Love* (1931), *There's Always Another Year* (1933), *The White Reef* (1934), *The Stone Field* (1937), *The Mandrake Root* (1938), *Love Passed This Way* (1942), and *O River, Remember* (1943). In addition to the novels, Ostenso and Durkin were turning out short formula fiction for the mass magazines and earning between $750 and $1250 for each of them. Financial records, which they kept scrupulously, suggest that their annual income between 1926 and 1939 fluctuated between thirty and forty thousand dollars, even in the depths of the Depression.

By all accounts, Ostenso and Durkin lived fully up to their income. In the fall of 1925 Ostenso made the first of three visits to her old home in Norway. Between 1926 and 1930 the couple maintained a house in Beverley Hills, California, as well as a residence in New Jersey, near Closter on the Hudson River Palisades. During the 1930s they moved back and forth between Hollywood and Minnesota, where they had a succession of homes in Minneapolis as well as a comfortable cabin they had built around 1930 at Gull Lake.[13] Even during the Depression they continued to live flamboyantly, driving expensive automobiles — Reos were their favourites — and travelling widely. Their circle of friends included actors such as Douglas Fairbanks and his wife Mary Pickford, John Barrymore, and Henry Fonda, who played Caleb Gare in the 1941 Hollywood remake of *Wild Geese*.[14] There were also connections with well known writers. They knew Louis Bromfield, Theodore Dreiser, and Thomas Wolfe. Carl Sandburg inscribed copies of at least two of his books to them, and family gossip has it that Sinclair Lewis desperately wanted to marry Martha, and on one memorable occasion he came to blows with Durkin over her.[15]

By the end of the Second World War the literary career of Ostenso and Durkin was in decline. *O River, Remember* had been chosen as a Literary Guild selection in 1943, but it was to be the last of their popular successes. They were married in 1944, a year after the death of Durkin's wife, and settled down to a relatively quiet life in Minnesota. Four more books appeared in the 1940s, one of them a collaboration with Sister Elizabeth Kenny on her "autobiography." The novels — *Milk Route* (1948), *The Sunset Tree* (1949), and *And the Town Talked* (1949) — tried with little success to chart the changing lifestyles of the post-war world. At best they were unremarkable, at worst, potboilers. In 1958 a final novel appeared. Entitled *A Man Had Tall Sons*, it was a throwback to earlier Ostenso work, set in the pre-war world of rural Minnesota. But the market had changed. Novels of life in rural America were no longer fashionable, and the Ostenso name no longer had the power to generate automatic sales. Martha Ostenso herself was now in failing health: the accumulated effects of three decades of indulgent living, and a growing tendency to alcoholism, had begun to take their toll (Buckley, p. 21). Late in 1963 she and Durkin decided to move to Washington to be close to two of Durkin's sons. The journey proved too much for her, however, and she collapsed on the train. On arrival in Seattle she was taken to hospital, where she died two days later on November 24. The cause of death "was cirrhosis of the liver" (Buckley, p. 21). Durkin survived her by nearly five years.

### NOTES

[1] Joan N. Buckley, "Martha Ostenso: A Critical Study of Her Novels," Diss. Univ. of Iowa 1976, p. 2. Further references to this work appear in the text.

[2] Although she was bilingual, and remained so throughout her life, Ostenso did all her creative work in English.

[3] Grant Overton, *The Women Who Make Our Novels* (New York: Essay Index Reprint Series, 1967), p. 247.

[4] Manuscript note dated 12 Jan. 1915 beside the poem entitled "The Price of War" in Ostenso's notebook. The only fiction it contains is an eight-page section from chapter III of *Wild Geese*, showing only minor variations from the printed text. The notebook was made available to me through the kindness of Stanley C. Stanko, London, Ontario, Ostenso's literary executor.

[5] Dates of Ostenso's teaching stint in Hayland (Sept.–Dec. 1918) are confirmed by Shirley Morrish, Manitoba Department of Education, in a letter to the author, 19 March 1982. Hayland was changed to Oeland in *Wild Geese*: the two words have similar pronunciations in Norwegian and Icelandic.

[6] University enrolment information supplied by J. Brian Salt, Director of Student Records, University of Manitoba, in a telephone conversation, 20 Aug. 1984.

[7] Information supplied by Columbia University and quoted in Brita Mickleburgh, "Martha Ostenso: The Design of Her Canadian Prose Fiction," *Alive*, No. 35 (1973), p. 17.

[8] See also Lyn Tallman, "Martha Ostenso: The Interesting Beginnings of a Writer," *The Western Home Monthly*, March 1927, p. 30.

[9] Martha Ostenso, *A Far Land* (New York: Thomas Seltzer, 1924). The collection includes forty-three short poems on a wide range of subjects. "Wasteland" (pp. 26–27) and possibly one or two others are worth anthologizing; the others are generally undistinguished.

[10] The document, dated 11 Feb. 1958, has to do with copyright, and was shown to the author by Stanko. It contains the following clause: "whereas, all of the literary works of Martha Ostenso commencing with the publication of 'Wild Geese' in 1925 were the results of the combined efforts of Douglas Leader Durkin and Martha Ostenso . . . . "

[11] The film in turn spawned one of the earliest "film editions" of a novel: the Grosset and Dunlap edition (New York, 1925) as "illustrated with scenes from the photoplay." The translations were in Danish, Dutch, Finnish, German, Norwegian, Polish, and Swedish: a separate English edition was entitled *The Passionate Flight*.

[12] Confirmed by administrative staff of Wittenberg University by telephone, 6 Aug. 1984. If Ostenso had been a man, the University would have given her a doctorate. This policy was abandoned a short time later.

[13] During this period they also helped to support Ostenso's extended family,

including her parents and siblings as well as Durkin's wife and children (Buckley, p. 17; confirmed by Stanko).

[14] The film was entitled *Wild Geese Flying* and is said to have taken great liberties with the novel.

[15] Information from Stanko, who has interviewed a number of family members at length. Presumably this was before 1928, when Lewis married his second wife, Dorothy Thompson.

# Morley Callaghan (1903–90)

GARY BOIRE

MORLEY EDWARD CALLAGHAN was born in Toronto on 22 February 1903. He grew up there in an ambience of literary and political awareness; both parents were active in liberal causes, read poetry to the family, and his father, Thomas, regularly contributed satirical verse to *The Telegram* [Toronto] and *The Moon.*[1] Callaghan was educated at Withrow Public School (1909–16), Riverdale Collegiate (1916–21), and St. Michael's College, University of Toronto (1921–25). In his last year, he entered Osgoode Hall, where he stayed until 1928 when he was admitted to the Ontario Bar. Although in the late 1920s Callaghan viewed Toronto as something of a cultural wasteland, it was nonetheless the locale of his own formative experiences, the inspiration for and scene in many of his stories and novels, and the place of initial contact with international magazines and writers. Despite the prestige of Paris, which he visited in 1929, and the publishing convenience of the

United States, where he lived briefly in 1930, Toronto was the home he accepted, when in 1952 he settled permanently in the neighbourhood of Rosedale.

Callaghan's early life might be viewed as a series of vocational and ideological flirtations, which in turn moved towards an undivided and passionate devotion to writing fiction. Most significant for Callaghan amidst the usual middle-class tangle of primary and secondary education, summer jobs (selling magazines in the Ottawa Valley), athletics (baseball, boxing, and hockey), hobbies (debating), and so on, were three principal influences: his Torontonian background; his seminal experience during university as a part-time reporter for the *Toronto Daily Star*, and his early interest and study in law. This interest did not develop into a career; Callaghan never practised law.

In many ways Toronto was Callaghan's own *fons et origo*. Edmund Wilson's 1960 description, "Morley Callaghan of Toronto," seems now paradoxical: odd, yet singularly apropos.[2] On one hand, Callaghan was resolutely international, hostile to what he saw as misguided definitions based solely on nationality. He stated bluntly in *That Summer in Paris*, Toronto "was a very British city. I was intensely North American. . . . Physically, . . . I was wonderfully at home in my native city, and yet intellectually, spiritually, the part that had to do with my wanting to be a writer was utterly, but splendidly and happily, alien."[3] And yet as a writer Callaghan chose to remain "alien" in Pound's "Tomato, Can." Prideful, at times sentimental quotations abound; in 1958 he remarked to Robert Weaver of the war years, ". . . in those ten years, God forgive me, I began to take a great interest in Canada. I mean, I say this with tears in my eyes and on my knees, but I began to think this was my country — to look at it for whatever it is — and God help me it's my country — and I began to take a great interest in it" (Weaver, p. 20). Such an ambivalence characterized Callaghan's entire career. He was at once a world writer, a compeer of Tolstoy, Flaubert, or Anderson; but he was also a Canadian writer whose life and work must also be considered in specifically *Canadian* contexts.

The importance of Callaghan's early avocations, journalism and the law, cannot be overemphasized. Both exerted artistic influence: stylistically the lean prose belied the journalism which in turn partly motivated his well-known assertion, "I'd be damned if the glory of literature was in the metaphor. . . . Tell the truth cleanly" (*TSP*, p. 20). Thematically the novels returned repeatedly to the question of real justice, natural versus legalistic, personal versus institutional. Equally important, moreover, is the fact that both interests provided the young Callaghan with a liberal dose of experience, the chance to use his Canadian training to develop international contacts, and the opportunity to explore those necessary intellectual flirtations preparatory to a writing career.

Concerning his experience as a part-time reporter for *The Toronto Daily Star*, Callaghan remarked, "[I was] vaguely aware that I might be coming to a turning point in my life" (*TSP*, p. 17). While on staff at *The Toronto Daily Star*, for example, Callaghan not only honed his distinctive reportorial style, but faced the grim task of distilling human experience (much of it painful) into a verbal form for public perusal. He began writing his first stories around 1923, and in 1924 met the first of his important literary contacts, Ernest Hemingway, who showed Callaghan's stories to both writers and publishers in Paris. During his Osgoode years, Callaghan continued to write (he began "An Autumn Penitent" in 1925 while articling under Joe Sedgewick), and in 1925 published his first story, "A Girl with Ambition," in *This Quarter*; with Art Kent in Toronto he opened the Viking Lending Library; he met Raymond Knister (one of the few Canadian writers who interested him); he began correspondence with Hemingway, Robert McAlmon, and Yvor Winters; and in both 1926 and 1928 he visited New York where he met American literati like Josephine Herbst and John Herman, Nathan Asch, William Carlos Williams, Allen Tate, and Katherine Ann Porter. In the latter year Callaghan met Max Perkins of Scribner's who accepted for publication the first of his novels, *Strange Fugitive* (1928) and commissioned a subsequent collection of stories, *A Native Argosy* (1929). Also in 1928 Callaghan appeared for the first of fourteen consecutive times in Edward J. O'Brien's *The Best Short Stories*.

Following this initial breakthrough, Callaghan established a publishing record impressive by any standard.[4] The 1930s, regarded by some critics as his most successful period, witnessed a spate of novels and stories; these include the early toyings with naturalism, *It's Never Over* (1930) and *A Broken Journey* (1932), the at-the-time risqué *No Man's Meat* (1931), privately printed by Edward W. Titus for his Black Manikin Press, the biblically titled triad, *Such Is My Beloved* (1934), *They Shall Inherit the Earth* (1935), and *More Joy in Heaven* (1937), as well as his second collection of stories, *Now That April's Here and Other Stories* (1936).

In 1939, depressed by recent events in Spain, political developments in Europe, and the certainty of world war, Callaghan entered what he has referred to as "the dark period of my life" (Weaver, p. 20). Fiction writing faltered. He wrote instead two plays, "Just Ask for George," and "Turn Again Home" (an adaptation of *They Shall Inherit the Earth*). Neither was staged until 1949 and 1950 respectively, under the titles *To Tell the Truth* and *Going Home*. Throughout the 1940s there appeared first sports and then editorial columns for E.P. Taylor's *New World Illustrated* (1940–48); there were only occasional published stories or essays.[5] In 1943 Callaghan turned to radio work with the CBC; from 1943 to 1947, he chaired the community series, *Of Things to Come* (later called *Citizen's Forum*); he then became a panel member for the quiz show, *Beat the Champs*; and in 1950 he hosted the series, *Now I Ask You*. His association with the CBC continued intermittently: through the 1950s Callaghan served as a panel member on the television series *Fighting Words*; in 1962 he narrated "A Tale of Three Cities" for *Camera Canada*. In 1963 he appeared for a literary discussion with Nathan Asch on *Quest* and in 1964 CBC Television presented a five-part serialization of *More Joy in Heaven*, directed by Ron Weyman. (This was later done over when Weyman re-made a two-hour feature film of the same novel.) The 1970s and 1980s saw Callaghan frequently on CBC Radio's *Anthology*, discussing (amongst others) such writers as Samuel Beckett and Gabriel García Marquez. In 1970 CBC Television produced four half-hour shows of Callaghan's short stories, "Very Special Shoes," "Rigmarole," "Father and Son," and "The Magic Hat." Finally, in 1971, CBC Television presented an hour-long documentary, *The Life of Morley Callaghan* — an honourable gesture repeated in 1986 on CBC's *Lifetime*.

The year 1948 saw a renaissance of sorts with the publication of two novels and the start of a third: *Luke Baldwin's Vow*, a novel for young readers based on a 1947 short story of the same name (later reprinted as "The Little Business Man" in *Morley Callaghan's Stories* [1959]); *The Varsity Story*, a fictional tale about the University of Toronto (a fund-raising gambit for the university); and *The Loved and The Lost* (1951). The subsequent three decades saw Callaghan experiment with both larger and more ambitious formats: the 1955 novella, "The Man with the Coat," was thoroughly recast in *The Many Colored Coat* (1960); and in 1961 there appeared the critically controversial *A Passion in Rome*. At wider intervals there followed the memoirs of 1929, *That Summer in Paris* (1963); a commentary on a book of John de Visser's Canadian photographs, *Winter* (1974); the amusing *roman à clef, A Fine and Private Place* (1975); a revised version of *Going Home, Season of the Witch* (1976); the mystical *Close to the Sun Again* (1977); and in 1978 a reprint of *No Man's Meat*, coupled with *The Enchanted Pimp*.

This latter text seemed to be something of an irresistible topic for Callaghan; he first began the story in 1963 under the working title of "Thumbs Down on Julien Jones." In 1973 he published a reworked excerpt in *Exile* as "The Meterman, Caliban, and Then Mr. Jones," and in 1974 CBC produced a film version entitled *And Then Mr. Jones*. In 1979 Callaghan published two further revised chapters of *The Enchanted Pimp* in *Exile*, this time as part of a projected new novella called *The Stepping Stone*. The most recent instalment was Callaghan's 1985 novel, *Our Lady of the Snows* — a book described on the dust-jacket as "A new novel, suggested by the story *The Enchanted Pimp*"!

During all of this revision Callaghan had time to produce three further books: in 1983 he published *A Time for Judas* (a revisionist look at the crucifixion); in 1985 *The Lost and Found Stories of Morley Callaghan* (an anthology of stories left out of the 1959 collection); and in 1988 *A Wild Old Man on the Road* (a thinly disguised blending of Callaghan's interviews, earlier novels, and reminiscences).

Despite the ebb and flow of Callaghan's critical reputation, his achievements did not go unrewarded. As well as having been nominated for the Nobel Prize in Literature, he received many awards, both honorary and highly remunerative. These included the Governor General's Award for Fiction in English for *The Loved and the Lost* (1951); the *Maclean's* novel prize of $5,000 for "The

Man with the Coat" (1955); the "Celebrity of the Day" from Celebrities Services International, New York (1960); the Lorne Pierce Medal of the Royal Society of Canada in recognition of distinguished services to Canadian literature (1960); the City Award of Merit, City of Toronto (1962); a D.Litt. from the University of Western Ontario (1965); an LL.D. from the University of Toronto (1966); an offer of the Medal of Service of the Order of Canada, which he rejected in 1967 as a second-class honour inferior to the Companion medal earlier awarded to other writers (like Hugh MacLennan); the $15,000 Molson Prize and the $50,000 Royal Bank Award (1970); and in 1973, a D.Litt. from the University of Windsor. Late in 1982 Callaghan was awarded the full Companion Medal by a repentant Canadian government and in 1983 received the Booksellers' Award as the Author of the Year for *A Time for Judas*.

Morley Callaghan died in Toronto on 26 August 1990, at the age of eighty-seven. At his death, he was at work on at least two projects: a book involving his early nonfiction about writers and writing and a further collection of "lost and found" stories.

## NOTES

[1] Biographical information included in this essay is derived from Robert Weaver, "A Talk with Morley Callaghan," *The Tamarack Review*, No. 7 (Spring 1958), pp. 3–29. Further references to this work appear in the text. Additional biographical information is drawn from Brandon Conron, *Morley Callaghan*, Twayne's World Authors Series, No. 1 (New York: Twayne, 1966); Donald Cameron, "Morley Callaghan: There Are Gurus in the Woodwork," in his *Conversations with Canadian Novelists — 2* (Toronto: Macmillan, 1973), pp. 17–33; and David Latham, "A Callaghan Log," *Journal of Canadian Studies*, 15 (Spring 1980), 18–29.

[2] Edmund Wilson, "Morley Callaghan of Toronto," *The New Yorker*, 26 Nov. 1960, pp. 224, 226, 228, 230, 233–34, 236–37.

[3] Morley Callaghan, *That Summer in Paris: Memories of Tangled Friendships with Hemingway, Fitzgerald and Some Others* (New York: Coward-McCann, 1963), p. 22. Further references to this work (*TSP*) appear in the text.

[4] For detailed bibliographical information, see David Latham, "A Callaghan Log," *Journal of Canadian Studies*, 15 (Spring 1980), 18–29; and David Staines, "Morley Callaghan: The Writer and His Writings," in *The Callaghan*

*Symposium*, ed. David Staines, Re-Appraisals: Canadian Writers (Ottawa: Univ. of Ottawa Press, 1981), pp. 111–21. These reference works are now superseded by Judith Kendle, "Morley Callaghan: An Annotated Bibliography," in *The Annotated Bibliography of Canada's Major Authors*, ed. Robert Lecker and Jack David, v (Downsview, Ont.: ECW, 1984), 13–177.

[5] For an account of Callaghan's work for *New World Illustrated*, see Judith Kendle, "Callaghan as Columnist, 1940–48," *Canadian Literature*, No. 82 (Autumn 1979), pp. 6–20.

# Thomas H. Raddall (1903– )

## ALAN R. YOUNG

THOMAS HEAD RADDALL was born on 13 November 1903, in Hythe, England, a small town on the southeast coast and the location of the British Army School of Musketry where his father was an instructor. Ten years later, on the eve of the First World War, Raddall's father was transferred to the Canadian army and posted to Halifax, Nova Scotia. During the war, two events occurred that deeply influenced the future writer. In December 1917, while Raddall's father was away at the front in Europe, a disastrous explosion occurred in Halifax Harbour as a result of a collision involving a French munitions ship. It was the largest man-made explosion prior to the atomic bomb, and, according to the official records, it killed almost 2,000 people, injured 9,000, and blinded 199. In addition, hundreds of people simply vanished. One of the postcards issued shortly after shows "The Morgue at Chebucto Road School." This was the young Raddall's neighbourhood school where he had been when the explosion blew out the windows. Here, too, later in the day he assisted in a minor way in setting up the temporary morgue. Raddall's mother and sisters, at home at the time of the explosion, escaped serious injury, but along with hundreds of other survivors, all in a state of shock, they and Thomas were forced to flee in the snow when warning was given of a second possible explosion. In his memoirs and in other writings, most notably his short story, "Winter's Tale,"[1] Raddall was to describe in telling detail the trauma and horror of these events. The immediate effect on the fourteen-year-old boy, the only son, was an increasing restlessness: "The truth was that enforced lessons of any kind now gave me a spirit of revolt, and school had become an ordeal . . . . the difficulty of home study in our battered and poorly lit house, the lasting effect of the stunning explosion and the macabre scenes that followed all gave me a desperate longing to get away and do something new somewhere else."[2]

Eight months later a second event, the death of his father, added to an already abundant experience of tragedy and suffering. It is at this time that Raddall seems to have begun to develop his characteristic faith in self-reliance since prayer seemed merely "like shouting down a drainpipe in the dark," and God was "invisible and aloof." It would be far better, he decided, "to face things on your feet and with eyes wide open, watchful for trouble and maybe a bit of luck here and there along the way" (*IMT*, p. 44). Here, in essence, is the origin of the kind of attitude that was later to be typical of a number of the protagonists in Raddall's fiction. However simply expressed, here too is the philosophical basis for Raddall's own later life.

Recognizing the need to become self-supporting, Raddall left school and began training in September 1918 as a radio telegrapher for the merchant marine service, pretending that he was eighteen, three years more than his actual age. From the spring of 1919, he served in coastal stations and a succession of small ships, rapidly acquiring a knowledge and love of the sea and a sometimes painful education in the ways of the world. In April 1921, he worked for a year at the radio station on Sable Island, the desolate and notorious "Graveyard of the Atlantic," some 175 miles east of Halifax, an experience that later provided the background for his novel, *The Nymph and the Lamp*.

Raddall then quit radio work to take a course in bookkeeping, and in 1923 found employment with a small wood-pulp firm in Milton, on the south shore of Nova Scotia, not far from the town of Liverpool. In this area, which became his permanent home, Raddall began to develop interests in local history, the local Native people, woodlore, hunting, and, with increasing seriousness, the craft of writing. While on Sable Island, Raddall had published a short story, "The Singing Frenchman," in a Halifax newspaper,[3] and earlier at sea he had become an assiduous journal-keeper. Now in Milton, to supplement an income somewhat meagre for a newly married man, Raddall began writing stories for magazines. After an initial success with *Maclean's*, he found a regular outlet in the prestigious British *Blackwood's*, which brought his work to the notice of Rudyard Kipling, John Buchan, Kenneth Roberts, and others whose subsequent praise and encouragement led him to resign his job with the mill in 1938 to work full time at writing.[4] With the success of his first published novel, *His Majesty's Yankees*, in 1942, Raddall's vocation was finally settled.[5] During a lengthy career remembered in his memoirs, *In My Time: A Memoir* (1979), he had published some eighty or so short stories; eight historical novels (best-known among these being *His Majesty's Yankees*, *Roger Sudden*, *Pride's Fancy*, *The Governor's Lady*, and *Hangman's Beach*); three novels with modern settings (*The Nymph and the Lamp*, *Tidefall*, and *The Wings of Night*); seven histories (best-known among these being *Halifax, Warden of the North* and *The Path of Destiny: Canada from the British Conquest to Home Rule, 1763–1850*); five collections of short stories; and numerous articles, many on historical topics.

Appreciation of Raddall's talents, which first came from the United States and Britain, in Canada came slowly. To date those who have sought to delineate the main traditions of Canadian literature have provided him with minor and often almost grudging notice, but, as already suggested, recognition of a sort has been his. Three of his books earned Governor General's Awards (for Fiction, for Creative Nonfiction, and for History, all in English), the most coveted of Canadian annual literary prizes. In 1949 he was elected to the Royal Society of Canada, and in 1956 he was presented with the Lorne Pierce Medal in recognition of his achievement as both novelist and historian; four Canadian universities have also awarded him honorary degrees. In 1968 Raddall was offered the Lieutenant-Governorship of Nova Scotia, an honour he declined, and in 1971 he was made a Companion of the Order of Canada. His status as not only an eminent Nova Scotian, but also as a self-educated historian and novelist was acknowledged by the opening of the Thomas Raddall Public Library near Halifax in 1989. For one with so unpretentious a beginning in life, with so minimal a formal education, and with such considerable obstacles to face before establishing himself as a professional author, Raddall's achievements must be seen as something of a triumph.

## NOTES

[1] Thomas H. Raddall, "Winter's Tale", *Blackwood's*, Jan. 1936, pp. 1–17.

[2] Thomas H. Raddall, *In My Time: A Memoir* (Toronto: McClelland and Stewart, 1976), p. 42. Further references to this work (*IMT*) appear in the text.

[3] Thomas H. Raddall, "The Singing Frenchman," *Halifax Sunday Leader*, 11 Dec. 1921, p. 3.

[4] "Three Wise Men" appeared in *Maclean's*, 1 April 1928, pp. 6–7, 56, 58, 61. Between September 1933 and December 1937, fifteen of Raddall's stories appeared in *Blackwood's*. From a third party, Raddall had heard that his stories in *Blackwood's* had been much admired by Kipling (author's interview with Raddall, 10 Aug. 1980). Buchan, too, also got to know Raddall in this way, and his admiration was expressed in the strongest terms in the preface he wrote for *The Pied Piper of Dipper Creek and Other Tales* in 1939. Kenneth Roberts, a leading American author of historical fiction, was the person who suggested to Raddall that he write an historical novel set in Nova Scotia, expanding upon the material of "At the Tide's Turn" (Letter from Roberts to Raddall, 4 April 1941 [Raddall Papers, Dalhousie Univ. Library, Mss.2.202.S. 915–19]).

[5] Officially, Raddall's first book-length publication was *Saga of the Rover* (Halifax: Royal Print & Litho, 1931), an historical novel published in a limited edition by the paper company that then employed Raddall. He later revised the novel for adolescent readers and published it as *The Rover: The Story of a Canadian Privateer* (1958; rpt. Toronto: Macmillan, 1966).

# Hugh MacLennan (1907–90)

HELEN HOY

JOHN HUGH MACLENNAN was born on 20 March 1907 at Glace Bay, Cape Breton Island, Nova Scotia. His parents, physician Samuel MacLennan (of Highland Scottish ancestry) and Katherine MacQuarrie (Scottish, Welsh, and United Empire Loyalist in background) had one other child, a daughter Frances, four years older. The family moved to Sydney in 1914, then settled in Halifax in 1915, where MacLennan experienced the devastating explosion of 1917. He demonstrated an unusual independence by sleeping in a backyard tent, summer and frosty Maritime winter, from age twelve to twenty-one. These sleeping arrangements suggest a need to gain distance from his demanding Calvinist father, whereas the thoughtful letters of political analysis that MacLennan continued to address to his father for months after Sam MacLennan's death in 1939 reveal an opposing need for parental approval.[1]

Upon completion of a B.A. in classics at Dalhousie University

(1928), MacLennan won a Rhodes Scholarship and began an exacting course of studies in this subject at Oxford (1928–32). Vacations took him to France, Italy, Switzerland, and Germany. For his Ph.D. in classics at Princeton (1932–35), he wrote a dissertation on the decline of an early Roman colony in Egypt, later published as *Oxyrhynchus: An Economic and Social Study* (1935). During these years, MacLennan was writing poetry and working on his two unpublished novels, "So All Their Praises" (completed in 1933) and "A Man Should Rejoice" (completed in 1937).[2] To support himself, he taught history and classics at Lower Canada College in Montreal from 1935 to 1945; for the following six years, he worked as a freelance writer and broadcaster. He joined the staff of McGill University in 1951, teaching in the English Department (part-time for the first thirteen years) until his retirement as full professor in 1979. He was professor emeritus at McGill until 1985 and, then, was writer-in-residence at Concordia University.

In 1936 MacLennan married Chicago writer Dorothy Duncan, whose rheumatic heart restricted her activity, especially from 1947 on, and led to her death in 1957. Two years after Dorothy's death, MacLennan married Frances (Tota) Walker. He had no children, a biographical note of interest for a writer haunted by father-son relationships.

MacLennan's published novels include *Barometer Rising* (1941), *Two Solitudes* (1945), *The Precipice* (1948), *Each Man's Son* (1951), *The Watch That Ends the Night* (1959), *Return of the Sphinx* (1967), and *Voices in Time* (1980). Interspersed among these are collections of essays — *Cross-Country* (1949), *Thirty & Three* (1954), *Scotchman's Return and Other Essays* (1960), *The Other Side of Hugh MacLennan* (1978) — and several other nonfiction works — *Seven Rivers of Canada* (1961) and *The Colour of Canada* (1967). Some of his best work, published and unpublished, has been collected by Douglas Gibson in *Hugh MacLennan's Best* (1991).

MacLennan's correspondence suggests the range of his interests and appeal. He corresponded with Canadian politicians Paul Martin, Leslie Roberts, Lester B. Pearson, and Pierre Elliott Trudeau; with historian A.R.M. Lower; with photographer Yousuf Karsh; and with scientists Wilder Penfield and Hans Selye. Among non-Canadian writers, C.P. Snow, Budd Schulberg, Edmund Wilson, and Bernard DeVoto were significant correspondents.[3]

Acknowledgement of MacLennan's contribution to Canadian literature has taken the form of five Governor General's Awards for Fiction and for Nonfiction, in English (more than awarded to any other writer), for *Two Solitudes*, *The Precipice*, *Cross-Country*, *Thirty & Three*, and *The Watch That Ends the Night*; a score of honorary degrees; the Lorne Pierce Medal (1952); the Molson Award (1966); the Royal Bank Award (1984); and Princeton University's James Madison Medal (1987). In 1943 MacLennan received a Guggenheim Fellowship in creative writing to assist completion of *Two Solitudes* and, in 1963, while working on *Return of the Sphinx*, a Canada Council award. He was made a Fellow of the Royal Society of Canada (1952), a Fellow (1956) and later a Companion (1967) of the Royal Society of Literature in England, and a Companion of the Order of Canada (1967).

Hugh MacLennan died at his Montreal home on 7 November 1990.

## NOTES

[1] Letters to Sam MacLennan, Hugh MacLennan Papers, Special Collections Division, Univ. of Calgary Library, 14.2.42 ff.

[2] "So All Their Praises" was accepted for publication by the New York publisher Robert O. Ballou, but the firm closed before the novel was published. See Elspeth Cameron, *Hugh MacLennan: A Writer's Life* (Toronto: Univ. of Toronto Press, 1981), p. 87.

[3] See Hugh MacLennan Papers, Special Collections Division, Univ. of Calgary Library, 14.2.70, 14.3.31, 14.3.43; and Hugh MacLennan Papers, Department of Rare Books and Special Collections, McGill Univ. Library, Box 1, Part 1, Files 2, 3, 5 and Part 2, Files 5–6.

# Ernest Buckler (1908–84)

JOHN ORANGE

ERNEST REDMOND BUCKLER was born on 19 July 1908 in Dalhousie West, Nova Scotia, the third of five children and the only son of Appleton and Mary (Swift) Buckler. Buckler's ancestors settled in the Annapolis Valley in Nova Scotia and can be traced back to a 1784 muster roll of Loyalists containing the name of Ernest's great-grandfather, John. Ernest's grandfather, Joseph, established a farm in the Annapolis Valley, so the family roots are deep into the soil of that region. Ancestors on his mother's side apparently go back to such illustrious figures as Jonathan Swift.

Accounts of Buckler's early family life in the country and his boyhood education can be found throughout his writing, notably in the early chapters of *Ox Bells and Fireflies: A Memoir* and in such articles as "Last Stop before Paradise," "School and Me," and "A Little Flag for Mother."[1] He has described his childhood as uneventful, "except for those terrific events of the spirit that come from living in the country, in a family where the tea canister had to be tipped from one end to the other to sort out every last penny when it was time to go to the store."² The landscape of the region around Dalhousie West, Annapolis Royal, and Bridgetown serves as the backdrop for most of Buckler's short stories and novels. The idyllic tone of a child's harmony with this natural surrounding is intense in Buckler's work.

Buckler completed his high-school training just before he turned thirteen. He spent the next five years working both at home and, during the summer, at a rather posh lodge in Greenwich, Connecticut, in order to earn money so that he could attend university. From 1925 to 1929 Buckler studied philosophy under Dr. Herbert L. Stewart and mathematics with Professor Murray Macneill at Dalhousie University in Halifax. He developed an interest in literature during those years. Hugh MacLennan attended Dalhousie in the same years, and the most influential literary figure there at the time was Archibald MacMechan. Visitors to the university included such notables as Bliss Carman, Wilson Mac-Donald, and Charles G. D. Roberts. In his final year, Buckler published an article and six poems in the student newspaper.³

In 1930 Buckler began studies at the University of Toronto for his M.A. in philosophy. He was required to write seven long essays and four shorter ones for his degree, and those essays, now in the manuscript collection at the Thomas Fisher Rare Book Library, indicate an interest in the works of Aristotle, Spinoza, Kant, and Croce. Some possibly significant titles from these essays are "Aristotle's Theory of Conduct," "Relations of Leibnitz to Locke," "Relative Merits of the Schools of Association and Apperception," "Spinoza's Conception of Experience and Its Evolution," and "Progress of Idealism from Kant to Lötze."⁴ Buckler lived in Trinity House and recalls happy, stimulating days at university (despite initial loneliness) under the tutelage of Professor George Brett.⁵ After he graduated, he accepted a job as an actuary with the Manufacturers' Life-Insurance Company in Toronto, where he worked for the next five years. He lived alone, and usually he ate out. He never fully adapted to big city living. At Trinity House he had made the acquaintance of J.K. Thomas, then editor of *The Trinity Review*, and in 1933–34 he had two short stories published in that little journal.⁶ He also tried writing poems in these years and spent some time reading current stories, especially those of such contemporaries as Ernest Hemingway, F. Scott Fitzgerald, John Dos Passos, and Morley Callaghan.

Buckler's father died in 1932. Partly because he was needed at home, partly because of his aversion to city living, and also because his own health was chronically delicate, Buckler decided to return to the Annapolis Valley in 1936 to live on the farm with his mother, his sister Nellie, and her husband. His interest in literature continued to grow and, noticing an advertisement in *Coronet* magazine for a writing contest, he decided to try for the $100 prize. He won first prize, the article was published, and in the same year, 1937, he began to write to the "Sound and Fury" column in *Esquire* magazine, commenting mostly on the quality of the fiction that the editors were publishing. Many readers wrote the magazine praising Buckler's letters, and eventually the editor, Arnold Gingrich, invited Buckler to submit articles of his own. Gingrich rejected these articles as "stiff and terribly self-conscious,"[7] but Buckler was obviously thinking about various kinds of stories, prose styles, and structures in fiction. Buckler's columns, articles, and reviews suggest that he developed as a theorist of literature at the same time that he was trying to write poems and stories. In fact he published a review in the *New York Herald Tribune Book Review* in April 1939 — the first article for which he was paid.[8]

That same year Buckler moved (with his mother) to Centrelea, about three miles southwest of Bridgetown, in order to help out an ailing aunt and uncle. He continued to work the family's 140-acre farm until 1980, supplementing his farm income with earnings from his writing. He began publishing articles in the "Back Page" section of *Saturday Night* in 1941 and continued to write for that magazine until 1948. His short story "One Quiet Afternoon" was published in *Esquire* in April 1940, and for the next three decades he published stories in a variety of magazines, including *Maclean's* (whose fiction editor, W.O. Mitchell, was an enthusiastic supporter of Buckler's work), *Chatelaine*, *The Atlantic Advocate*, *Weekend*, and *Reader's Digest*.[9] He also sold radio plays to the CBC.[10] In 1948 he won a *Maclean's* fiction contest for his story "The Quarrel,"[11] and in 1957 and 1958 his short stories won the President's Medal from the University of Western Ontario.[12]

His first novel, *The Mountain and the Valley* (1952), was published in New York and sold 7,000 copies in hardcover. It was well received and attracted a good deal of attention. CBC Radio adapted it a number of times, and the book has since gone through a number of paperback editions.[13] The next novel, *The Cruelest Month*, was not very successful when it was published in Canada in 1963, but *Ox Bells and Fireflies: A Memoir* (1968) was an immediate success. All three novels have been reproduced in McClelland and Stewart's New Canadian Library series.

Buckler continued to publish articles and book reviews (the latter in New York and Los Angeles) throughout the 1960s, but his writing slowed down somewhat in the next decade. However, he did collaborate with the photographer Hans Weber to produce a descriptive study called *Nova Scotia: Window on the Sea* (1973), and a retrospective collection of his short stories, *The Rebellion of Young David and Other Stories*, was published in 1975. Readers were surprised in 1977 by *Whirligig*, a selection of witty articles and verse, though Buckler had been writing that sort of thing for the "Mermaid Inn" column in *The Globe and Mail* [Toronto]. *Whirligig* won the Stephen Leacock Medal for Humour in 1978. In the same year he also won the Hudson's Bay Company Award.

Buckler's quiet dedication to writing has also been honoured by a Canada Council Scholarship (1960–61) and Fellowships (1964–65, 1966–67); a Centennial Medal (1967); honorary degrees from the University of New Brunswick (1969), Dalhousie University (1971), and Acadia University (1978); and an Order of Canada award (1974). He attempted to carry on two professions at once. He wrote painstakingly slowly; consequently, his total canon is not large. He became a speaker for a community and a region, and, though he lived in relative isolation, he felt this was good for his writing. In his lifetime, he was very much aware of what the rest of the world had to offer, but he chose to stay close to his traditions and to be faithful to his regional roots. His writing is a testament to the wisdom of that decision.

In the fall of 1982, a tribute to Buckler was organized by Claude Bissell. About one hundred friends gathered at Mountain Lea Lodge, a retirement home in Bridgetown where the author had been obliged to move in 1981 because of failing health. Letters from admirers, such as Margaret Laurence and Margaret Atwood, were read, and Bissell read passages from Buckler's novels. Buckler's eyesight had deteriorated so that he could not write, but he had the company of two of his three sisters, Nellie and Olive, who lived in Bridgetown. Buckler died on Sunday, 4 March 1984, at the age of 75, and is buried in All Saints Parish Cemetery, Gibson's Lake, Nova Scotia.

NOTES

[1] Ernest Buckler, "Last Stop before Paradise", *Maclean's*, 1 June 1949, pp. 22–23, 49; "School and Me," *Maclean's*, 1 Sept. 1949, pp. 30, 44, 47–48; and "A Little Flag for Mother," *Farm Journal*, 87 (May 1963), 69–70.

[2] Ernest Buckler, quoted in "The Winners of the *Maclean's* Fiction Contest," *Maclean's*, 1 Jan. 1949, p. 3.

[3] Ernest Buckler, "Others Support Compulsory P.T.," *Dalhousie Gazette*, 10 Feb. 1928, p. 3; "The Chase," *Dalhousie Gazette*, 18 Jan. 1929, p. 2; "What Price Freedom?", *Dalhousie Gazette*, 15 Feb. 1929, p. 2; "Why?", *Dalhousie Gazette*, 22 Feb. 1929, p. 2; "Music," *Dalhousie Gazette*, 15 March 1929, p. 2; "Visions," *Dalhousie Gazette*, 15 March 1929, p. 2; and "Thought," *Dalhousie Gazette*, 22 March 1929, p. 2.

[4] Handwritten versions of these essays are part of the Ernest Buckler Manuscript Collection, Thomas Fisher Rare Book Library, University of Toronto.

[5] Ernest Buckler, "The Best Place To Be," *Graduate* [Univ. of Toronto], 4, No. 3 (1977), 32–33.

[6] Ernest Buckler, "No Second Cup," *The Trinity Review*, 46 (Dec. 1933), 74–76; and "Always Old Ending," *The Trinity Review*, 46 (June–July 1934), 246–49, and 46 (Oct. 1934), 16–21.

[7] Arnold Gingrich, *Nothing but People: The Early Days at Esquire: A Personal History* (New York: Crown, 1971), p. 253.

[8] Ernest Buckler, "Notable Spring Fiction," rev. of *They Wanted to Live*, by Cecil Roberts, *New York Herald Tribune Book Review*, 2 April 1939, p. 16. A notation on the author's copy of this review in the Ernest Buckler Manuscript Collection reads: "My first paid for article."

[9] Ernest Buckler, "One Quiet Afternoon," *Esquire*, April 1940, pp. 70, 199–201. For a complete listing of Buckler's published stories, see John Orange, "Ernest Buckler: An Annotated Bibliography," in *The Annotated Bibliography of Canada's Major Authors*, ed. Robert Lecker and Jack David, III (Downsview, Ont.: ECW, 1981), 18–21.

[10] For a listing of Buckler's plays broadcast on CBC Radio, see Orange, pp. 27–28.

[11] Ernest Buckler, "The Quarrel," *Maclean's*, 15 Jan. 1949, pp. 5–6, 26–27; rpt. in *Chatelaine*, July 1959, pp. 65–68; rpt. in *Maclean's Canada*, ed. Leslie F. Hannon (Toronto: McClelland and Stewart, 1960), pp. 146–51; rpt. in *The Rebellion of Young David and Other Stories*, ed. Robert D. Chambers (Toronto: McClelland and Stewart, 1975), pp. 41–53.

[12] Ernest Buckler, "Anything Can Happen at Christmas," *Chatelaine*, Dec. 1957, pp. 66–68; and "The Dream and the Triumph," *Chatelaine*, Nov. 1956, pp. 12, 33–36, 38, 40–44; rpt. in *The Rebellion of David and Other Stories*, pp. 67–80.

[13] For a short history of the publication of the novel, see Gregory M. Cook's Introduction in *Ernest Buckler*, ed. Gregory M. Cook, Critical Views on Canadian Writers, No. 7 (Toronto: McGraw-Hill Ryerson, 1972), pp. 4–5. For a record of dramatic adaptations of this novel for broadcast on CBC, see Orange, pp. 46–47.

# Sinclair Ross (1908–   )

## MORTON L. ROSS

IN ORDER to rescue Sinclair Ross from what one reviewer called "the prominent obscurity"[1] granted him by readers, three investigators sought him out during his years of retirement in Spain — Myrna Kostash in 1972, William French in 1974, and Lorraine McMullen in 1977. Each reported that while Ross was cooperative and friendly during the interviews, his discussions of his life and work were modest, unassuming, and finally reticent, and there seems general agreement with French's summary: "He's a reclusive bachelor, a loner who cherishes his privacy."[2] Never seeking the public eye except for his fiction, and persistently discouraged by its public reception, Ross may deserve the biographer's tact more than those writers following the model of Norman Mailer's *Advertisements for Myself* (1959).

James Sinclair Ross was born, the third child and second son, on 22 January 1908, to Peter Ross and Catherine Foster Fraser Ross

on a 160-acre homestead twelve miles from Shellbrook, Saskatchewan. Catherine Fraser, her father a university-educated clergy-
man, had been born in Edinburgh and had come to Prince Albert,
Saskatchewan, with her mother and stepfather. There she married
Peter Ross who had come west from the Owen Sound area of
Ontario. They permanently separated when Sinclair was about
seven years old, and he alone of the three children remained with
his mother, who supported them by working as a housekeeper on
various farms. He completed grade eleven at age sixteen in 1924
at Indian Head, Saskatchewan, and began his long career with the
Royal Bank of Canada, first at the Union Bank of Abbey, then in
1928 at Lancer, and in 1929 at Arcola, until transferred to Winnipeg in April of 1933. He joined the Canadian Army in 1942, was
sent overseas with the Ordnance Corps, and served with Army
Headquarters, London, until he was demobilized and returned to
Winnipeg and the Royal Bank in 1946. In April of that year, the
bank transferred him to its headquarters in Montreal where he
lived and worked until his retirement on 31 January 1968. In
March of 1968, he moved to Athens, Greece, living there for three
years, then in 1971 to Barcelona, and in 1973 to Malaga, on Spain's
Costa del Sol. Ross returned to live in Montreal in 1980.[3] Since
1986 he has lived in an extended-care ward at Shaughnessy Hospital, Vancouver.[4]

McMullen records Ross's interest in writing fiction as early as his
tenth year and an unsuccessful submission of a story for publication at age sixteen. Ross was twenty-six before his first story,
"No Other Way," was published in the English *Nash's Pall-Mall* in
October of 1934, after it had received third prize in their short-
story competition for previously unpublished writers from a
reported eight thousand entries. Over the next eighteen years, Ross
published fifteen stories, all but three of them in the *Queen's
Quarterly*. Ten of these were carefully revised to form *The Lamp
at Noon and Other Stories* in 1968, and since that date two more
stories have been published, the last in 1972. In 1982 his previously
uncollected short stories, along with a chapter from *Whir of Gold*,
were published as *The Race and Other Stories*, edited and introduced by Lorraine McMullen. Ross's first novel, *As for Me and My
House*, was published in 1941 in New York to a North American
audience deeply preoccupied with yet another world war; the

result, as French reports, was a few hundred copies sold and "exactly $270" for Ross, all in advance royalties.[5] A review of *As for Me and My House* in *The New Yorker* noted the book in four sentences, concluding that "Some good things here, but the book is very gloomy."[6] Another New York critic persisted in referring to the author as Miss Ross.[7] The public's response to *The Well* in 1958 and *Whir of Gold*, rewritten in Greece and published in 1970, was little better.

During the decade of the seventies, Ross's work was beginning to receive belated critical attention. *As for Me and My House* became a standard on Canadian literature syllabi across the country. One consequence may have been a more sympathetic reception for *Sawbones Memorial* when it appeared in 1974, but there has been nothing since. Ross is working on a new novel, about what he calls "the worst voyage of my life," travelling to Europe with 2300 troops in 1942. It remains to be seen whether he will complete this work, or destroy it as he has done with all of his work that he does not like. Seventeen years between his first and second novels, twelve between it and his third, and four years of productive retirement issuing in his fourth and shortest novel, and then silence — these long intervals may be mute testimony to Ross's repeated frustrations and disappointments, perhaps another reason for his career-long concern with the figure of the outsider or exile struggling to maintain his independence and self-respect in a particularly obdurate world. But the intervals may also testify to Ross's persistent need for expression, a need captured in *Sawbones Memorial* by Harry Hubbs's memory of his own behaviour in isolation: "I'd get a feeling sometimes that I had to tell somebody, write a letter, tell what it was really like, the prairie and the Pims and the horses with their sores, but there was nobody to write to, not a letter telling those things. So I'd get a piece of paper and just sit looking at it for a while, sort of wondering, and then not knowing what else to write I'd make a list . . . things I'd no intention of doing, couldn't do, but just writing them down sort of gave me a feeling I was still all right."[8]

## NOTES

[1] Mark Sarner, "Whore with a Heart of Golda," *Books in Canada*, Nov. 1974, p. 9.

[2] William French, "Too Good Too Soon, Ross Remains the Elusive Canadian," *The Globe and Mail* [Toronto], 27 July 1974, p. 25.

[3] Ken Mitchell, *Sinclair Ross: A Reader's Guide* (Moose Jaw: Thunder Creek Publishing Co-operative, 1981), p. iii.

[4] Liam Lacey, "The 'Cosmopolitan' Prairie Boy," *The Globe and Mail* [Toronto], 16 Feb. 1991, p. C11.

[5] French, p. 25.

[6] Rev. of *As for Me and My House*, *The New Yorker*, 22 Feb. 1941, p. 72.

[7] Rose Feld, rev. of *As for Me and My House*, *New York Herald Tribune Book Review*, 23 Feb. 1941, p. 14.

[8] Sinclair Ross, *Sawbones Memorial* (Toronto: McClelland and Stewart, 1974), p. 89.

# Sheila Watson (1909–   )

STEPHEN SCOBIE

THE MAJOR FACT about Sheila Watson's biography is that she does not have one; or, rather, that she would regard it as irrelevant. She would doubtless prefer that this section not be included. Like T.S. Eliot, the "invisible poet,"[1] she has cultivated a style of impersonality, and, though biographical elements do enter into her writing, she would hold to the principle that only the text itself is of legitimate interest to the critic.

Her life has been fascinating, not in terms of any major dramatic events, but in terms of the people she has known and the periods of Canadian intellectual history she has been a part of. But it is a story that she can only tell herself — as, indeed, all her friends have been urging her to do for years. Once, over an excellent meal of Pacific salmon cooked by her husband, Wilfred, I heard her embark on a series of personal anecdotes, until Wilfred remarked, "Now, now, Sheila, you're getting biographical." It was a joke, but the

SHEILA WATSON

caution and reticence which the joke implies have been fundamentally characteristic of Sheila Watson's attitude towards any biographical criticism of her writing.

The facts of her life may be briefly stated — and in this account I am deeply indebted to the short biography prepared by Diane Bessai and David Jackel for their tributary volume *Figures in a Ground: Canadian Essays on Modern Literature Collected in Honor of Sheila Watson* (1978). Sheila Watson was born on 24 October 1909 in New Westminster, British Columbia, where her father, Dr. Charles Edward Doherty, was Superintendant of the Provincial Mental Hospital. Her childhood on the grounds of the hospital is reflected (and, of course, changed, mythologized) in some of her short stories, notably "Antigone." Her upbringing was strictly Roman Catholic, her primary and secondary schooling being with the Sisters of Saint Anne in New Westminster, and her first two years of university being at the Convent of the Sacred Heart in Vancouver. She studied English at the University of British Columbia, graduating with Honours in 1931; in 1932 she obtained an Academic Teaching Certificate; and in 1933 she completed an M.A. with a thesis on Addison and Steele.

Over the next two years, Sheila Watson taught school in New Westminster, Langley Prairie, Duncan, Mission City, and — most significantly, from the point of view of her writing — in Dog Creek, a tiny community on the Fraser River between Ashcroft and Williams Lake. "I didn't choose," she recalled later, "it chose me. It was the only place in 1934 that said, 'Come, and teach our children.' "[2] Years later, it was to become the model for the setting of *The Double Hook*.

In 1941 Sheila Doherty married Wilfred Watson, playwright, poet, teacher and literary theorist, a marriage that has lasted to this day. "To be with Sheila and Wilfred Watson," Henry Kreisel has written, "is to be in the presence of two of the most original, the most stimulating minds in the country."[3] After the war, the Watsons lived in Toronto, Powell River, and Calgary before settling in Edmonton, where they both held positions in the Department of English at the University of Alberta.

In Toronto, Sheila Watson pursued her academic interest in the works of Wyndham Lewis, the English painter, novelist, and polemicist, under the direction of Marshall McLuhan, "who had known

Lewis while he lived in Toronto and Windsor during the war years, and was the only professor of English in Canada who had any extensive knowledge of Lewis's work at that time" ("Sheila Watson: A Biography," p. 3). Her doctoral study, "Wyndham Lewis and Expressionism," supervised by McLuhan, was completed in 1955.

During the 1950s, Sheila Watson began publishing a small number of short stories, and was also working on her novel, *The Double Hook*. According to Bessai and Jackel, the novel was completed during her residence in Calgary between 1951 and 1953, but it was not published until 1959.[4] A Swedish translation appeared in 1963 and a French one in 1976.[5]

From 1961 until 1975, Sheila Watson taught at the University of Alberta. "In the winter, on very cold days, you can see her small figure, wrapped up in a huge, yellowish fur coat of indeterminate ancestry, walking across the snow-covered campus," Henry Kreisel recalls. "She seems vulnerable, fragile almost. A strong gust of wind might blow her away. But that's an illusion. The small figure creates a space of its own, asserts itself, and yet seems an integral part of the landscape."[6] For generations of staff and students in Edmonton, Sheila Watson was indeed "an integral part of the landscape." She and Wilfred formed the unquestioned centre around which the literary life of the city revolved. Wilfred was writing prolifically — plays, poems — but even Sheila's silence commanded attention and respect. Endlessly generous in devoting time to her students, she illuminated the lives and the studies of all those privileged to work with her.

In 1971 she was instrumental in founding *White Pelican: A Quarterly Review of the Arts*, whose initial editorial board consisted of Sheila Watson, Stephen Scobie, Douglas Barbour, John Orrell, Norman Yates, and Dorothy Livesay.[7] The magazine ran for eighteen issues, four and a half years, during which time it published some of the best work in writing and graphics being done in Canada. *White Pelican* also published two books of poetry, Wilfred Watson's *The Sorrowful Canadians* and Miriam Mandel's *Lions at Her Face*, which won the Governor General's Award for Poetry in English in 1973.

In 1974 a special issue of *Open Letter* [Sheila Watson: A Collection], 3rd ser., No. 1 (Winter 1974–75) collected all of Sheila Watson's published writing outside of *The Double Hook*. Apart from two translations of stories by Madeleine Ferron in Philip Stratford's *Stories from Québec*,[8] this collection represented the total of her new publications until the appearance of the startling short story *And the four animals* in May 1980.[9] In 1984 *Five Stories* was published, re-issuing the contents of *Four Stories* (1979), along with one new story. *Figures in a Ground: Canadian Essays in Modern Literature Collected in Honor of Sheila Watson* was published by Western Producer Prairie Books in 1978. After her retirement from the University of Alberta, a special prize in Canadian literature was inaugurated in her name by the Department of English.

Sheila Watson retired from the University of Alberta, at the rank of full professor, in 1975, and Wilfred Watson retired two years later. In 1980 they left Edmonton and returned to Vancouver Island, just north of Nanaimo, on the coastline where Wilfred had spent much of his childhood. Retirement has dulled nothing of the sharpness of Sheila Watson's mind, or of the energy of her contribution and commitment to the continuing cause of contemporary Canadian literature. *Deep Hollow Creek* was published by McClelland and Stewart in 1992.

## NOTES

[1] Hugh Kenner, *The Invisible Poet: T.S. Eliot* (New York: Citadel, 1964).

[2] Sheila Watson, "What I'm Going to Do," *Open Letter* [Sheila Watson: A Collection], 3rd ser., No. 1 (Winter 1974–75), pp. 182–83.

[3] Henry Kreisel, "Sheila Watson in Edmonton," in *Figures in a Ground: Canadian Essays on Modern Literature Collected in Honor of Sheila Watson*, ed. Diane Bessai and David Jackel (Saskatoon: Western Producer Prairie Books, 1978), p. 4.

[4] "Sheila Watson: A Biography," in Bessai, ed., p. 2.

[5] *Dubbelkroken* , trans. Artur Lundkvist (Stockholm: Tidens Verlag, 1963); and *Sous l'oeil du coyote*, trans. Arlette Francière (Montréal: La Presse, 1976).

[6] Kreisel, p. 4.

[7] These names are as they appear on the masthead of the first issue: *White Pelican*, 1, No. 1 (Winter 1971).

[8] "Sugar Heart" and "Be Fruitful and Multiply," in *Stories from Québec*, ed. Philip Stratford (Toronto: Van Nostrand Reinhold, 1974), pp. 11–19.

[9] Sheila Watson, *And the four animals*, MS Editions [First Draft May 1980] (Toronto: Coach House, 1980).

# Robertson Davies (1913– )

## JOHN MILLS

ROBERTSON DAVIES was born on 28 August 1913 in Thamesville, Ontario, the son of Florence (Mackay) and William Rupert Davies, publisher of the Thamesville *Herald*, later the owner of *The Whig-Standard* [Kingston] and *The Peterborough Examiner*, and senator. Davies grew up in relatively affluent circumstances and was educated accordingly: at Upper Canada College, and later, Queen's University in Kingston — a city that he disguised as "Salterton" to form the locale of his first two novels. Davies' inability to cope with mathematics led him to be admitted to Queen's as a "special student," a course that did not lead to a degree. After three years at Queen's, Davies went on to Oxford, where he received a B.Litt. in 1938, writing, as his thesis, a study of Shakespeare's boy actors.

During his residence at Oxford, Davies was a stage manager for the Oxford University Drama Society. Later he toured the English

provinces with an acting company and then worked for a year for
the Old Vic Repertory Company, where one of his colleagues was
Tyrone Guthrie — a founder, in post-war years, of the Stratford
Festival. In 1940 he married Brenda Mathews, to whom he is still
married over fifty years later. That year he returned to Canada to
become literary editor of *Saturday Night* and, in 1942, editor of
*The Peterborough Examiner*. In 1960 he began teaching English
at the University of Toronto and in 1962 was appointed first
Master of Massey College, where he is now Professor Emeritus.

Davies started his career as an actor and producer of plays and
began writing his own plays during the 1940s. By the end of that
decade, he had established himself as a dramatist and essayist —
two collections of articles for the *The Peterborough Examiner*,
written by his alter ego, "Samuel Marchbanks," appeared during
1947–49, as well as the plays *Overlaid, Eros at Breakfast*, and
*Fortune, My Foe*. He published three novels during the 1950s
(*Tempest-Tost, Leaven of Malice*, and *A Mixture of Frailties*), three
plays (*At My Heart's Core, A Masque of Aesop*, and *A Jig for the
Gypsy*), and innumerable articles, reviews, and essays. During this
period, he found the time to serve on the board of governors of the
Stratford Festival, an experience that informs the unpromisingly
titled *Twice Have the Trumpets Sounded* and *Thrice the Brinded
Cat Hath Mew'd*, accounts of the festival for 1954 and 1955
respectively, both written in collaboration with Tyrone Guthrie.
Teaching, journalism, and academic administration kept Davies
busy for a number of years, and he did not publish another novel
until *Fifth Business* appeared in 1970. *The Manticore* and *World
of Wonders* followed within five years, and in 1981, Davies published his seventh novel, *The Rebel Angels*. This has been followed
by *What's Bred in the Bone* (1985), *The Lyre of Orpheus* (1988),
and *Murther and Walking Spirits* (1991). Davies says that *Murther*
is his last novel, but he continues to be involved in theatre,
including the dramatization of *World of Wonders*, which will be
presented next year at the Avon Theatre in Stratford. He also
continues to speak out on a variety of issues, particularly the
preservation of Canadian culture — a commitment that led him to
be one of the most vociferous opponents of the Canada-United
States free trade agreement.

Honours and awards have come early and easily to Robertson

Davies, and in many respects he seems an "establishment" figure: his family background is upper-class, his schooling very nearly impeccable, and the number of honorary degrees to his name prodigious. These include degrees from McMaster, Bishop's, and McGill universities, from the universities of Windsor, Manitoba, and Western Ontario, and many more. He was made a Fellow of the Royal Society of Canada in 1967 and a Companion of the Order of Canada in 1972. He has won the Stephen Leacock Medal for Humour for *Leaven of Malice*, and the Governor General's Award for Fiction in English for *The Manticore*. In 1988 he was awarded the Canada Council Molson Prize in the Arts. The posts and honours accorded him have placed him at the very top of his nation's cultural life, and at the same time he is admired internationally, certainly as a novelist. This is evidenced by the awards bestowed on him such as the National Arts Club of New York's Medal of Honor for Literature (1987), the Scottish Arts Council's Neil Gunn International Fellowship (1988), and by the fact that *What's Bred in the Bone* was short-listed for the Booker Prize in 1986.

Despite all these accolades, it is by no means possible to categorize Davies' work as "establishment." It is singularly "unstuffy" and colloquial; thematically it supports values that can be characterized as liberal, including a rejection of small-town narrowness, criticism of the institution of the family, and a commitment to self-evaluation and personal growth. His presence in our literature is somehow, even after we have looked closely at individual works, greater than the sum of its parts, and his influence has been a good one — on the side of the "Eros men," as a character in his *A Mixture of Frailties* puts it, as opposed to the followers of Thanatos.

# Hugh Garner (1913–79)

## PAUL STUEWE

HUGH GARNER was born in England on 22 February 1913 in the Yorkshire town of Batley, a working-class community whose residents found employment in the area's woollen mills and coal mines.[1] His parents' marriage seems to have been of the "shotgun" variety, with his father absent from the household for most of Garner's early childhood, and he was raised in the home of his maternal grandmother. In 1919 his mother followed his father to Canada with Garner and his younger brother Ronald and settled in Toronto, but the marriage continued to be one in name only and eventually broke down completely when Mrs. Garner sued her husband for nonsupport.

Garner's autobiography, *One Damn Thing after Another* (1973), the primary source of information about his life, is fairly reticent concerning his early years in Toronto, although its brief descriptions of what it was like to be poor and without close friends suggest that this must have been a trying period for him. Whatever these tribulations, however, Garner was a consistently better-than-average student who had no difficulty with most of his courses, and only the failure to pass the grammar portion of his high-school entrance examination kept him from attending a collegiate rather than a technical school.

Garner did not enjoy his three years at Danforth Tech, in Toronto's east end, where his conviction that he was not cut out for a vocational education and his after-school job as a delivery boy tended to isolate him from his fellows. He did submit sentimental poetry to the school newspaper, but otherwise distinguished himself only by some creditable performances as a long-distance runner. He left Danforth Tech on his sixteenth birthday in 1929 and immediately went to work as a copy boy on the *Toronto Daily Star*.

At the *Star* Garner learned the rudiments of daily journalism before he was fired in November of the same year. He credited the experience with teaching him how to write pointed and economical prose. After a period of odd jobs and hoboing around the North American continent, he began to try his hand at short stories and sketches, and in 1936 he had a nonfiction piece called "Toronto's Cabbagetown" accepted by *The Canadian Forum*.[2] A concurrent interest in radical and socialist politics led to military service on the Loyalist side in the Spanish civil war in 1937–38. After returning to Toronto, Garner again applied himself to writing. Except for the acceptance of another short sketch by the *Forum* in 1938,[3] he was largely unsuccessful, although some of the short stories he wrote during this period would eventually be published in the early 1950s.

When World War II began in September 1939, Garner joined the army, but he was soon discharged for alleged communist sympathies. During the brief period before he enlisted in the navy, he wrote the story "The Conversion of Willie Heaps," but from then until the end of the war, his only further brush with authorship was an abortive attempt at a novel during a short spell of shore duty in 1944. Meanwhile, he had in 1940 met, and in 1941 married, the former Alice Gallant, and was soon the father of a daughter and a son.

After being discharged from the navy in October 1945, Garner began to write the novel that would eventually be published as

*Cabbagetown* (1950) while working at various clerical and factory jobs to support his family. *Cabbagetown* was finished by 1948, and, while waiting for it to find a publisher, Garner completed another novel, *Storm Below* (1949), and wrote several of the stories that would be collected in *The Yellow Sweater* (1952). *Storm Below* was immediately accepted for publication, and Garner now felt able to embark on the professional writing career that, supplemented by occasional odd jobs, he pursued for the remainder of his life.

Although Garner's literary reputation rests upon his short stories and novels, he was also a prolific journalist whose nonfiction pieces provided the major part of his income for much of his writing life. Two "quickie" paperback novels, *Waste No Tears* (published in 1950 under the pseudonym Jarvis Warwick) and *Present Reckoning* (1951), exhibited this facility in the production of fiction, and until the early 1960s most of Garner's work was written under the pressure of deadlines and immediate economic needs. In 1956 he began to write dramatic adaptations of his stories and novels, and this soon became an important source of additional income.

Garner deliberately avoided the social life of the Toronto literary scene, although he was close to various individuals (including Morley Callaghan, Farley Mowat, Irving Layton, Robert Weaver, and Doug Fetherling) whose company he chose for personal reasons rather than professional ones. His relationships with the academic world were tenuous and often mutually suspicious, and throughout his life a penchant for heavy drinking combined with a somewhat abrasive personality made it difficult for him to function in anything resembling polite society. Although Garner sometimes complained about being ignored by "serious" writers and critics, it is clear from his autobiography that his pride in being a loner from the wrong side of the tracks was the primary reason why he did not become a member of any literary coterie.

Despite his isolation from the mainstream of literary life, Garner did receive a Canada Council grant to write *The Silence on the Shore* (1962, *Silence on the Shore* in subsequent editions), and in 1963 *Hugh Garner's Best Stories* won the Governor General's Award for Fiction in English. An anthology of humorous nonfiction pieces, *Author, Author!* (1964), was followed by the short-story collection *Men and Women* (1966), and in 1968 an uncut version of *Cabbagetown* appeared. The novel *A Nice Place to Visit* was published in 1970, and in the same year *The Sin Sniper* introduced Police Inspector Walter McDumont, also the protagonist of *Death in Don Mills* (1975) and *Murder Has Your Number* (1978). The short-story collection *Violation of the Virgins* (1971), the autobiography *One Damn Thing after Another* (1973), the trilogy of one-act plays *Three Women* (1973), the novel *The Intruders* (1976), the short-story collection *The Legs of the Lame* (1976), and the anthology *A Hugh Garner Omnibus* (1979) round out the list of his book publications. He died in 1979, at the age of sixty-six, after an eventful and productive career that is itself one of the most interesting stories in the history of Canadian literature.

## NOTES

[1] Biographical information in this section has been taken from Hugh Garner, *One Damn Thing after Another* (Toronto: McGraw-Hill Ryerson, 1973).

[2] Hugh Garner, "Toronto's Cabbagetown," *The Canadian Forum*, June 1936, pp. 13–15. This essay was reprinted in *Canadian Life and Letters 1920–70: Selections from* The Canadian Forum, ed. J.L. Granatstein and Peter Stevens (Toronto: Univ. of Toronto Press, 1972), pp. 145–48.

[3] Hugh Garner, "Christmas Eve in Cabbagetown," *The Canadian Forum*, Jan. 1938, pp. 354–55.

# W.O. Mitchell (1914– )

## DICK HARRISON

W.O. MITCHELL'S life invites comparison with his fiction to an extent uncommon among major Canadian authors. This is in part because Mitchell is a public figure, probably familiar to more Canadians on radio and television than on the page. His first widespread popularity was not as novelist but as writer of the *Jake and the Kid* radio dramas. His public readings, in the tradition of Dickens, Twain, and Leacock, are performances; he acts his way into his fiction in the eyes of his audience. The public persona he often affects — the old prairie gopher — is carefully chosen to complement his writings. Within Mitchell's fiction there are circumstances which parallel his Prairie childhood, and his theories of artistic creation further encourage the comparison. Mitchell stresses the importance to the artist of the vivid experiences of childhood, the "litmus" years that colour the imagination, and in his advice to young writers he speaks of the need to draw from the well of subconscious memory, which is replenished by the flow of personal experience.

William Ormond Mitchell was born in Weyburn, Saskatchewan, 13 March 1914, second of four sons of Ormond S. Mitchell, a druggist from Waterdown, Ontario, and Maggie MacMurray, a nurse from Clinton, Ontario. In 1921 his father died, and his grandmother MacMurray moved in with the family. The boy was strongly influenced by her and by an uncle who farmed nearby.[1] Even these basic facts are a strong temptation to a biographical reading of Mitchell's first novel and of his *Jake* stories. But though Mitchell's Prairie childhood does undoubtedly underlie his fiction in an enduring way, the rest of his early life should alert the reader to the usual dangers of making simple biographical connections. From 1927 to 1931, Mitchell was sent to school in Long Beach, California, and St. Petersburg, Florida. This adolescent period of usually turbulent growth is almost untouched in his fiction until *Ladybug, Ladybug* . . . (1988). His next three years, spent in the study of philosophy and psychology at the University of Manitoba, 1931 to 1934, have yet to appear in fictional form, though they must have been important to his intellectual development. Since he spent some time there developing a talent for acting earlier discovered in St. Petersburg, the years could be seen as preparation for Mitchell as playwright, and they included the publication of his first piece of writing, "A Panacea for Panhandlers," excerpts from a diary kept while working his way around Europe in the summer of 1932. Mitchell's next six years, 1934 to 1940, look like the stock preparation of a young man of his generation for a writing career: an assortment of jobs in Seattle and, after 1936, in Calgary, predominantly in sales (insurance, magazines, and encyclopedias), journalism, and radio. His taking a course in play writing and the short story at the University of Washington suggests that the jobs were intended to be temporary.

By the time Mitchell enrolled in the University of Alberta in 1940, he was writing but not publishing. He received a B.A. and a teaching certificate in 1943, but the importance of his Edmonton years was personal and artistic. He continued his acting; he met and, in 1942, married Merna Hirtle, who has been a mainstay of his life. He also came under the guidance of Professor F.M. Salter, a celebrated teacher of creative writing who had a strong influence on a number of Alberta writers. Salter encouraged Mitchell in the discovery of his subject and the development of his craft and theories of creation. As part of an association that was to continue after Mitchell left the university, Salter helped to arrange for the publication of three of Mitchell's short stories in 1942: "But as Yesterday" in *Queen's Quarterly* and "You Gotta Teeter" and "Elbow Room" in *Maclean's*.[2] It was with the stimulation of Salter's teaching that Mitchell began the series of *Jake and the Kid* stories and conceived his first and most popular novel, *Who Has Seen the Wind*.[3]

From 1942 until 1947, Mitchell combined his writing with teaching in a number of small Alberta communities: Castor, New Dayton, High River, and the Eden Valley Reserve west of High River (where he also acted as Indian agent). In these communities he gathered experience that would serve him in *The Alien* (1953) and *The Vanishing Point* (1973). During this period his and Merna's sons Ormond (1943) and Hugh (1946) were born, and Mitchell's writing culminated in the publication in 1947 of *Who Has Seen the Wind*.

With the success of *Who Has Seen the Wind*, Mitchell moved out into a wider world, which in Canada in 1948 meant Toronto, serving for three years as fiction editor for *Maclean's* and beginning the *Jake and the Kid* radio series. The series ran through some 320 episodes from 1950 to 1956, with twelve of the episodes adapted for television.[4]

In 1951, Mitchell returned to settle in High River, where he would make his home base for the next seventeen years. They were years of great productivity but mixed success. The continuing *Jake and the Kid* episodes were immensely popular, and the selection published in 1961 won the Stephen Leacock Medal for Humour. Dozens of other Mitchell radio dramas were produced, including *The Black Bonspiel of Wullie MacCrimmon* (1951). The musical, *Wild Rose*, was performed in Calgary for the 1967 Centennial Celebration by the semi-professional group, Mac 14, which became Theatre Calgary. Mitchell also wrote at least twenty-one television plays and programs and three screenplays as well as articles for magazines. A novel, *The Alien*, won the *Maclean's* award for fiction in 1953 and was serialized in an abridged version in *Maclean's* in 1953 and 1954, but Mitchell himself regards it as an artistic failure. Another novel, *The Kite* (1962), enjoyed little of the popular success or critical recognition accorded to *Who Has Seen the Wind*. A third novel of this period, *Roses Are Difficult Here*, was only published in 1990. All of this while Mitchell was cultivating an active home life (and various strains of orchids) in his foothills home. His and Merna's daughter, Willa, was born in 1954.

The latest phase of Mitchell's career, 1968 to the present, is characterized by a succession of university appointments, four novels, *According to Jake and the Kid: A Collection of New Stories* (1989), writing for the stage, and numerous honours and awards, including the 1990 Stephen Leacock Medal for Humour for *According to Jake and the Kid*. He has taught creative writing at the University of Alberta (1971–73) and been writer-in-residence at the University of Calgary (1968–71), Massey College (1973–74), and the University of Windsor (1979–87). The novels represent significant developments in his fiction. *The Vanishing Point* (1973), which incorporates portions of the unsuccessful *The Alien*, has earned critical acclaim, if not general popularity, to rival *Who Has Seen the Wind*. In *How I Spent My Summer Holidays* (1981), Mitchell departs from the comic form, though not the humour, of his earlier novels. In *Since Daisy Creek* (1984) and *Ladybug, Ladybug . . .* (1988), Mitchell explores his fundamental themes with older protagonists.

With the production of *The Devil's Instrument* in Peterborough in 1972, Mitchell began moving his dramatic writings to the live stage and attracting increasing recognition as a playwright. Just as many of his early radio dramas were adapted from his fiction, Mitchell's plays have usually moved from one medium to another. The five plays the author selected for *Dramatic W.O. Mitchell* (1982), *The Devil's Instrument*, *Back to Beulah*, *The Black Bonspiel of Wullie MacCrimmon*, *The Kite*, and *For Those in Peril on the Sea*, all had a previous form or precursor in radio, television, or fiction.

Official recognition of W.O. Mitchell's contribution to Canadian culture has included honorary degrees from the universities of Ottawa, Brandon, Regina, Calgary, and Windsor, and appointment as an Officer of the Order of Canada. As he approaches eighty, Mitchell remains a prolific and intensely active artist.

## NOTES

[1] My main source of data was biographical notes provided by Catherine McLay of the University of Calgary, confirmed and corrected by the author's wife, Merna Mitchell, and his son and biographer, Ormond Mitchell.

[2] The earliest acceptance, again by Salter's arrangement, was actually "Owl and the Bens," a segment of *Who Has Seen the Wind* published in *The Atlantic Monthly*, though it did not appear until 1945.

[3] A new edition of *Who Has Seen the Wind*, with illustrations by William Kurelek, was published in 1991 by McClelland and Stewart. This edition is the first since 1947 to use Mitchell's full text; all other editions since 1947 have used the American publisher's text, about 5,000 words shorter than the original.

[4] The tally of episodes varies. I take the figure 320 from Sheila Latham, "W.O. Mitchell: An Annotated Bibliography," *The Annotated Bibliography of Canada's Major Authors*, ed. Robert Lecker and Jack David, III (Downsview, Ont.: ECW, 1981), 334.

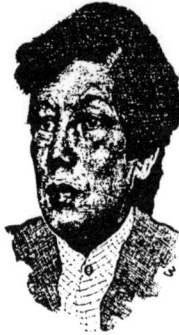

# Mavis Gallant (1922– )

JUDITH SKELTON GRANT

BORN 11 AUGUST 1922 in Montreal, Mavis Gallant lived until she was eight on Sherbrooke Street opposite McGill University in a grey stone house with a bow window.[1] This is one of the places etched in her memory. Another is Châteauguay, Quebec, where she summered from her seventh through tenth years in a white clapboard house with a gallery. Her father was British (Scots and English); her mother, Canadian (but raised in the United States) of mixed heritage — German, Breton, Rumanian. She spoke German and some French. Gallant herself learned to speak French from her French-Canadian nurse at the same time as she learned to speak English from her parents. An important result of her parents' attitudes was that she became "European-minded"[2] and ended up with "no national or religious prejudice whatever."[3]

Two aspects of Gallant's childhood made her an observer, a person acutely aware of differences, a quick study in new situations. One was her father's occupation. Stewart Young was a painter (and remittance man) "at a time in Canada when if you said your father painted, people would say, 'Yes, but what does he *do*?' "[4] The other was her schooling. By the time she completed high school, she had attended seventeen different schools in Quebec, Ontario, Connecticut, New York State, and one other state. Of the French schools, where she "was the only English Canadian and the only Protestant," and where she "suffered enormously" though not "in a tragic way" (Markle), the Pensionnat Saint-Louis-de-Gonzague, a convent boarding school of "an extremely severe Jansenist kind,"[5] which she entered at the age of four, looms large in her memory. Her father disappeared from her life when she was about nine (he died at the age of thirty-two or thirty-three, possibly a suicide[6]). After her mother (who was a musician, though not professionally) remarried and moved to Toronto and then to New York, Gallant viewed school as a place where she was dumped.[7] Not surprisingly, she was unhappy there. Yet these recurrent plunges into new school situations "did something positive for me — there's no milieu I don't feel comfortable in, that I don't immediately understand" (Hancock, p. 23).

In 1941, disliking her stepfather and unwilling to depend on him financially any longer, Gallant returned on her own to Montreal. She worked briefly as a woman's social secretary, then helped in the woman's real-estate business, before taking the job with Canadian National Railways described in "Between Zero and One" (first published in 1975 and reprinted in *Home Truths: Selected Canadian Stories*). Next she worked for the National Film Board in Ottawa in the negative-cutting room before becoming a staff writer for *The Standard* [Montreal] from 1944 to 1950. From 1943 through 1946, she was married to John Gallant, a Winnipeg musician. The marriage, which ended in divorce, was briefer than the dates suggest since her husband was in the armed forces overseas for much of the time.

The matter of vocation was settled early. Gallant says that she always wanted to be a writer (Hancock, p. 21). She recalls dictating well-known carols and nursery rhymes as a little girl of four to her father, who would write them out for her. Then for years she would build a city called Marigold using books and furniture and peopling it with figures cut from newspapers. She would push them around quickly with her finger, making them perform, as she spoke all the dialogue for their long adventures to the background music of opera records. By the time she was twelve or thirteen, she was writing. She tried little stories but didn't get far with them. What did flow easily was poetry, but eventually "la poésie m'a quittée."[8] Then, from eighteen or nineteen until she was twenty-five, she wrote little scraps of plays, learning to work with dialogue. At the same time, she began to write short stories.

Getting her work published proved surprisingly easy. Soon after she joined *The Standard* [Montreal] in 1944, she gave (after being asked) two stories to Kit Shaw, the paper's librarian. F.R. Scott (a friend of Shaw's) promptly published them in *Preview*. The fiction editor of *The Standard* asked for a story, liked what she gave him, and published it in December of 1946. He sent it to CBC Radio; it was read on the air. Though Gallant found such ready publication reassuring, she didn't pursue these avenues because they were not what she wanted — to succeed as a writer in the larger English-speaking world.

In 1950 she was ready to leave her job at *The Standard*. She was disillusioned by her discovery that she was not paid as much as men in comparable positions and by the fact that, though she had helped to establish a press club, the men promptly voted to exclude women from it.[9] She'd had her brush with commercial reality: she was taken off film criticism because a chain of art theatres objected to her impact on theatre-goers, and her radio column was taken from her because advertisers did not like her views. Her job had come full circle: assignments she'd done when she first joined the paper had begun to recur. She felt that she must make her move before her thirtieth birthday, and before contributing to the paper's new compulsory pension plan psychologically inhibited her from leaving.

Montreal was also becoming less attractive. It was the place where her ex-husband lived and where she suffered the stigma of divorce. She liked neither the current political climate in North America nor the increasing materialism. There was a strong pull outward too. She was yearning to travel, to get to Europe, to try her wings now that her writing had matured, and was afraid that travel might be restricted because of the Korean War. She preferred to go abroad to write, take a cut in living standards, than to live in Montreal on a good salary.

She gave notice in 1950. Challenged by a fellow reporter (envious of her willingness to make a leap of faith or perhaps just concerned that she might not be able to sell her stories), she typed up one of her manuscripts and sent it to the The New Yorker. The New Yorker found the story too Canadian, asked for a second story, and accepted it. Thus began a long, fruitful relationship. The New Yorker has been the first publisher of most of Gallant's stories, having published more than one hundred of them by 1990, and has had a first reading contract with her at least since 1964.[10] Gallant has published with the magazine longer than any of their other current writers of fiction.[11]

Reassured by The New Yorker's reaction to her work, Gallant set off for Europe and has lived there ever since. Between 1950 and 1954, she spent time in London, Paris, Salzburg, Italy, Spain, Yugoslavia, Alsace, and Sicily. She was not a tourist merely passing through; she lived in those places, taking a flat, doing her own cooking, meeting people. In 1954 she leased a gardener's cottage in Menton-Garavan near the French-Italian border. Here she found the colonies of foreigners (mostly English) left over from before the war who became the subject of many of her stories. Then in 1960 she took a Paris flat in the sixth arrondissement as her permanent base. She kept her cottage for a time and subsequently, from the early 1960s until the mid-1970s, leased a villa in the south of France instead. She frequently travelled to Germany during the 1960s. She has also returned to Canada on more than a dozen occasions in the last forty years, including a year as writer-in-residence at the University of Toronto during 1983–84. She has said that she never writes about a place she has not visited.[12]

Only a little can be said about her friendships, which include both francophone and anglophone Canadians. Mordecai Richler is among the latter, as was the late Morley Callaghan. Most of her Paris friends are French-speaking, though they come from many different countries. In spite of Geoff Hancock's statement to the contrary,[13] Roland Barthes and Simone de Beauvoir were not among them. That many of her friends are painters is a legacy from her father, for she feels "completely at home as soon as I walk into someone's studio" (Markle). Joe Plaskett is one such friend in Paris.

Some of the people who matter deeply to Gallant have had books or a story dedicated to them. Her first collection, The Other Paris:

*Stories* (1956), names Elaine Hennessy, a close English friend who is no longer living. Her first novel, *Green Water, Green Sky* (1959), is dedicated to Diarmuid Russell, her agent in New York for a time, now dead. She singles out William Maxwell, a good friend and her first editor at *The New Yorker*, in *My Heart Is Broken: Eight Stories and a Short Novel* (1964). Doyle Klein, the dedicatee of her second novel, *A Fairly Good Time* (1970), and a writer at *The Standard* [Montreal] during Gallant's time there, stood as an older sister to her. Neither *The Pegnitz Junction: A Novella and Five Short Stories* (1973) nor *The End of the World and Other Stories* has a dedication, but *From the Fifteenth District: A Novella and Eight Short Stories* (1979) names "H.T.," a Paris friend who appears in Gallant's two-part essay "The Events in May: A Paris Notebook" (first published in 1968 and reprinted in *The Pegnitz Junction*). *Home Truths: Selected Canadian Stories* (1981) cites Nellie McMillan, Gallant's "oldest and closest and dearest Canadian friend"[14] who died of cancer in 1983. The story "With a Capital T" (first published in 1978 and reprinted in *Home Truths*) is "For Madeleine and Jean-Paul Lemieux," Québécois friends she mentions several times in interviews. Gallant wanted her play *What Is to Be Done?* (1983) to be dedicated to the British critic and documentary film producer Edgar Anstey, but didn't make her wish known in time. *Overhead in a Balloon: Stories of Paris* (1985) is for "G. de D.M.," and *Paris Notebooks: Essays and Reviews* (1986), for Josie Peron.

Gallant has won awards for several individual stories.[15] She is an Officer of the Order of Canada (1981), received the Governor General's Award for Fiction in English for *Home Truths* (1981), was given the 1983 Canada-Australia Literary Prize, and in 1984 was awarded two honorary degrees, a doctor of letters by York University in Toronto and a *doctorat en lettres* by l'Université Sainte-Anne in Nova Scotia. In 1989 Gallant was made an honorary member of the American Academy and Institute of Arts and Letters and a Fellow of the Royal Society of Literature. Obviously, Gallant's fear as she ventured forth in 1950 to try her luck as a writer that, like her father, she might have the vocation but not the talent, was unfounded. Her own assessment of her achievement is characteristically modest and blunt: "I never thought that I had a very large talent. I thought that I went to the limit of what I could do. I never made the mistake of thinking of myself as a Dostoevsky. I've not neglected anything, I don't think, that I could [have developed]."[16] Gallant continues to develop her craft; her latest project is a novel with the working title "Clowns and Gentlemen," to be told from the point of view of a Canadian diplomat reflecting upon his career.

## NOTES

[1] Biographical details were culled from many interviews and places where Gallant has written about her life. There were two important sources in addition to those mentioned in the notes: Joanne Philpott, "The Writing Comes First," *The Globe and Mail* [Toronto], 26 July 1984, p. L6; and Mavis Gallant, "Profile — Mavis Gallant," in *Writers and Writing* (Toronto: Ontario Educational Communications Authority, 1981), pp. 61–67.

[2] Earl Beattie, "Interview with Mavis Gallant," *Anthology*, CBC Radio, 24 May 1969.

[3] Judith Skelton Grant, personal interview with Mavis Gallant, 26 Jan. 1984.

[4] Fletcher Markle, "Interview with Mavis Gallant," *Telescope*, CBC Radio, 22 Jan. 1965. Further references to this interview appear in the text.

[5] Geoff Hancock, "An Interview with Mavis Gallant," *Canadian Fiction Magazine* [A Special Issue on Mavis Gallant], No. 28 (1978), p. 28. Further references to this work appear in the text.

[6] Marci McDonald, "Exile in Her Own Write," *Maclean's*, 19 Nov. 1979, p. 12.

[7] Howard Engel, "Interview with Mavis Gallant," *Stereo Morning*, CBC Radio, 28–29 Oct. 1981.

[8] Jean Royer, "Mavis Gallant: 'La vie n'est pas un roman,' " *Le Devoir* [Montréal], 21 mai 1983, p. 19.

[9] See Karen Lawrence, "From the Other Paris: Interview with Mavis Gallant," *Branching Out*, Feb.–March 1976, pp. 18–19.

[10] Robert Fulford, "On Mavis Gallant's Best Fiction Yet: The Memoirs of a WASP in Wartime Montreal," rev. of *My Heart Is Broken*, *Maclean's*, 5 Sept. 1964, p. 45.

[11] Anne-Marie Girard and Claude Pamela Valette, "Entretien avec Mavis Gallant," *Les Cahiers de la nouvelle: Journal of the Short Story in English*, No. 2 (Jan. 1984), p. 83.

[12] Zoe Bieler, "Visiting Writer Finds Montreal Changed in the Past Five Years," *The Montreal Star*, 30 Aug. 1955, p. 26.

[13] Geoff Hancock, "Mavis Tries Harder," *Books in Canada*, June–July 1978, pp. 5–6.

[14] Grant, personal interview with Mavis Gallant.

[15] "The Other Paris" (first published in 1953 and reprinted in *The Other Paris*) was chosen by Harvard University as the Best Short Story of 1953; "With a Capital T" (first published in 1978 and reprinted in *Home Truths*) won the *Canadian Fiction Magazine*'s Annual Contributor's Prize in 1978; and "Luc and His Father" (first published in 1982 and reprinted in *Overhead in a Balloon*) was selected as the best short story published in *The New Press Anthology: Best Canadian Short Fiction 1* (1984).

[16] Graeme Gibson, "Interview with Mavis Gallant," *Anthology*, CBC Radio, 31 Aug. 1974.

# Robert Harlow (1923–   )

## LOUIS K. MACKENDRICK

ROBERT HARLOW was born on 19 November 1923 in Prince
Rupert, British Columbia. His father had emigrated there from
Maine in 1909 when the town was the end of the track for the
Grand Trunk Pacific Railroad. His mother's family, Scottish and
Huguenot in background, had moved there from Alberta in 1914.
He was brought up in Prince George after 1926. For a long time,
he wanted to be a musician and performed in a small band from
1936 to 1941. Harlow left Prince George at nineteen to join the
RCAF and was a Bomber Command pilot in Britain from 1943 to
1945; he was discharged as Flying Officer, having been awarded
the Distinguished Flying Cross.

After his military service, Harlow attended the University of
British Columbia from 1945 to 1948, a period when he began to
write in earnest, working on stories during summer jobs. He joined
Earle Birney's creative-writing class in 1947, then in its second year;

formed a short-lived big band at the university; and became a member of Vancouver's "Authors Anonymous," a social-literary group dedicated to writing and criticism. Birney recommended Harlow to Paul Engle, director of the Writers' Workshop at the University of Iowa, and subsequently he became the first Canadian invited to participate. He received his B.A. from the University of British Columbia in 1948 and attended the Workshop from 1948 to 1951, holding a sessional lectureship in communication skills in the Department of English. Harlow studied prose with Ray B. West, Jr., and took Hanford Martin's workshop on the short story. His thesis was a novel, "But Frail Clay"; it appears as a war novella of the same title in his novel *Scann*. He was married in 1949 and was granted the M.F.A. in 1950. He taught in Iowa's rhetoric program the next academic year.

Harlow sold his first story to CBC Radio in the fall of 1948 and joined its Vancouver studio as assistant talks producer in September 1951. He rose to station manager and, from 1954 to 1964, was director of radio for the British Columbia region. In the early 1950s, Harlow attempted several novels, which he discarded. He was divorced in 1955 and remarried in 1958. He figured in the birth of CBC Radio's literary program *Anthology*. In 1962 his first novel, *Royal Murdoch*, was published by Macmillan of Canada.

In 1964 the creative-writing program at the University of British Columbia was separated from the Department of English, and in 1965 it was made a formal department. Harlow had been teaching occasionally for the university's continuing education division since 1952, and in 1964 Earle Birney asked him to fill in as a sessional lecturer when an appointee failed to appear. Harlow was asked to stay on permanently, and in 1965 he was appointed head of the new department. That year Macmillan of Canada released his next novel, *A Gift of Echoes*. He was associated with the university group that founded *Prism*, and, when this magazine was renamed *Prism International* in 1964, he served as prose editor. Harlow was an associate dean of the University of British Columbia from April 1968 to April 1969, after which he obtained a leave of absence to work on *Scann*. In 1970 he received a special Canada Council grant to work on the novel and finished the book while living in Mallorca. Sono Nis published *Scann* in 1972. He was divorced for the second time in the spring of 1975.

In 1977 Harlow retired from his position as head of the Department of Creative Writing; he remained on faculty there as a
professor, retiring in 1988 while retaining the title of professor
emeritus. His papers and manuscripts were acquired by the
National Library (Ottawa) in 1984. He has an enduring interest in
jazz. He has a large farm near White Rock, British Columbia, and
he has always wanted to breed thoroughbred racing stock, a
fascination reflected in his novel *Making Arrangements* (1978).
Other interests include theatre and opera. He is a founding member
of the Writers Union of Canada. In 1980 he married for the third
time. That year he travelled to Poland while researching a story
about World War II and then travelled on to Austria, Italy, Sardinia,
Greece, and Costa Rica, where he worked on *Felice: A Travelogue*.
*Paul Nolan* was published in 1983, followed in 1985 by *Felice*. A
novel set in 1939, *The Saxophone Winter*, was also finished in
1985, but only published in 1988.

Harlow writes early each morning, recognizing his responsive-
ness to routine. Geoff Hancock, a former student in Harlow's
writing workshop in Vancouver, has described him as

not as serious as he looks. His conversation is crowded equally
with jokes, bad puns, shaggy dog stories, literary bits and
paternal advice. He chuckles constantly, especially at his own
jokes and often looks down at his hands, whether embarrassed
or discovering another story palmed away is hard to say.[1]

Harlow resists any autobiographical identification in his fiction,
though elements of *Felice* appear to be based on his experiences
while travelling in Poland. He has described himself as a "modestly
respectable" writer and as a "good journeyman novelist."[2]

NOTES

[1] Geoff Hancock, Editorial, *Canadian Fiction Magazine* [Robert Harlow
issue], No. 19 (Autumn 1975), p. 4.
[2] Letter from Robert Harlow, Nov. 1986; and Geoff Hancock, "An Interview
with Robert Harlow," *Canadian Fiction Magazine* [Robert Harlow issue], No.
19 (Autumn 1975), p. 49.

# Norman Levine (1923– )

## LAWRENCE MATHEWS

ALBERT NORMAN LEVINE was born in Ottawa on 22 October 1923, the son of Annie (Gurevich) and Moses Mordecai Levine, Jews who had emigrated from Poland. The family was part of the small Jewish community in Ottawa's mainly French-speaking Lower Town. Moses Levine was a fruit pedlar.

Norman Levine's first language was Yiddish. He spoke no English until the age of five, when he began to attend York Street Public School. Later he studied at the High School of Commerce but left at sixteen to become an office boy at the Department of National Defence. He joined the Royal Canadian Air Force in 1942 and became a flying officer, piloting Lancaster bombers with the 49th Squadron, based in Leeming, Yorkshire.

After the war, Levine attended McGill University, taking a B.A. (first-class honours in English) in 1948 and an M.A. in 1949, with a thesis entitled "Ezra Pound and the Sense of the Past." He also edited *Forge*, the university literary magazine, and wrote poetry, some of which was collected in *Myssium*, a 1948 Ryerson Press chapbook. Under the informal supervision of Professor H.G. Files, he began the first draft of a novel, *The Angled Road*.

In June 1949 Levine returned to England, his home for the next thirty-one years. He had won a Beaver Club Fellowship to go to King's College, London, but had already decided to become a writer rather than an academic. He never started his dissertation on Hardy, Lawrence, and Eliot (to have been entitled "The Decay of Absolute Values in Modern Society"). Instead he moved to St. Ives, Cornwall, where he lived for most of his years in England, and began to write full time. He has done so ever since, except for a one-year term as head of the English Department at Barnstaple Boys' Grammar School in Barnstaple, Devon (1953–54).

Two books appeared during the early years in St. Ives. *The Tight-Rope Walker*, a slim volume of poetry, was published by Totem Press of London in 1950.[1] *The Angled Road* was published by Werner Laurie in Great Britain in the fall of 1952 and by McClelland and Stewart in Canada in the spring of 1953. Levine was also beginning to publish stories, poems, travel articles, and reviews, at first in obscure periodicals like *The Norseman*, later in more prestigious ones such as *Harper's Bazaar*, *Vogue*, and *Encounter*.

In 1952 he married Margaret Emily Payne, an Englishwoman, who was born in Blackheath, London. They had three daughters.

St. Ives was a leading centre of British painting from just after the Second World War until the mid-1960s, so it is not surprising that many of Levine's friends have been painters: Francis Bacon, Peter Lanyon, Alan Lowndes, Patrick Heron, Terry Frost, Bryan Wynter. He has never considered himself part of any literary group or movement; writers who have been his friends include Charles Causley, Philip Oakes, and Mordecai Richler.

In 1956 Levine returned to Canada for three months, making a cross-country journey that furnished the material for his next book, *Canada Made Me* (1958) — part autobiography and part obser-vations of contemporary Canadian life. Much of this work is harshly critical of his native land. Putnam was the British publisher, but there was no simultaneous Canadian edition, although McClel-land and Stewart distributed five hundred copies in Canada. Jack

McClelland thought the book gave "a misleading picture of the country"² and did not want his name associated with it. Levine found himself at the centre of a national controversy. At the same time, *Canada Made Me* established his reputation as a mature literary artist.

His next three books were first published in Great Britain, with a Canadian firm subsequently taking copies of the British edition: *One Way Ticket* (1961), a collection of stories; *From a Seaside Town* (1970) republished in 1975 as *She'll Only Drag You Down*, a novel; and a second volume of stories, *I Don't Want to Know Anyone Too Well* (1971). During this time, Levine's growing artistic stature was recognized in various ways: he received three Canada Council grants (a Fellowship in 1959, arts awards in 1969, and 1971); he was appointed writer-in-residence at the University of New Brunswick (1965–66); he edited an anthology of Canadian fiction (*Canadian Winter's Tales* [1968]); and he was the first writer commissioned by CBC Radio to write a short story for the *Anthology* series (1971).

In 1975 Levine published *Selected Stories*, one of which, "In Lower Town," was published together with photographs by Johanne McDuff as a separate book in 1977. *I Walk by the Harbour* (1976) is a very slim volume of poetry; most of its contents were written, according to Levine's prefatory note, in 1949 and 1959. *Thin Ice* (1979) is a collection of stories, published by Deneau & Greenberg in Canada and by Wildwood House in Great Britain. The Canadian firm — now called simply Deneau — has also brought out paperback editions of *Canada Made Me* (1979; the first Canadian edition), *From a Seaside Town* (1980), *Thin Ice* (1982), and *I Don't Want to Know Anyone Too Well* (1982). In 1984 Deneau published *Why Do You Live So Far Away?* and Penguin published *Champagne Barn*, collections consisting almost entirely of previously published work. In 1991 a collection of stories, *Something Happened Here*, was published.

A remarkable feature of Levine's career has been his popularity in Europe. His work has been translated into many languages. He is especially well known in Germany, partly because his West German translators were Heinrich Böll and Anne-Marie Böll. But collections of his stories appeared in the former East Germany in editions of thirty thousand and twenty thousand. By contrast, *Thin*

*Ice* was published in Canada in an edition of five thousand.

Levine's first wife, Margaret, died in 1978. He returned to Canada in 1980 and in 1983 married Anne Sarginson in Toronto. He now lives there but still has his residence in St. Ives, to which he returns from time to time. He continues to write.

## NOTES

[1] Norman Levine informed me, in a letter of 23 December 1981, that the title should be *The Tightrope Walker* but that the printer made a mistake. (The printer was Guido Morris, one of the most distinguished in Britain; he printed the book by hand at his Latin Press in St. Ives.)

[2] Jack McClelland, quoted in "One Man's Canada," rev. of *Canada Made Me, Time* [Canadian ed.], 19 Jan. 1959, p. 9.

# Margaret Laurence (1926–87)

## J.M. KERTZER

A novel based on a writer's experience is no less a work of true fiction than a novel which has nothing to do with the writer's own life. The art of fiction lies in the ability to bring to life on the printed page a whole range of characters and events, and to explore meaningful and universal themes. In this sense, it has nothing to do with simply recording the events of anyone's life.[1]

MARGARET LAURENCE'S fiction is neither autobiographical nor confessional, though it does incorporate many features from her own life: her youth, family heritage, and upbringing in Manitoba; her travels throughout Canada, Europe, and Africa; her struggles as a Canadian woman writer. But as her comment shows, she regarded a novel, not as a disguised recording of its author's experience, but as a separate creation with a life of its own. It is "a work of true fiction," a well-crafted story whose truth is in its telling and in the vitality of its characters, not in its correspondence to fact. She warns us, therefore, about interpreting novels biographically by seeking conformity between an author and her work. Nevertheless, we are justified in considering Laurence's life for its own interest — it was eventful and even adventurous — and for the light it casts on her aims, convictions, interests, and habits as a novelist. It helps us to understand the temperament of a temperamental writer, that is, of a writer whose main interest lay in the complexities and nuances of human character.

Jean Margaret Wemyss was born on 18 July 1926 in Neepawa, Manitoba, the daughter of Verna Simpson Wemyss and Robert Wemyss. She came from a family of respectable lawyers, artisans, and merchants who were of Scottish and Irish background. Of her Celtic heritage she has written both affectionately and critically, finding it colourful, proud, clannish, snobbish, and Presbyterian. She notes its obsession with hard work, discipline, guilt, and with the "Black Celt" feeling "that things could hardly be worse in the world, and that we are on the brink of a precipice."[2] She has also written of Neepawa, which became her fictional Manawaka, as a town at once protective, splendid, and stultifying. It first directed her vision of the world and therefore "would form the mainspring and source of the writing [she] was to do, wherever and however far away [she] might live."[3]

After her mother died in 1930, and her father in 1935, she was raised by her maternal grandfather, John Simpson, and by her aunt, Margaret Simpson Wemyss, who had married her widowed father. Both were strong influences on the young girl. The spirit of John Simpson, a repressive, authoritarian figure who was a cabinet-maker and an undertaker, haunts many of Laurence's novels. He appears as Timothy Connor in *A Bird in the House*. The fictional Vanessa says of him, as did Laurence of her grandfather: "I had feared and fought the old man, yet he proclaimed himself in my veins."[4] Her aunt and stepmother was also an intelligent woman, a teacher, and founder of the Neepawa Public Library. She encouraged Laurence to read, and the girl started writing by the age of six or seven, though it was not until she was about twenty-three that she took herself seriously as a writer.

She lived in Neepawa through the Depression and the Second World War until 1944, when she attended United College in Winnipeg. There she studied English, published her first poems and stories in the college journal, *Vox*, and later worked as a reporter for *The Winnipeg Citizen*. In these formative years, according to Clara Thomas, she responded to the "powerfully positive, liberal idealism" of the college and to the optimism of the "Winnipeg Old Left," with its confidence in reform, brotherhood, and social justice.⁵ Laurence later questioned her easy liberal attitudes, which were tested in Africa, but retained her indignation with forms of injustice, exploitation, and dispossession, even though she grew sceptical of social solutions. She kept the compassionate, moral outlook that pervades her novels.

In Winnipeg she also met her husband, Jack Laurence, a civil engineer. They married in 1948 and proceeded first to England and then in 1950 to the British Protectorate of Somaliland in East Africa. In often dangerous conditions, Jack Laurence supervised the construction of a series of reservoirs in the desert. Meanwhile Margaret immersed herself in Somali culture, as far as was permissible for a foreign woman; she later recorded and interpreted her experiences in *The Prophet's Camel Bell* (1963). At the time, her main project was to study the oral tradition of Somali literature and to prepare a book of translations, *A Tree for Poverty* (1954). This was her first published volume, and it is hard to imagine anything further from Neepawa in place and spirit than the *belwo* and *gabei*, the lyrical and narrative poems in this book. Between 1952 and 1957, the Laurences lived in the Gold Coast, later Ghana, where they had two children, Jocelyn (born 1952) and David (born 1955). Her career as a writer of fiction began at this time as she wrote stories about the life that she observed around her. She published her first African story, "The Drummer of All the World," in *Queen's Quarterly* in 1956 and wrote several others that were later included in *The Tomorrow-Tamer* (1963). She also began her first and only African novel, *This Side Jordan* (1960). These years in Africa were of enormous importance to her development as a writer. They affected her long after she left Africa because she continued to read and learn from the work of talented Nigerian novelists and dramatists. Her critical study of them, *Long Drums and Cannons: Nigerian Dramatists and Novelists 1952–1966*

(1968), while valuable in itself, is also interesting because it offers insight into her own books and displays her views of the art of fiction.

In 1957 the Laurences moved to Vancouver, where Margaret completed *This Side Jordan* — which won the Beta Sigma Phi Award for the best first novel by a Canadian — and began *The Stone Angel*. In her second novel, she returned to her native ground and took the most important step in her career:

> When I stopped writing about Africa and turned to the area of writing where I most wanted to be, my own people and background, I felt very hesitant. The character of Hagar had been in mind for quite a while before I summoned enough nerve to begin the novel. Strangely enough, however, once I began *The Stone Angel*, it wrote itself more easily than anything I have ever done. I experienced the enormous pleasure of coming home in terms of idiom.[6]

In her own life, however, she had not yet come home. She seems to have needed a more distant view of herself, her country, and her art, and so in 1962, after separating from her husband, she took her manuscript and her children to England. She lived at Elm Cottage in Buckinghamshire. Here she created the world of Manawaka, completing *The Stone Angel* (1964) and writing *A Jest of God* (1966), which won the Governor General's Award for Fiction in English, *The Fire-Dwellers* (1969), and *A Bird in the House* (1970). She also wrote her first children's book, *Jason's Quest* (1970). It was in England that she established herself as a major Canadian novelist and as a woman of letters, reading widely in Canadian literature, writing reviews, essays, and articles, and meeting other Canadian writers who visited her at Elm Cottage. "Her house," recalls Margaret Atwood, "was a rambling country-village cottage outside London whose chief characteristics were its multitude of books and its resemblance to Canada House at the height of the tourist season."[7]

Eventually Laurence was lured back to Canada. Through the 1970s she was awarded honorary degrees from eleven Canadian universities; she became a Companion of the Order of Canada; she served as writer-in-residence at Trent University and at the universities of Toronto and Western Ontario. She returned, first in summers to a cottage on the Otonobee River in Ontario, where she wrote much of *The Diviners* (1974), which won the Governor General's Award for Fiction in English, and then permanently to the nearby town of Lakefield. A collection of articles previously published in various newspapers and magazines, *Heart of a Stranger*, was published in 1976. She wrote three more children's books: *The Olden Days Coat* (1979), *Six Darn Cows* (1979), and *The Christmas Birthday Story* (1980). She spoke publicly on social issues, especially nuclear disarmament, proclaiming herself "a Christian, a woman, a writer, a parent, a member of humanity and a sharer in life itself, a life I believe to be informed and infused with the holy spirit."[8] In 1981 she was appointed Chancellor of Trent University, which is located in the very city, Peterborough, where a few upright citizens declared *The Diviners* to be an immoral book that should be removed from the high-school curriculum.

Margaret Laurence died on 5 January 1987. Since her death she has received many tributes, perhaps the most important of which was the creation of the Margaret Laurence Fund for the Promotion of Peace and the Environment. This fund is administered by the Energy Probe Research Foundation, where Laurence served as director for five years, and awards research grants every year on the anniversary of her death.[9] Laurence's childhood home in Neepawa was bought by a group of citizens in 1986, who restored and converted it into an historical site and cultural centre in 1987.[10] Her last work and life story, *Dance on the Earth: A Memoir* was published in 1989. Laurence began it in 1984, and, by the time she had finished the first draft, she knew she was dying. The manuscript was almost complete when Laurence died; her daughter Jocelyn prepared it for publication.[11]

NOTES

[1] Margaret Laurence, Introd., *House of Hate*, by Percy Janes, New Canadian Library, No. 124 (Toronto: McClelland and Stewart, 1976), p. x.

[2] Donald Cameron, "Margaret Laurence: The Black Celt Speaks of Freedom," in *Conversations with Canadian Novelists — 1* (Toronto: Macmillan, 1973), p. 100.

[3] Margaret Laurence, "Where the World Began," *Maclean's*, Dec. 1972,

pp. 23, 80; rpt. (revised) in her *Heart of a Stranger* (Toronto: McClelland and Stewart, 1976), p. 217.

⁴ Margaret Laurence, "Jericho's Brick Battlements," in her *A Bird in the House* (Toronto: McClelland and Stewart, 1970), p. 270. See also "Sources," *Mosaic*, 3, No. 3 (Spring 1970), 80–84; rpt. (revised — "A Place to Stand On") in her *Heart of a Stranger*, p. 17.

⁵ Clara Thomas, *The Manawaka World of Margaret Laurence* (Toronto: McClelland and Stewart, 1975), pp. 13, 15. For a fuller account of Laurence's life, see this book and Susan J. Warwick, "A Laurence Log," *Journal of Canadian Studies*, 13, No. 3 (Fall 1978), 75–83.

⁶ Margaret Laurence, "Ten Years' Sentences," *Canadian Literature*, No. 41 (Summer 1969), pp. 10–16; rpt. in *Margaret Laurence: The Writer and Her Critics*, ed. William H. New (Toronto: McGraw-Hill Ryerson, 1977), p. 20.

⁷ Margaret Atwood, "Face to Face," *Maclean's*, May 1974, pp. 38–39, 43–46; rpt. in New, ed., *Margaret Laurence*, p. 34.

⁸ Margaret Laurence, "A Statement of Faith," in *A Place to Stand On: Essays by and about Margaret Laurence*, ed. George Woodcock, Western Canadian Literary Documents, No. 4 (Edmonton: NeWest, 1983), p. 56.

⁹ H.J. Kirchhoff, "Environmentalists Win First Awards from Laurence Fund," *The Globe and Mail* [Toronto], 6 Jan. 1989, p. C9.

¹⁰*The Gazette* [Montreal], 26 June 1987, p. C2.

¹¹ William French, "A Fruitful Life," *The Globe and Mail* [Toronto], 4 Nov. 1989, p. C19.

# Robert Kroetsch (1927- )

## PETER THOMAS

ROBERT KROETSCH published his first novel, *But We Are Exiles*, in 1965, at the age of thirty-eight. *The Words of My Roaring* followed in the next year, and, when *The Studhorse Man* (1969) received the Governor General's Award for Fiction in English, Kroetsch first achieved wide recognition. *Gone Indian* (1973), *Badlands* (1975), *What the Crow Said* (1978), and *Alibi* (1983) have appeared since. Kroetsch has not limited himself to fiction, publishing several books of poetry: *The Stone Hammer Poems, 1960–1975* (1975), *The Seed Catalogue* (1977), *The Sad Phoenician* (1979), *Field Notes* (1981), *Advice to My Friends* (1985), *Excerpts from the Real World* (1986), and *Completed Field Notes* (1989); a journal, *The Crow Journals* (1980); and a book of essays, *The Lovely Treachery of Words* (1989). Formally innovative, indeed restlessly inventive, Kroetsch seems compelled to deconstruct the narrative structures he employs, pressing their aesthetic terms by parody, inversion, and sophisticated word play. He is, to the point of self-consciousness, a contemporary writer, seeking in particular the authentic voice of that essentially international literary sensibility that calls itself postmodern.

Yet he is also — perhaps increasingly — aware of the energies and obligations of place. From his Prairie origins, he went out, like so many other artists seeking the community of the imagination, to discover an elusive self-justification: the writer's life. And what he discovered enabled him to return to make his own land the scene of his fiction.

He was born on a large farm southwest of the little town of Heisler in central Alberta on 26 June 1927, the first of the five children of Hilda Weller and Paul Kroetsch. At the time of his birth, Kroetsch's parents were living in a homestead shack while their large farmhouse was being built (completed, fortunately, a few months before the Crash of 1929). The farm specialized in wheat and cattle, and during Kroetsch's boyhood his family cultivated up to two sections of land with horses, a very large acreage for the time. As a result, there were usually a number of hired men on the farm (so that W.O. Mitchell's "Jake" stories spoke very directly to Kroetsch). As an adolescent, he began to ask how one might write about rural life and about the Battle River region in particular — a place about which he had never read anything in books.

The deep valley of the Battle, with its miniature badlands, stirred him even then, and he traces his later fascination with the major badlands of the south to that early experience. The valley had strange coal mines and unfamiliar plant life. There were eagles and birds he could not name. When his family rented a section on the river, one of Robert's favourite yearly rituals was the round-up, entering mysterious coulees to gather in cattle each fall.

The home farm did not dry out during the 1930s; indeed, there was a story current in Heisler of how Kroetsch's father was almost wiped out by a good crop. The wheat cost him thirty cents a bushel to harvest. He sold it for twenty-five. During this period, hired men drifted in from all across North America and Europe, bringing with them an enormous range of experience and education. There was a Swede, for instance, who landscaped the yard: a big, knowledgeable, articulate individualist. These men told stories and sang songs in the bunkhouse in the evenings. "In a small way," Kroetsch writes, "the world came to us, on the prairies, in the Thirties."[1] He remembers the hobo jungle in the fall, where the harvesters set up camp by the railroad tracks, waiting to be hired.

Because of allergies to grain dust, Kroetsch spent little time in the granaries or barns, becoming instead the family gardener, working alone in the plot or tending the many trees he planted. He was around the house most of the time. "In fact I spent my life surrounded by women rather than men." He had four younger sisters (Patricia, Sheila, Jane, and Kay), and his mother often hired girls or women from the community. When he was five, an unemployed schoolteacher came to work for his mother; in the mornings she taught him.

Kroetsch's mother died when he was thirteen. Some of his father's sisters then stood in — two were widows, one "what we called an old maid," Kroetsch reports. According to family legend, Kroetsch was prodigiously spoiled by his mother. After her death, his sisters and aunts followed that lead with concerted zeal. He grew up in a household of loving women, while, at the same time, his allergies placed him in some ways outside the traditional farm role for men. It is this, he believes, that has led him to parody obsessively that role in his novels, to write of male heroes who swim and flounder in an engulfing female sea of existence. As Kroetsch explains, "I was treated to a version of the male role that has made me endlessly dependent, I suspect, along with my passion for independence."

He thrived in school. There was no grade twelve at Heisler during the war years. Grades one to four were in one room; grades five to eight in the next. In grade four he was allowed to enter the second room to fetch more books (having exhausted his first supply):

> As a result I read two novels that astonished me, perplexed me, fascinated me, because I realized they were somehow different, did something different with words and said something different about life. Only many years later, in graduate school, did I discover that they were in fact Conrad's *The Nigger of the Narcissus*, and Henry James' *The Turn of the Screw*.

He consumed books and, since his parents demanded so little work from him, lived in an imagined world. Sports held little interest, though during the war he played first base for the community baseball team; when the ball players returned from military service, however, his sporting career ended abruptly. Sometimes he went out hunting, mostly to be able to walk the countryside, explore the poplar bluffs, and study the life around the sloughs. But after wounding a mallard, which flew until it seemed to fall unwontedly dead out of the sky, he shot nothing, though he continued to "hunt."

Kroetsch went away to Red Deer High School to complete grade twelve. There he was told by his English teacher, Miss Aylesworth, that he should think about becoming a teacher. For Kroetsch, Miss Aylesworth was "fierce, intense, beautiful"; he reports that her "intelligence somehow inspired a kind of love in me." Patiently, she explained what he had hardly noticed, that he was always writing. When he enrolled as a first-year arts student at the University of Alberta, he was, in his own words, "the first student ever from the Heisler district to be that impractical."

Graduating in 1948, he missed the graduation ball to fly North. It held him for six years. He worked as a purser on MacKenzie River boats and later spent two and a half years at the United States Air Force camp at Goose Bay, Labrador, where he was the Information and Educational Specialist, editing the base newspaper, writing a radio program, and running teaching projects. His familiarity with the American educational system, gained through advising airmen, was perhaps part of the reason he later went to the United States to attend graduate school. The United States Air Force offered him an even better job, but, as Kroetsch reflects, "I realized I had to get out or become rich and settled."

At first he only tested the new waters, attending McGill University in 1954 to study with Hugh MacLennan and, then, trying a summer at Middlebury College, Vermont:

I discovered a new addiction. I delighted in the intellectual life. After six years in the North, I turned from the physical, sometimes, violent life of the frontier to the intense life of the mind.

Kroetsch received his M.A. from Middlebury in 1956; then he moved on to the Writers' Workshop at the University of Iowa, where he received a Ph.D. for an unpublished novel, "Coulee Hill," in 1961.

In Vermont, he had met Mary Jane Lewis, another graduate student, from Wilmington, North Carolina. They eloped to Mexico in 1956. Their two daughters were born while Kroetsch was teaching at the State University of New York at Binghamton — he joined the Department of English in 1961, remaining until 1975. Soon after leaving this position, he was divorced. He married Smaro Kamboureli in 1982. That marriage has also ended.

Early in the 1960s, he began to teach a course in American poetry, which developed, over a few years, into the study of the modern long poem. He also joined with his colleague William V. Spanos in founding *Boundary 2: A Journal of Post-Modern Literature*. This commitment to the theory of contemporary writing remains essential to Kroetsch's intellectual life, as absolute as his need to recover for formal narrative the spontaneity and freedom of the oral tale. If there is an apparent contradiction between these aspects of his literary personality, it provides a continuing imaginative tension to his novels.

His return to Canada began in 1975, when he was writer-in-residence at the University of Manitoba. In 1978 he accepted a permanent position as professor of English at the same institution; in 1985 he was made a Distinguished Professor. For several years he also taught summer school at the Saskatchewan School of the Arts, in the Qu'Appelle Valley. These experiences he found "instructive and beautiful," drawing him back to life on the Canadian prairies:

I have now returned to live on these prairies and to write. But the distancing process asserts itself again — now I find myself reading books in translation — novels and books of poetry from South America, from Italy, from Germany and France. The dialectic of space continues.

### NOTE

[1] Letter from Robert Kroetsch, 3 March 1981. Unless otherwise stated, subsequent biographical information given in the text is derived from a set of autobiographical notes included in this letter from Kroetsch.

# Hugh Hood (1928– )

## KEITH GAREBIAN

HUGH JOHN BLAGDON HOOD was born of mixed ethnic ancestry in Toronto on 30 April 1928. He has strong historical connections to Quebec, eastern Ontario, Nova Scotia, and, more remotely, to Britain. His mother's grandmother, a Quebecker named Aubeline Lemieux, married a sea captain named Blagdon from Lévis. Hood's maternal grandfather, Alfred Esdras Blagdon, married Eugénie Sauriol from eastern Ontario and settled in Toronto. Hood's paternal grandfather, John, was born in Shelburne, Nova Scotia, and was a descendant of Admiral Samuel Hood, member of a famous naval family from Bridport, England. He married Katherine MacDonald from Antigonish and lived in Nova Scotia. It is therefore not surprising to find in Hood a sense of a single, yet bilingual, Canada. Hood remembers hearing French spoken around his home from earliest childhood.

He received his formal education in English, attending Catholic parish and high schools where he received his grounding in Catholic doctrine and liturgy and in Scripture. He went on to obtain a Ph.D. from the University of Toronto in 1955 with a thesis on "Theories of Imagination in English Thinkers 1650–1790." After teaching in Hartford, Connecticut, for six years (1955–61), he settled in Montreal and has taught English literature ever since in the French milieu of the Université de Montréal. He is fluently bilingual, and several of his books create a bicultural ambience that bears witness to his perception of Canada as a dual nation in which a minority French culture still possesses a strong sense of self.

Hood is proud of Canadian biculturalism. In a letter to Naïm Kattan in *Le Devoir* [Montreal] in 1964, following the publication of his first novel, he articulated his aim to unite the whole of Canadian bilingual culture in his work, however imperfect the style of his written French or however vulnerable he would become to the charge of opportunism in his writing:

> J'ai l'ambition de devenir un romancier ni anglais ni français mais tout à fait et simplement canadien. Je veux réunir les consciences de mes parents en la mienne. Et je me propose à écrire dans mon français très imparfait des phrases et de temps en temps même des pages entières dans mes romans et nouvelles afin d'unir dans mon oeuvre la totalité de notre culture, la culture la plus intéressante du monde.[1]

Hood is not material for sensationalism. He lives with his wife, the artist Noreen Mallory, with whom he has two sons and two daughters, in Notre Dame de Grace, a quiet, aging section of Montreal. Although he has a circle of artist-friends (such as painters Seymour Segal and Louise Scott, photographer Sam Tata, and writer John Metcalf), he is not a social creature given to gossip or glittering trivia around the cocktail circuit.

After numerous short stories and two false starts as a novelist, he set aside his unpublished manuscripts ("God Rest You Merry" in 1958, and "Hungry Generations" in 1960) to produce a collection of short fiction, *Flying a Red Kite*, in 1962. This brought him a $200 award from the Toronto Women's Canada Club in 1963. His short fiction continued to appear in numerous journals such as *Esquire, The Tamarack Review, The Canadian Forum, Prism*

*International, The Fiddlehead, Queen's Quarterly, The Montrealer*, and *Saturday Night,* while he was exercising his scope and style in the 1960s with novels such as *White Figure, White Ground* (1964), *The Camera Always Lies* (1967), and an urban pastoral, *Around the Mountain: Scenes from Montreal Life* (1967). Citations came in "The Yearbook of the American Short Story" and "Distinctive Short Stories in American Magazines" in 1961 and 1967.[2] Moreover, Hood twice won the President's Medal from the University of Western Ontario: in 1963 in the short story category for "The End of It"; and in 1968 for a general article, "It's a Small World." *White Figure, White Ground* won the Beta Sigma Phi Award in 1965 for the best first novel by a Canadian.

The 1970s bore five new novels: *A Game of Touch* (1970); *You Cant Get There From Here* (1972); *The Swing in the Garden* (1975); *A New Athens* (1977); and *Reservoir Ravine* (1979). The last three, along with *Black and White Keys* (1982), *The Scenic Art* (1984), *The Motor Boys in Ottawa* (1986), *Tony's Book* (1988), and his latest novel, *Property and Value* (1990), comprise two-thirds of Hood's serial epic *The New Age/Le nouveau siècle,* which is designed as a twelve-part philosophical fiction that will use all the materials of Hood's life in order to tell a massive story of Canada's "ranges of behaviour" or "moral possibilities."[3] *The Swing in the Garden* won the City of Toronto Book Award for 1975 and was much touted to win the Governor General's Award for Fiction in English that year, though it failed to do so. *The Motor Boys in Ottawa* won the first annual QSPELL award in 1988 for the best novel written in English in Quebec. Hood has also published a short novel, *Five New Facts About Giorgione* (1987).

More of Hood's short stories were collected in *The Fruit Man, The Meat Man & The Manager* (1971), *Dark Glasses* (1976), *Selected Stories* (1978), *None Genuine Without This Signature* (1980), *August Nights* (1985), *Flying a Red Kite: The Collected Stories,* I (1987), *A Short Walk in the Rain: The Collected Stories,* II (1989), and *The Isolation Booth: The Collected Stories,* III (1990). A new collection of stories, *You'll Catch Your Death,* was published in 1992. Hood remains a virtuoso, turning briefly to sports biography with *Strength Down Centre: The Jean Béliveau Story* (1970), essays with *The Governor's Bridge Is Closed* (1973), a commentary on Seymour Segal's painting in *Scoring: Seymour*

*Segal's Art of Hockey* (1979), and more essays with *Trusting the Tale* (1983) and *Unsupported Assertions* (1991).

Hood's prodigious production will, no doubt, continue. If destiny permits, he aims to complete his millenial *New Age* series by the year 2000. With so much material to his credit, Hood is anything but that familiar Canadian phenomenon — the one-shot success. His contribution to Canadian literature was recognized in 1988 when he was made an Officer of the Order of Canada.

## NOTES

[1] Hugh Hood, letter to Naïm Kattan, *Le Devoir* [Montreal], 12 Dec. 1964, p. 15.

[2] Martha Foley and David Burnett, eds., *The Best American Short Stories 1962* (Boston: Houghton Mifflin, 1962), p. 428; and Martha Foley and David Burnett, eds., *The Best American Short Stories 1968* (Boston: Houghton Mifflin, 1968), pp. 354, 359.

[3] Geoff Hancock, "Hugh Hood's Celebration of the Millennium's End," *Quill & Quire*, Nov. 1980, p. 40.

# Adele Wiseman (1928–92)

## MICHAEL GREENSTEIN

PETER AND CLARA WAISMAN emigrated in the early 1920s from Ukraine to Winnipeg, where their daughter, Adele Wiseman, was born on 21 May 1928. Her most important education took place in her home during the years of the Depression. Biblical legends and tales of the old country, the immigrants' cultural baggage, echoed through her household providing the oral inspiration and rhythm for fictional dialogue. Complementing this oral expression, her parents' artisanship as tailor and dressmaker furnished her with a strong visual sense. Biblical mythology, nineteenth-century Eastern European history, immigrant settlement on the Prairies, and second-generation acculturation to the Canadian mainstream form the biographical pattern that Adele Wiseman shapes into the four historical stages of her fiction.

Her elementary education was divided between public school, with its authoritarian teachers who appear as Miss Flake and Miss

Bolthumsup in *Crackpot*, and the Jewish Peretz School with its liberal spirit, where teachers like Mr. Polonick in *Crackpot* instilled leftist ideals and individualism in the minds of their young charges. Later, the unpleasant years at Saint John's Technical High School made her critical of overly structured education that stultifies creativity. "Thank you, formal education, thank you, herd standards, but no thank you, too. Long is the unlearning of your learning, glad the return to vision."[1] Like e.e. cummings' "nonlecture," her "UNLESSON" proposes that "Children who learn too well are those most cheated by their education."[2]

The University of Manitoba was much more to her liking: majoring in English (studying with Malcolm Ross) and psychology, she graduated with honours in 1949. Though she always knew she wanted to be a writer, she began to write seriously while at university, where she found the atmosphere conducive to creativity. She contributed to the university's literary journal, which had previously been edited by Jack Ludwig, and eventually won the Chancellor's Prize for a short story.

After leaving university, Wiseman became friends with Margaret Laurence, who helped her get a job in England as a social worker with the Stepney Jewish Girls' Hospital in London. In 1951 she moved to Rome to teach for the Overseas School of Rome, and returned to Winnipeg the following year. During the next three years she finished *The Sacrifice*, worked as a lab technician, and became executive secretary to the Royal Winnipeg Ballet. Upon completion of *The Sacrifice*, she returned to London for a writers' conference and remained for the year to research her play "The Lovebound," which remains unpublished. During the period 1957–60, she won a Guggenheim Fellowship and moved to New York city; during 1961–63 she lived in London and wrote children's stories; and for the rest of the 1960s she lived in Montreal lecturing in English at Sir George Williams University, Macdonald College, and McGill University.

After several years of revision, *The Sacrifice* was published in 1956, winning the Governor General's Award for Fiction in English and the annual Beta Sigma Phi Award. In 1964 Wiseman collaborated with Joe Rosenthal, who provided the drawings for *Old Markets, New World*; in her text, she reminisces about her childhood experiences in the market. Her second novel, *Crackpot*, appeared in 1974 after being rejected by many publishers. Her most autobiographical work, *Old Woman at Play*, published in 1978, combines descriptions of her mother's doll-making and the author's reflections on the creative process. Wiseman received a Senior Arts Award from the Canada Council to finish *Memoirs of a Book-Molesting Childhood and Other Essays* (1987). Her last book is a children's story, *Kenji and the Cricket* (1988). She privately published a play, *Testimonial Dinner* (1978), and wrote many reviews, critical articles, and short stories. Wiseman was writer-in-residence at the University of Toronto during 1975–76, and in the last decade she was writer-in-residence at the University of Prince Edward Island and the University of Windsor.

An important interview with her friend Roslyn Belkin is featured in the *Journal of Canadian Fiction*;[3] it surveys most of Wiseman's work and draws the distinction between the use of myth in *The Sacrifice* and the use of metaphor in *Crackpot*. The same issue contains a previously unpublished short story, "The Country of the Hungry Bird," and excerpts from "The Lovebound."

Adele Wiseman died of cancer on 1 June 1992 in Toronto.

### NOTES

[1] Adele Wiseman, *Old Woman at Play* (Toronto: Clarke, Irwin, 1978), p. 24.

[2] Wiseman, p. 24.

[3] Roslyn Belkin, "The Consciousness of a Jewish Artist: An Interview with Adele Wiseman," *Journal of Canadian Fiction*, Nos. 31–32 (1981), pp. 148–76.

# Alice Munro (1931–  )

## HALLVARD DAHLIE

ALICE ANNE MUNRO was born on 10 July 1931, in Wingham, Ontario, the eldest of three children of Anne Chamney Laidlaw and Robert Eric Laidlaw. Her father was a farmer, raising silver foxes during the Depression years, switching to turkey farming during the 1940s, and augmenting the fluctuating family income by working as a night watchman in the local foundry. At a fairly advanced age, he began writing articles and sketches about his own life, and just before his death in 1976 he completed a novel about a pioneer Southwestern Ontario family, which was edited and published after his death as *The McGregors: A Novel of an Ontario Pioneer Family* (1979). Alice's mother had been an elementary-school teacher in Alberta and Ontario before her marriage, an occupation she was not permitted to pursue in the Ontario of the Depression. Like many of the unfulfilled and despairing mothers of Munro's fiction, she expended her energies during the formative years of the three Laidlaw children in the nurturing of a family under conditions of deprivation and hardship. She fought a long and painful battle with Parkinson's disease, to which she succumbed in 1959, a situation poignantly evoked in such stories as "The Peace of Utrecht" and "The Ottawa Valley."

Undoubtedly the Laidlaw family suffered its share of hard times during the Depression, but those years seemingly have had no adverse effect on the three children: Alice's sister, Sheila, has become an artist in Toronto, and her brother, William, a professor of chemistry at the University of Calgary. And Alice recalls that, though her childhood was at times lonely and isolated, it was on the whole a rich and satisfying one:

> I thought my life was interesting. There was always a great sense of adventure . . . . We lived outside the whole social structure because we didn't live in the town and we didn't live in the country. We lived in this kind of little ghetto where all the bootleggers and prostitutes and hangers-on lived. Those were the people I knew. It was a community of outcasts. I had that feeling about myself. . . . I didn't belong to any nice middle class so I got to know more types of kids. It didn't seem bleak to me at the time. It seemed full of interest.[1]

That kind of environment, together with her voracious and indiscriminate reading, enabled her early in life to develop a curiosity and excitement about herself and her world that helped to direct her towards a writing career.

Beginning her schooling in a two-room country school, Alice completed her elementary and secondary education in the Wingham public schools, and she recalls that she was an above-average and highly competitive student. She tended towards being a loner, losing herself in books with romantic and fantastic plots, and around the age of fourteen or fifteen started turning her hand to writing short stories. She even confesses to writing a somewhat melodramatic novel during this adolescent period, the manuscript of which she is happy to record has long since ceased to exist. After graduation from the Wingham and District High School, she attended the University of Western Ontario from 1949 to 1951, where she majored in English and began her serious writing, publishing three stories in the university's *Folio*, and selling a story entitled "The Strangers" to Robert Weaver's CBC program *Canadian Short Stories*.

In December 1951 she married a fellow student at Western, James Munro, and they soon moved to Vancouver, where she continued intermittently with her writing, worked for a couple of years at the Vancouver Public Library, and began to raise a family (they have three daughters, born in 1953, 1957, and 1966). In 1963 the Munros moved to Victoria, where they established the still flourishing Munro's Books, and where Alice found it possible to return to regular writing. Her first marriage ended in 1972, whereupon she returned to Ontario. Today she lives on a farm on the outskirts of Clinton in Huron County with her second husband, cartographer Gerald Fremlin, whom she married in 1976.

As indicated above, Alice Munro's writing career began in earnest during her university years, but her first commercial story, "A Basket of Strawberries," appeared in the now defunct Canadian magazine *Mayfair* in November 1953. She continued to publish slick stories intermittently over the next few years in *Chatelaine* and, more recently, in such magazines as *Redbook*, *Ms.*, and *McCall's*. Simultaneously, however, her serious stories were being picked up by *The Montrealer*, *The Canadian Forum*, and *The Tamarack Review*, and later by such journals as *Queen's Quarterly* and *Ploughshares*. Within the last decade or so, she has joined Mavis Gallant as one of Canada's regular contributors to *The New Yorker*, and her stories have been included in virtually every anthology of Canadian short stories published in the last twenty years.

Though Alice Munro has now been writing for some thirty years, she is not a prolific writer and to date has published in book form six collections of short stories and one novel. Her latest short-story collection, *Friend of My Youth* (1990), was the 1991 Canada/Caribbean regional winner of the Commonwealth Writers Prize as well as Ontario's Trillium Book Award and was short-listed for the International Irish Times-Aer Lingus Fiction Prize. Her first collection, *Dance of the Happy Shades* (1968), won the Governor General's Award for Fiction in English, as did her third collection, *Who Do You Think You Are?* (1978) (published in the United States and England as *The Beggar Maid: Stories of Flo and Rose*), and also her fifth, *The Progress of Love* (1986). Her other collections are *Friend of My Youth* (1990), *The Moons of Jupiter* (1982), and *Something I've Been Meaning to Tell You* (1974). Her only novel to date, *Lives of Girls and Women* (1971), won the Canadian Booksellers Association International Book Year Award. In 1986 Alice Munro was the first winner of the Marian Engel Award, given to a woman writer for an outstanding body of work, and in 1991 she was awarded the Canada Council's Molson Prize for her contributions to Canadian writing. Munro has served as writer-in-residence at the University of Western Ontario and the University of British Columbia and, in 1980, spent a term at Queensland University in Brisbane as the first Canadian winner of the Canada-Australia Literary Prize.

### NOTE

[1] Alan Twigg, "What Is: Alice Munro," in *For Openers: Conversations with Twenty-Four Canadian Writers* (Madeira Park, B.C.: Harbour, 1981), p. 18.

# Mordecai Richler (1931– )

KERRY MCSWEENEY

THE 1931 census revealed that the total population of the greater Montreal area was just over one million, of whom almost fifty-eight thousand were Jewish. Comparison with the 1921 census showed that within the Montreal area Jews had already begun to move from the inner-city wards of Saint Louis and Laurier to the more affluent districts of Westmount and Outremont.[1] This migration accelerated during the next two decades but never included the parents of Mordecai Richler. It was the predominantly Jewish, working-class ghetto — "an all but self-contained world made up of five streets, Clark, St. Urbain, Waverley, Esplanade, and Jeanne Mance, bounded by the Main, on one side, and Park Avenue, on the other"[2] — into which the future novelist was born on 27 January 1931 and in which he grew up.

Richler's forebears had immigrated to Canada from Russia and Poland early in the century. One grandfather was a Hassid and a scholar who translated the Zohar into modern Hebrew and wrote religious tracts and speeches for rabbis.[3] In Montreal he became a pedlar. Richler's father was a junk dealer, and his mother, after her divorce in the early 1940s, rented rooms and cooked meals for neighbourhood bachelors.[4] The son attended the Talmud Torah primary school and Baron Byng High School (called Fletcher's Field in his novels). Since his grades were sufficiently mediocre to keep him out of McGill University, it was while attending Sir George Williams College that Richler discovered that he wanted to be a writer.

This discovery ended his formal education. At the age of nineteen, Richler left for Europe, where he remained for two years, living in London, on the Spanish island of Ibiza, and in Paris, where his literary acquaintances included Terry Southern, Mason Hoffenberg, Mavis Gallant, Alan Temko, and James Baldwin.[5] When Richler returned to Canada in 1952, he worked as a news editor for the CBC and began revising his first novel, *The Acrobats*, for which André Deutsch Ltd., the London publisher, had made an offer (one of their advisers was the distinguished British critic Walter Allen).[6] In 1954 Richler returned to London, where he was to live for the next eighteen years, and where in 1959 he married Florence Wood, with whom he has five children.

*The Acrobats* came out in 1954. In the next five years, Richler published three more novels: *Son of a Smaller Hero* (1955), *A Choice of Enemies* (1957), and his best-known work, *The Apprenticeship of Duddy Kravitz* (1959). His later novels have been much slower in coming: *The Incomparable Atuk* (*Stick Your Neck Out* is the title of the American edition) appeared in 1963; *Cocksure*, in 1968; *St. Urbain's Horseman*, in 1971; *Joshua Then and Now*, in 1980; and *Solomon Gursky Was Here*, in 1989. To this list should be appended *The Street* (1969), a medley of stories and memories that nostalgically but unsentimentally recreates the Saint Urbain Street world of Richler's childhood and adolescence.

In addition to his novels, Richler has written frequently (some would say indiscriminately) on cultural subjects for a wide variety of magazines and journals.[7] It is this body of writing that established Richler as an *enfant terrible* of Canadian letters and raised the hackles of literary and cultural nationalists. The best of his reviews and periodical essays were collected in *Hunting Tigers*

*Under Glass: Essays and Reports* (1968) and *Shovelling Trouble* (1972). Their contents are rearranged and recycled in *Notes on an Endangered Species and Others* (1974) and *The Great Comic Book Heroes and Other Essays* (1978). Most recently, Richler published *Broadsides: Reviews and Opinions* (1990). Richler started a storm of controversy with a 21,000-word article published in *The New Yorker* in 1991, on contemporary politics in Quebec, in which he mocked the province's language legislation and accused Quebec nationalists, past and present, of anti-semitism.[8] Richler edited *Canadian Writing Today* for Penguin Books in 1970 and *Writers on World War II* for Viking in 1991. His children's book *Jacob Two-Two Meets the Hooded Fang* appeared in 1975 and was followed by *Jacob Two-Two and the Dinosaur* in 1987. In 1977 he supplied a text for *Images of Spain*, a collection of photographs by Peter Christopher. Richler has also written film scripts: his credits include *No Love for Johnnie* (1961), *Life at the Top* (1965), and *The Apprenticeship of Duddy Kravitz* (1974), the last two of which were directed by Richler's close friend Ted Kotcheff.[9] *O Canada, O Quebec* is a 1992 nonfiction book about Quebec (from which his controversial article in *The New Yorker* was excerpted).

In 1972 Richler returned to live in Montreal and settled his family in Westmount, premier emblem of the Canadian WASP establishment and the epitome of the social goals of many of his Saint Urbain Street contemporaries. He now spends most of his time in Magog, in Quebec's Eastern Townships. In his sixties now, Richler would seem to have attained most of his own worldly goals: he is one of Canada's better known contemporary writers and one of the more distinguished. His honours and awards include a Guggenheim Fellowship in creative writing, a Canada Council Senior Arts Fellowship, the 1968 Governor General's Award for Fiction in English and Essays in English (*Cocksure* and *Hunting Tigers Under Glass*), and the 1971 Governor General's Award for Fiction in English (*St. Urbain's Horseman*). *Jacob Two-Two* won two awards, as did the film version of *Duddy Kravitz*. In 1990 *Solomon Gursky Was Here* won the Commonwealth Writers Prize and the QSPELL award for English-language fiction in Quebec and was a finalist for the Booker Prize. Richler has also been writer-in-residence at Sir George Williams University and Carleton University. His appointment in 1976 to the editorial board of the Book-of-the-

Month Club and the 1986 NFB film about him, *The Apprenticeship of Mordecai Richler*, are reminders that Richler has maintained a high profile and that over the years he has cultivated his talents as an entertainer as well as his skills as a novelist. It is as much the former as the latter that has won Mordecai Richler a wide audience, not only in Canada but in the United States and Britain as well.

## NOTES

[1] Louis Rosenberg, *Canada's Jews: A Social and Economic Study of the Jews in Canada* (Montreal: Bureau of Social and Economic Research, Canadian Jewish Congress, 1939), p. 31.

[2] Mordecai Richler, *The Street* (Toronto: McClelland and Stewart, 1969), p. 10.

[3] Nathan Cohen, "A Conversation with Mordecai Richler," *The Tamarack Review*, No. 2 (Winter 1957), pp. 6–23; rpt. in G. David Sheps, ed., *Mordecai Richler*, Critical Views on Canadian Writers, No. 6 (Toronto: McGraw-Hill Ryerson, 1971), p. 24.

[4] "The Expatriate Who Has Never Left Home," *Time* [Canadian ed.], 31 May 1971, pp. 8–9.

[5] See Mordecai Richler, "A Sense of the Ridiculous: Notes on Paris 1951 and After," in his *Shovelling Trouble* (Toronto: McClelland and Stewart, 1972), pp. 23–46.

[6] Mordecai Richler, "How I Became an Unknown with My First Novel," *Maclean's*, 1 Feb. 1958, p. 40.

[7] The most complete listing of Richler's periodical writings is Michael Darling, "Mordecai Richler: An Annotated Bibliography," in *The Annotated Bibliography of Canada's Major Authors*, ed. Robert Lecker and Jack David, I (Downsview, Ont.: ECW, 1979), 161–78.

[8] Mordecai Richler, "Inside/Outside," *The New Yorker*, 23 Sept. 1991, pp. 40–41.

[9] For information on the Richler-Kotcheff friendship and on the filming of *The Apprenticeship of Duddy Kravitz*, see Martin Knelman, "You See, Daddy, You See?" in *This Is Where We Came In: The Career and Character of Canadian Film* (Toronto: McClelland and Stewart, 1977), pp. 99–114.

# Marian Engel (1933–85)

## ELIZABETH BRADY

MARIAN RUTH (PASSMORE) ENGEL was born in Toronto on 24 May 1933 to Mary Elizabeth and Frederick Searle Passmore. Although she has described herself as "a kind of placeless person,"[1] in reality she is a person of many different places who has permanent roots in none. Her father was a First World War pilot who became a trade-school auto-mechanics teacher; his itinerant employment during the Depression and war years took the family to a succession of Southwestern Ontario towns — Port Arthur, Brantford, Galt, Hamilton, and Sarnia. "Moving a lot," she once remarked, "of course, puts you at an angle to your circumstances."[2] Inheriting no privileges based on birth, Engel belonged to a class of people who stressed education, hard work, practicality, moral responsibility, and respectability as the true measures of one's place in society. Her family were "Orange-Irish, extremely conservative, long-livers, and church-goers with a tendency to belong to Temperance societies."[3] From them she learned the importance of self-discipline and application; her non-conformist irreverence for bourgeois social values is self-taught.

In a bittersweet reminiscence called "The Girl from Glat: Memories of a Town That's Been Wiped Off the Map," she has written about the influential wartime years from age five to ten, when her family lived in Galt, a town representative of the provincial environment that figures so prominently in her fiction: ". . . your home was your family, you went where it went. If it went to a strange, gritty place full of dour people and beautiful buildings, fine. But now I know that if there's iron in my soul, it came from Galt."[4] This vein of "iron" she traces back to the small community's acute consciousness of class, nationality, and religious affiliation. The town's overriding Puritanism — equally manifest in her own family — taught her "to pay for joy" ("The Girl from Glat," p. 6) and that "every choice was a moral choice."[5] She credits the work ethic for her rigorous writing habits and the "bleak environment" for provoking her to use her imagination: "We had those big flat fields . . . . I guess the tendency is to people them in your head" (Gibson, p. 108). In a tone implying limited victory over the ancestral antagonist, she records her retrospective thoughts about her background: "I walk along Beverly [the street she lived on] with interest, but not nostalgia, and a feeling of relief. I am finally grown up. I have survived . . . . and if I can't run fast under trains any more I have five books to defend myself with" ("The Girl from Glat," p. 7).

From Sarnia Collegiate Institute and Technical School, Engel entered McMaster University — then a Baptist institution — graduating in 1955 with a B.A. in language studies. She went on to McGill University, receiving her Master's degree in Canadian literature in 1957; her thesis, "A Study of the English Canadian Novel since 1939," was supervised by Hugh MacLennan, who was then working on *The Watch That Ends the Night*. Her brief teaching career included posts as English lecturer at Montana State University in Missoula (1957–58) and as geography mistress at a private girls' school, The Study, in Westmount, Montreal (1958–60). A Rotary Foundation Fellowship then took her to the Université d'Aix-Marseille in Aix-en-Provence (1960–61), where she studied French literature. Following a year-long stint working as a translator of foreign credit reports in London, England, and her marriage in 1962 to Howard Engel, who was then a freelance CBC Radio broadcaster, she moved to Cyprus. She taught for a year at St. John's School (RAF) in Nicosia.

She returned to Canada in 1964; from that time on, she was based in Toronto. One year later, in the midst of completing her fourth unpublished novel, Engel became the mother of twins, Charlotte and William. In the early 1970s she broke with her housebound, domestic existence to begin a phase of active political work. She became the first chairperson of the Writers Union of Canada in 1973. Two years later she was appointed a trustee of the Toronto Public Library Board. Of her three-year trusteeship, Engel observed: ". . . it taught me a very great deal about the workings of power structures and how social change is brought about."[6] She separated from her husband, who was by then a prominent CBC Radio producer, in 1975; they were divorced two years later. During this period, she also served as a member of the City of Toronto Book Prize Committee and of the Canadian Book and Periodical Development Council. In 1977 she moved to Edmonton as writer-in-residence at the University of Alberta; she stayed on for another year to teach creative writing. During 1980–81 Engel was the University of Toronto's fourteenth writer-in-residence.

Marian Engel died of cancer on 16 February 1985 at the age of fifty-one. Although the disease had been diagnosed six years earlier, she maintained an active life and continued to write — in spite of diminishing energy, frequent hospitalization, and great pain.

Marian Engel began writing shortly after she learned the alphabet. Her first published article, "The Postman," appeared on 20 April 1947 in *The Canadian Girl*, a United Church Sunday-school paper, to which she became a regular contributor. Over the next five years she published twenty-five articles and nineteen poems in the paper.[7] Her first published short story, "A Summer's Tale," appeared in *Seventeen*, winning honourable mention in the magazine's annual fiction contest; the following year, her story "Al" (Jan. 1953) won her third prize in the same contest. While still a high-school and university student, she worked as a reporter for *The Sarnia Observer*. At McMaster she belonged to the group that published the student newspaper (*Silhouette*; she served as associate editor), the literary magazine (*The Muse*, which she edited), and the yearbook. During her undergraduate years, her poetry and short stories appeared in *Silhouette* and *The Muse*.

What she calls her "apprentice work" (Gibson, p. 106) includes four novels — "stinkers that naturally weren't published."[8] The first, an "academic spoof" called "The Pink Sphinx," was written in 1958, when she was teaching at Montana State University, in collaboration with a friend, Leslie Armour, who provided the plot. While living in England, she wrote "Women Travelling Alone," a "big scrappy novel with time and everything out of perspective," a premature attempt to write the memoirs of a forty-year-old woman: it "had some lovely ... pieces of writing, but it didn't hang together or know enough of time and space" (Gibson, p. 106). She collaborated on a "terrible" detective novel, "Death Comes for the YaYa,"[9] with her husband, who "made up the plot," while they were living in Cyprus: "I wrote it in order to get down a lot of information, a lot of sensations I wanted to keep" (Gibson, p. 106). Some of the material from this manuscript was later incorporated into her Cyprus novel, *Monodromos*. A fourth unpublished novel, "Lost Heir & Happy Families," was written during 1964–65.

Engel's *No Clouds of Glory* was published in 1968. Six more novels followed: *The Honeyman Festival* (1970); *Monodromos* (1973); *Joanne: The Last Days of a Modern Marriage* (1975); *Bear* (1976); *The Glassy Sea* (1978); and *Lunatic Villas* (1981). A collection of nineteen short stories, *Inside the Easter Egg*, appeared in 1975; a second collection, *The Tattooed Woman*, was published posthumously in 1985. She also wrote two children's books, *Adventure at Moon Bay Towers* (1974) and *My Name Is Not Odessa Yarker* (1977), and the text for a nonfiction "coffee table" book, *The Islands of Canada* (1981). At the time of her death, she left uncompleted an historical novel she had worked on intermittently for twelve years.

From 1968 until her death, she published numerous book reviews in leading Canadian and American newspapers (she was a regular contributor to *The Globe and Mail*'s [Toronto] book pages) and articles on a wide range of topics in magazines (*Chatelaine* was her biggest outlet), newspapers, professional journals, and books. From November 1981 through to September of 1982, she contributed a weekly column, entitled "Being Here," to *The Toronto Star*.

Engel was the recipient of three Canada Council Senior Arts

Fellowships (1968, 1973, 1976). In 1977 *Bear* won the Governor General's Award for Fiction in English. *The Glassy Sea* was awarded the 1978 Canadian Authors Association Silver Medal for Fiction. She travelled to Australia in March 1980 to participate as the Canadian representative in the biennial Adelaide Festival. In May 1980 she was awarded the 1979 McClelland and Stewart Award for fiction writing in a Canadian magazine for her short story "Father Instinct," published in *Chatelaine* (Aug. 1979). On 24 February 1982 she was awarded the City of Toronto Book Award (1981) for *Lunatic Villas* — a prize she shared with Claude Bissell, author of *The Young Vincent Massey*. Later that same year, she was appointed an Officer of the Order of Canada. In 1984 Marian Engel was named Metro Toronto YWCA's Woman of Distinction in Arts and Letters.

## NOTES

[1] Doris Cowan, "The Heroine of Her Own Life," *Books in Canada*, Feb. 1978, p. 9.

[2] Carroll Klein, "A Conversation with Marian Engel," *Room of One's Own*, 9, No. 2 (June 1984), 5.

[3] Carole Corbeil, "Marian Engel: U of T Writer-in-Residence Continues to Mention the Unmentionables," *The Globe and Mail* [Toronto], 14 Feb. 1981, Sec. E, p. 3.

[4] Marian Engel, "The Girl from Glat: Memories of a Town That's Been Wiped Off the Map," *Weekend Magazine*, 26 July 1975, p. 6. Further references to this work appear in the text.

[5] Graeme Gibson, "Marian Engel," in his *Eleven Canadian Novelists Interviewed by Graeme Gibson* (Toronto: House of Anansi, 1973), p. 109. Further references to this work appear in the text.

[6] Aritha van Herk and Diana Palting, "Marian Engel: Beyond Kitchen Sink Realism," interview, *Branching Out*, 5, No. 2 (1978), 40.

[7] See Annette Wengle, "Marian Engel: A Select Bibliography," *Room of One's Own*, 9, No. 2 (June 1974), 96–98.

[8] Du Barry Campeau, "Women Writers Are on a Literary Cloud of Glory," *The Telegram* [Toronto], 13 Feb. 1968, p. 37.

[9] Klein, p. 8.

# Leonard Cohen (1934–    )

## LINDA HUTCHEON

IN THE NFB FILM *Ladies and Gentlemen . . . Mr. Leonard Cohen,* family movies of the incipient poet's childhood are viewed to the accompaniment of readings by Cohen from his first novel, *The Favorite Game,* a work that is, by implication, at least somewhat autobiographical. Like his fictional protagonist, Leonard Cohen grew up in Montreal's Westmount district, one of two children in a relatively prosperous Jewish family. Again like Lawrence Breavman, Leonard Cohen would find his formal education considerably less significant, in his own mind, to his development as an artist than a summer at camp: the socialist camp he attended as a teenager was where he first played guitar, allegedly with the intention of impressing women. While singing and playing in Mountain Street cafés in the early 1950s, Cohen managed at the same time to pay off his old debts to his family and to his society, as he later put it,[1] by attending first McGill University (which recognized his abilities by awarding him the MacNaughton Prize in creative writing) and later, briefly, Columbia University.

Freed of these familial and social obligations, Cohen then proceeded to divide his time among Montreal, New York, and the Greek island of Hydra. In Greece he lived comfortably, if not luxuriously, on a small inheritance, in the company of a beautiful Norwegian woman named Marianne and her son. Cohen's own two children, Adam Nathan and Lorca Sarah, were born later of his relationship with Suzanne Elrod, a relationship whose dissolution is acknowledged, lamented, and exulted in throughout the pages of *Death of a Lady's Man*. From his songs to his books, all of Cohen's work revolves around his own personality as artist, his "life is art."

It is tempting to see in Cohen, one of Canada's most public and most publicized writers, the incarnation of the spirit of the 1960s: the man who went from vegetarianism (until he decided he felt too arrogant about it) to Eastern mysticism, from drugs to spiritual renewal through fasting and meditation. If Cohen has been seen as a counterculture model, it is surely a role he has fostered, at least since 1967 when Judy Collins began recording his music and taking him along to her concerts. In the summer of that year, he appeared in his own right at the Newport Folk Festival. A brief appearance in September 1967 on CBS–TV's *Camera Three* met with an enthusiastic response that helped launch Cohen's new career — as a popular singer. Columbia Records, over the next twenty years, was to issue ten albums: *Songs of Leonard Cohen, Songs from a Room, Songs of Love and Hate, Live Songs, New Skin for the Old Ceremony, The Best of Leonard Cohen, Death of a Ladies' Man* (the product of a much-debated collaboration with Phil Spector),[2] *Recent Songs, Various Positions, I'm Your Man*, and *The Future*. When not on the road or in Nashville, Cohen has tended to use Montreal as a base, having moved to the Saint Dominique Street flat celebrated in Harry Rasky's 1980 CBC film, *The Song of Leonard Cohen*.

Cohen's success as a performer, documented by the near-idolatrous reviews of his European concert tours, has almost eclipsed his career as a poet and novelist. His first collection of verse, *Let Us Compare Mythologies*, inaugurated Louis Dudek's McGill Poetry Series in 1956. Cohen's later Canadian publisher,

McClelland and Stewart, did not reprint the volume until 1966. Cohen's first real Canadian success was to come in 1961 with *The Spice-Box of Earth*. Viking, his American publisher, did not release this book until 1965, that is, until it had discovered Leonard Cohen the novelist. In 1963 *The Favorite Game* appeared in London and New York; in Canada, however, Cohen was presumably still only a poet, since the Canadian edition come out only four years after Cohen's second novel, *Beautiful Losers* (1966). Between the two novels came two controversial collections of verse, *Flowers for Hitler* (1964) and *Parasites of Heaven* (1966). After producing his *Selected Poems 1956–1968*, Cohen disappeared onto the public stage, reappearing in print with *The Energy of Slaves* in 1972 and, after even longer "silences," with *Death of a Lady's Man* (1978) and *Book of Mercy* (1984).

There is little doubt that Cohen's recording and performing career has interfered with the quantity — and some would say the quality — of Cohen's poetic and novelistic production. Nevertheless, he has not gone unrecognized as a literary artist. Besides winning awards from the Canada Council, Cohen has received the Quebec Award in 1964 and even a Litt.D. from Dalhousie University in 1971. His refusal of the Governor General's Award for Poetry in English in 1968 was carried off with typically ironic Cohen aplomb: he claimed that, although much in him strove for the honour, the poems themselves forbade it absolutely. Cohen was named to the Juno Hall of Fame in 1990 and accepted the title of Officer of the Order of Canada in 1991. Other tributes, less official but no less revealing, have taken the form of stage performances based on Cohen's music and verse. In 1970 the Royal Winnipeg Ballet took a new work, *The Shining People of Leonard Cohen*, on its European tour. Three years later a show entitled *Sisters of Mercy* was staged at Niagara-on-the-Lake. Cohen's songs and poems have also been translated into several languages; the appearance of his second novel in France in 1972, under the title *Les Perdants magnifiques*, gives testimony to Cohen's vast European following. Cohen's songs were recorded in 1987 by Jennifer Warnes on her hit album, *Famous Blue Raincoat*. Cohen is recording a new album that should be completed in 1992. Although he has not published fiction or poetry in several years, concentrating on his music, he says that he is doing a lot of writing besides his songwriting.[3]

## NOTES

[1] Michael Harris, "Leonard Cohen: The Poet as Hero: 2," interview, *Saturday Night*, June 1969, p. 27.

[2] Note the difference in spelling between the title of the record and that of the book (*Death of a Lady's Man*).

[3] Philip Marchand, "Leonard Plays Prophet for Irving the Messiah," *The Toronto Star*, 25 Oct. 1991, p. D20.

# Leon Rooke (1934–   )

KEITH GAREBIAN

BORN 11 SEPTEMBER 1934 in Roanoke Rapids, North Carolina, Leon Rooke is yet another expatriate writer of the first rank now living and working in Canada. The third and final child of Louise Gray, a farmer's daughter, and Jesse Lofton Rooke, a farmer's son, he has dim childhood memories of his parents, largely because he was separated from them in 1940, when he went with his brother and sister to live on his grandparents' farm outside Garysburg, North Carolina. Poverty provided an education of sorts, as did Rooke's encounters with Black playmates. This farm life lasted for six years, after which young Rooke moved back to town. Too shy for his own good, he nevertheless excelled in baseball, became sports editor of his school newspaper, and began writing poems and stories about 1948.

His graduation from Roanoke Rapids High School in 1952 was marred by an incident with a teacher who insulted him by implying that, owing to his father's low-income level, Rooke would never achieve much in life. Rooke reacted by working for a year in a bank and trust company in Charlotte, North Carolina, so that he could pay his way through college. He has said of the school incident: "The possibility of going to college had not occurred to me. But I was mortally offended by this remark and said to myself, 'By God I *will* go to college.' "[1] Between 1953 and 1955 he attended Mars Hill College, wrote and directed his first play, and won the Betty Smith Award, a state drama-festival prize. In 1955 he entered the University of North Carolina at Chapel Hill to study journalism. In his senior year, however, he switched to drama and won the Frederick H. Koch Playwriting Award. It was at this time he first began to be seriously interested in fiction, as he pounded away at short stories on a secondhand typewriter. Nevertheless, he did not abandon his drama writing, and he worked two summer sessions as technician and actor in *Unto These Hills*, an outdoor drama, staged at Cherokee, North Carolina.

Army service pulled him away from university in 1957, and, when he returned after his compulsory stint to the University of North Carolina in 1960, it was to study screenwriting at graduate school on the basis of a Screen Gems Graduate Writing Fellowship. Academic life did not carry much appeal for him, and Rooke did not complete his degree, dropping out after the first term and working as a writer for the University News Bureau. Writing was a preoccupation. He produced several stage and radio plays (of which only *Evening Meeting of the Club of Suicide* [1972], *Krokodile* [1973], *Sword/Play* [1974], and "Cakewalk" [1980] were published, later in his career). "My first writings were aimed at the stage," he has said, "And when some of those first plays were produced and I heard actors returning the words it probably had the effect of making me listen more attentively to how the voices sounded on the page."[2] Despite his evident dramatic talent, he was haunted by the literary ghost of fiction.

Rooke can remember thinking, his first evening on campus as thick fog swirled around old lampposts: "God, this is a dream, something is going to happen to me here!"[3] The great literary ghost at Chapel Hill was Thomas Wolfe, whom Rooke read and loved. The South was populated by writers destined to be the great names of the century: William Faulkner and Eudora Welty in Mississippi;

Carson McCullers and Flannery O'Connor in Georgia; Tennessee Williams and Truman Capote of New Orleans; William Styron in Virginia; and Shirley Ann Grau in Louisiana. All this did something to Rooke's sense of loyalty to the region, although he dissociates himself from regionalism as a writer, claiming in a biographical note that "place (locale) in fiction" is "a vastly over-rated virtue."[4]

His Uncle Donald Gray, a chronic knockabout who detested living in a small town and had travelled across the United States, exerted a special influence on him. Rooke, identifying with his uncle's spirit of rebellion and adventure, decided to become a traveller himself and visited Alaska, San Francisco, New Orleans, and Virginia between 1957 and 1964. Yet his were not really leisurely adventures. He went to Alaska when he was drafted into the army in 1958 and had to serve for eighteen months with an infantry battalion in Anchorage — perhaps the source for his novella "Brush Fire," in *Last One Home Sleeps in the Yellow Bed*. New Orleans entered his life when he went there to work a third summer on *Unto These Hills*.

From 1963 to 1965 he was engaged by The North Carolina Fund for a pilot project to combat poverty, although he himself was not exactly affluent. His luck increased when he was appointed writer-in-residence at the University of North Carolina. A short sojourn in Fancy Gap, Virginia, was followed by journalistic and editorial work on *The North Carolina Anvil* [Durham, North Carolina], a weekly newspaper of politics and the arts, and then by romance with Constance Merriam Raymond, whom he married in 1969.

The new partnership arrived in Victoria, British Columbia, soon after the wedding because Constance had a position teaching English at the University of Victoria. Rooke attained a certain amount of respect through his own writing and teaching, although he was regarded by many critics as being a "grim, unbalanced, keyhole guy — too obsessed with evil, death, weirdness, etc."[5] — for his works such as *Last One Home Sleeps in the Yellow Bed* (1968), *Vault: A Story in Three Parts* (1973), *The Broad Back of the Angel* (1977), *The Love Parlour* (1977), and *Cry Evil* (1980). Rooke was too strange, too idiosyncratic a virtuoso for many Canadian critics. Nevertheless, their critical attitudes modulated into cautious admiration for *Fat Woman* (1980), Rooke's first full-length novel, which was nominated for both the *Books in*

*Canada* First Novel Award and, more importantly, the Governor General's Award for Fiction in English. Although Rooke did not win either, he did win the Periodical Distributors of Canada Award for the best paperback novel and, in the following year, the $20,000 Canada-Australia Literary Award, given on the basis of overall literary contribution instead of a single work. The award, which included a trip to Australia, came the same year in which he brought out *Death Suite*, his sixth collection of short fiction, and *The Magician in Love*, a fabulistic and satiric novella. A special issue of *Canadian Fiction Magazine* (No. 38) was devoted exclusively to his work, and it seemed that his reputation was in high gear. In 1982 Rooke published *The Birth Control King of the Upper Volta*, a short-story collection about people who meet their joys and misfortunes head-on. His second novel, *Shakespeare's Dog* (1983), won the Governor General's Award for Fiction in English. In 1984 Rooke produced two more short-story collections, *A Bolt of White Cloth* and *Sing Me No Love Songs I'll Say You No Prayers*, the latter a volume of selected stories that contained ten hitherto unpublished ones.

Since 1988 Rooke and his wife Constance have lived in Eden Mills, Ontario (population about 350); Constance is a professor of English at nearby University of Guelph. Rooke teaches and conducts writers' workshops and is the founder and organizer of the Eden Mills Writers' Festival, held annually since 1989. Since the move, Rooke has published three books, *How I Saved the Province* (1989), *A Good Baby* (1989), and *The Happiness of Others* (1991), as well as many short stories. His writing continues to win recognition and awards: the Author's Award for the Short Story in 1987, the Pushcart Prize in 1988, and the Okanagan Fiction Prize in 1989. *Who Do You Love?* appeared in 1992.

## NOTES

[1] Leon Rooke, quoted in Anne Collins, "A Canine's Search for Poetic Justice," *Maclean's*, 16 May 1983, p. 44.

[2] Clint Burnham, "Reading Foreign Writers: An Interview with Leon Rooke," *Waves*, 14, No. 3 (Winter 1986), 6.

[3] Geoff Hancock, "An Interview with Leon Rooke," *Canadian Fiction Magazine*, No. 38 (1981), p. 120.

4 "Leon Rooke," in *Canada Writes!: The Members' Book of the Writers Union of Canada*, ed. K.A. Hamilton (Toronto: Writers Union of Canada, 1977), p. 295.

5 Leon Rooke, "Leon Rooke: The Authorized Biography," *Canadian Fiction Magazine*, No. 38 (1981), p. 146.

# Rudy Wiebe (1934–  )

SUSAN WHALEY

RUDY WIEBE: novelist, short-story writer, playwright, anthology editor, professor of creative writing, and Canadian historian and myth maker. A remarkable diversity has informed this Western writer's literary career, which shows no signs of abating.

Rudy Henry Wiebe was born on 4 October 1934 in Fairholme, Saskatchewan, the second child of Tena (née Knelson) and Abram J. Wiebe. Rudy Wiebe's first childhood visions were shaped by the surrounding bush and prairie, and his imagination was fired by his parents' stories "of Russia, of czars and villages and Bolsheviks and starvation and anarchists and war and religious fights: all very good in their way because they kept the childish story-necessity alive. . . ."[1] As Mennonites, the elder Wiebes had been subjected to religious persecution in Russia and had fled to Canada in 1930, only a few years before Wiebe's birth. The Wiebe family spoke a Friesian dialect of Low German at home, and they were concerned with preserving the religious precepts for which they had been obliged to leave Russia. They were pioneers in the tiny community of Speedwell-Jackpine, Saskatchewan, which remained the family home for the first thirteen years of Rudy Wiebe's life. Wiebe remembers the harsh climate and difficult working conditions to which his family was subjected, and, even now, he vividly recalls the three long miles he had to trek to a one-room schoolhouse. "Towns and cities," says Wiebe, "with their paved streets, department stores, motor vehicles, electric lights and spacious bedrooms ... inhabited the segment of my imagination reserved for Grimm's fairy tales and the Greek myths," and Canada itself seemed "a miracle" by virtue of the fact that "... we could work and we had something to eat. ..."[2] Initially, it was the emptiness and loneliness of his environment that impressed Wiebe; together with his historical sense of the land, these early impressions continue as the main catalysts for his writing.

The Wiebe family moved to Coaldale, Alberta, in 1947, and Rudy began studies at the Alberta Mennonite High School. He entered the University of Alberta in Edmonton in 1953 as a first-year medical student but switched to the study of English literature during his second year. Encouraged in his writing by F.M. Salter, who had also been W.O. Mitchell's mentor, Wiebe won first prize in the National Federation of Canadian University Students' short-story contest, for "Scrapbook,"[3] when he was twenty-one years old. Wiebe graduated in 1956 with a Bachelor of Arts, and, in the same year, his short story "The Power" was chosen by Earle Birney to appear in *New Voices: Canadian University Writing of 1956*. During the year following his graduation, Wiebe worked as a research writer for the Glenbow Foundation in Calgary, Alberta. Then, presented with a Rotary International Fellowship for 1957–58, he spent the year studying at the University of Tübingen in West Germany. This prestigious award was followed by his being named an International Nickel Graduate Fellow (1958–59) and a Queen Elizabeth Graduate Fellow (1959–60). After his return to Canada, Wiebe married Tena F. Isaak in March 1958, and recommenced studies at the University of Alberta, from which he received his Master of Arts in 1960. That same year, he also worked in Ottawa as a foreign-service officer for the Government of Canada. In 1961 he completed theological studies at the Mennonite Brethren Bible

College in Winnipeg, to earn his Bachelor of Theology, and began his career as an English teacher in a high school in Selkirk, Manitoba. He combined this vocation with further studies at the University of Manitoba during 1961 and worked as editor of *The Mennonite Brethren Herald* in Winnipeg from 1962 to 1963.

His first novel, *Peace Shall Destroy Many*, originated as his Master's thesis and was published in 1962. The novel presents a bleak look at a Mennonite community in Saskatchewan, and its publication raised no small amount of controversy in Canadian and American Mennonite circles. As a result, Wiebe resigned his position as editor of the Mennonite paper. He eventually left Manitoba to teach at Goshen College, Indiana, as assistant professor of English from 1963 to 1967. In 1964 he studied creative writing at the University of Iowa and received a Canada Council bursary. With 1966 came the publication of his second novel, *First and Vital Candle*, a tale of the Canadian North, which was adapted for radio in 1967. The following year, Wiebe and his family returned to Alberta. Since then, Wiebe has taught at the University of Alberta in Edmonton, where he has been a full professor of creative writing since 1976. From 1978 to 1979 he was writer-in-residence at the University of Calgary.

With the publication of *The Blue Mountains of China* in 1970, it was quite evident that Wiebe's writing had taken a new and mature direction. His next novel, *The Temptations of Big Bear* (1973), brought him the coveted Governor General's Award for Fiction in English. This book, which meticulously delineates the conflict between Native people and whites, and the final demise of Native freedom, had taken him six years to research and write. His next novel, *The Scorched-Wood People* (1977), is a testament to the vision of Louis Riel and the Métis people.

Aside from his novels, Wiebe has produced a number of short stories and edited many short-story anthologies, which include: *The Story-Makers: A Selection of Modern Short Stories* (1970, rev. ed. 1987), *Stories from Western Canada* (1972), *Stories from Pacific and Arctic Canada* (1974, with Andreas Schroeder), *Double Vision: An Anthology of Twentieth-Century Stories in English* (1976), *Getting Here* (1977), *More Stories from Western Canada* (1980, with Aritha van Herk), *West of Fiction* (1983, with Leah Flater and Aritha van Herk), and *War in the West: Voices of the*

*1885 Rebellion* (1985). The first collection of his own short stories, *Where Is the Voice Coming From?*, was published in 1974, and his first play, written in conjunction with Theatre Passe Muraille and entitled *Far as the Eye Can See*, was published in 1977. Wiebe has also written the script for a film version of his novel *The Mad Trapper* (1980), entitled *Death Hunt*. These works have been followed by another collection of short stories, *The Angel of the Tar Sands and Other Stories* (1982), and a novel, *My Lovely Enemy* (1983). His essays have been collected in *A Voice in the Land: Essays by and about Rudy Wiebe* (1981; edited by W.J. Keith) and *Playing Dead: A Contemplation Concerning the Arctic* (1989). Wiebe was one of the founders of the Baffin Writers' Project, a workshop for northern Native writers.

A family man, a teacher, and still very much a writer, Wiebe continues to reside in Edmonton with his wife, Tena, and their three children: Adrienne, Michael, and Christopher. Wiebe thinks of himself as "someone who's trying to live what the original Anabaptists were about," which means being "a radical follower of the person of Jesus Christ."[4] The 320 acres of bush, swamp, and rock that Wiebe owns, fifty miles southwest of Edmonton, attest to his devotion to the land and his intense awareness of it as both living presence and historical force. The majority of his fiction arises from his long-cultivated interest in Native peoples, while the thematic bent and lyrical rhythm of much of his best work reveal Wiebe's religiousness and his natural musical inclination. Wiebe is highly conscious of his responsibility as an artist, and it is his integrity as a writer that most clearly defines him.

### NOTES

[1] Rudy Wiebe, "A Novelist's Personal Notes on Frederick Philip Grove," *University of Toronto Quarterly*, 47 (Spring 1978), 189–99; rpt. in *A Voice in the Land: Essays by and about Rudy Wiebe*, ed. W.J. Keith, Western Canadian Literary Documents, No. 2 (Edmonton: NeWest, 1981), p. 217.

[2] Rudy Wiebe, "Tombstone Community," *Mennonite LIfe*, 19, No. 4 (Oct. 1964), 15–53; rpt. in Keith, ed., *A Voice in the Land*, pp. 19–20, 21.

[3] "Scrapbook" was originally published as "The Midnight Ride of an Alberta Boy," *Liberty*, 33 (Sept. 1956), 22, 64, 66; rpt. (revised) in *Where Is the Voice Coming From?* (Toronto: McClelland and Stewart, 1974), pp. 13–18.

[4] Donald Cameron, "Rudy Wiebe: The Moving Stream Is Perfectly at Rest," in *Conversations with Canadian Novelists* — 2 (Toronto: Macmillan, 1973), p. 148.

# Audrey Thomas (1935–  )

## BARBARA GODARD

AUDREY GRACE (CALLAHAN) THOMAS was born in Binghamton, New York, on 17 November 1935 to Frances (Corbett) and Donald Earle Callahan. Her father, a teacher, returned to graduate school, putting the family in straitened circumstances. Like many middle-class families in that "Presbyterian"[1] city, this one espoused the work ethic and stressed intellectual attainments as a measure of social position. Indeed, several of its members were notable advertisements for these values; one of Thomas' aunts was a professor of mathematics, while her maternal grandfather was an engineer and inventor with IBM in nearby Endicott. He provided the thread of gold in an otherwise drab, brown life. His big summer place in the Adirondack Mountains of northern New York, with a private, sandy beach on a well-wooded lake, afforded idyllic memories, while his punning and philology stimulated Thomas' interest in words. His practical jokes, Thomas remembers, provided lessons in "reality and illusion,"[2] another encouragement for a budding writer.

Elsewhere, this encouragement was lacking. Her ill-matched parents quarrelled, and the family was isolated. Despite this, in later years they expected Thomas to write "stories that ended happily."[3] But this sat ill with Thomas' sense of herself as a misfit, which developed from early loneliness, augmented by a feeling of being completely left out when she started school at four, small and with bad eyesight. Growing up during the war years, with radio bulletins announcing heavy casualties, Thomas was preoccupied with death. Nor did this preoccupation diminish, as polio scares and a car crash that killed fellow students kept green its possibility.[4] All these experiences nourish Thomas' fiction, despite her revolt against the rigid, narrow philistinism of her milieu that prompted her adult wanderings.

Thomas escaped in an acceptable way, helped by a scholarship to a girls' private school in New Hampshire when she was fifteen. This was followed by a scholarship to Mary A. Burnham School, a finishing school in Northampton, Massachusetts. Some of the money for her education was earned by summer work at the insane asylum in Binghamton when she was seventeen. In 1953 she entered prestigious Smith College, also in Northampton, on a tuition scholarship. Here, in the company of other bright young women, she was challenged intellectually for the first time. Majoring in English, she made the dean's list when she graduated with a B.A. in 1957.

Thomas embarked on a year abroad to complete her sentimental education when she followed her best friend to St. Andrew's University in Scotland for her junior year (1955–56). There she enjoyed a taste of independence in boardinghouse living and in an academic system of large lectures at a cosmopolitan university attended by many commonwealth students. During her holidays she took the usual grand tour to Spain, Italy, Belgium, Switzerland, and Scandinavia. Upon graduation from Smith College, she returned to Britain, finding employment as a teacher in the Birmingham slums at Bishop Rider's Church of England Infant and Junior School.

In 1958 she met and married Ian Thomas, a sculptor and art teacher at Birmingham College of Art. With their first child, they moved in 1959 to Vancouver, where Ian taught. After supply teaching for a year, Thomas enrolled in an M.A. program in English and became a teaching assistant at the University of British Columbia. Her thesis, "Henry James in the Palace of Art: A Survey and Evaluation of James' Aesthetic Criteria as Shown in His Criticism of Nineteenth Century Painting," was completed in 1963, at which point she began doctoral work with the support of a Canada Council award. "An Archetypal Reading of Beowulf," the thesis she wrote, was more like a novel than a dissertation. The thesis was not accepted, and Thomas opted out of academia.

Her first published story appeared in *The Atlantic Monthly* while she was in Africa, where her husband taught at the University of Science and Technology in Kumasi, Ghana, from 1964 to 1966. In 1969 she took up writing full-time and bought a house on Galiano Island, in the Gulf of Georgia, British Columbia, where she has lived since. In 1971 she returned to Africa — to Senegal and Mali, as well as Ghana again — for three months of research. She separated from her husband the following year; they were divorced in 1979. To support herself, she returned to teaching, alternating years of writing with posts in university creative-writing departments — at the University of British Columbia (1975–76 and 1981), Concordia University (1978), the University of Victoria (1978–79), and Simon Fraser University (1982), and most recently, the University of Ottawa. Further travels abroad took her to Greece for a year during 1976–77 and to France in the summer of 1979 to try out the French she had been learning the preceding year.

During the 1970s Thomas was involved with a number of Canadian literary institutions, serving on the Arts Advisory Board of The Canada Council and on its Reading Tours Committee. As well as being a member of Amnesty International and ACTRA, Thomas is a member of the Writers Union of Canada, on whose national executive she has served, and of PEN. These commitments reflect a putting down of roots manifested in her taking out Canadian citizenship in 1979.

As a child Thomas had a romantic dream of being "A Writer," wanting "to be *known* and all those things,"[5] to compensate for being small and shy. She was an avid reader, alerted by her grandfather to the magic of words, and a listener of her "Shanty Irish" father's storytelling.[6] She wrote some poetry when she was about twelve, adding fiction at about nineteen.[7] None of her apprentice works has been published, and Thomas considers them "really terrible stories."[8] Juggling babies, graduate school, and teaching, she had little time for writing, though the stimulation of the University of British Columbia "turned [her] on to words again" (Coupey et al., p. 95). She submitted about a dozen stories to *Prism* and other periodicals and collected rejection slips. The shock of Africa, amplified by the experience of a miscarriage, placed her under a compulsion to order the chaos of her life. "Words were all I had . . ." in that state of despair, says Thomas (Coupey et al., p. 94), to "organize the pain and turn it into art" (Wachtel, p. 5). "I realized that it wasn't going to kill me. So I really began to write, to go down deeper" (Wachtel, p. 5). "If One Green Bottle . . . ," a story from that experience, was published in *The Atlantic Monthly* in 1965 and won an invitation from editor Bob Amussen to submit a manuscript to Bobbs-Merrill.

Thomas' collection of stories *Ten Green Bottles* was published in 1967. Then followed what Thomas has called "the glass slipper technique of getting published."[9] The contract stipulated a novel as well. While writing her doctoral thesis and awaiting the birth of a third daughter, Thomas struggled with a novel that failed to click. She put it aside to write *Mrs. Blood* (1970) and *Munchmeyer and Prospero on the Island* (1971) before revising the novel as *Songs My Mother Taught Me* (1973). These were followed by another novel, *Blown Figures* (1974), and a second collection of stories, *Ladies and Escorts* (1977). *Latakia* (1979), a novel, was in turn succeeded by more stories, *Real Mothers* (1982) and *Two in the Bush and Other Stories* (1982), a selection from her two earlier collections. In 1984 she published the novel *Intertidal Life*, and in 1986 a collection of short stories, *Goodbye Harold, Good Luck*. Her latest work is another collection of short stories, *The Wild Blue Yonder* (1990). Over the past decade, Thomas has published or had broadcast on CBC Radio's *Anthology* another half-dozen uncollected pieces, including a children's story. She has also published more than a dozen book reviews in periodicals such as *Canadian Literature* and *Books in Canada* and has contributed essays to academic journals on subjects such as art criticism and women writers. She has written plays for CBC Radio's *Stage* and has contributed a number of travel articles to newspapers and magazines.

Thomas is the recipient of several Canada Council arts awards

(1969, 1971, 1972, 1979). Her story, "If One Green Bottle . . ." won a "Firsts" Award in 1965 from *The Atlantic Monthly*. Other stories have won more recent competitions: "Harry and Violet," second prize in the National Magazine Awards fiction category, 1979; "Natural History," second prize in the CBC Literary Contest fiction division, 1979–80; "Real Mothers," second prize in *Chatelaine*'s Fourth Annual Fiction Competition, 1981; and "Untouchables: A Memoir," second prize in the CBC Literary Contest memoir division, 1981. *Intertidal Life* was short-listed for the 1984 Governor General's Award for Fiction in English, and it was the first winner of the Ethel Wilson Fiction Prize in 1985 offered by the Association of Book Publishers of British Columbia and the Federation of British Columbia Writers. Thomas won this prize again in 1991 for *The Wild Blue Yonder*. She has also won the Canada-Australia Literary Prize and the Marian Engel Award, given to a woman writer for an outstanding body of work. Together, these honours and awards support Priscilla Galloway's contention that Audrey Thomas has moved definitely into the "top rank of Canadian novelists."[10]

## NOTES

[1] Alison Appelbe, "Female Loners . . . and the Broken Marriage Syndrome," *Leisure* [*The Vancouver Sun*], 31 Aug. 1973, p. 34A.

[2] Don Stanley, "Stories Audrey Told Me," *Leisure* [*The Vancouver Sun*], 9 Sept. 1977, p. 7A.

[3] Appelbe, p. 34A.

[4] Graeme Matheson, "Below the Surface," *Quill & Quire*, Oct. 1974, p. 3.

[5] Pierre Coupey et al., "Interview/Audrey Thomas," *The Capilano Review*, No. 7 (Spring 1975), p. 94. Further references to this work appear in the text.

[6] John Hofsess, "A Teller of Surprising Tales," *The Canadian* [*The Toronto Star*], 6 May 1978, p. 16.

[7] There are several different versions of Thomas' beginning to write. This one comes from Eleanor Wachtel, "Interview with Audrey Thomas," *Sunday Morning*, CBC Radio, 24 Jan. 1981. She also said to David Watmough in an interview (*Anthology*, CBC Radio, 1 May 1971) that she had been writing since she was a young child. To George Bowering, she stated that she began writing stories in England ("Songs and Wisdom: An Interview with Audrey Thomas," *Open Letter*, 4th ser., No. 3 [Spring 1979], p. 7). In the Coupey et al. interview,

she said that she began writing again as a graduate student at the University of British Columbia (p. 95).

[8] Eleanor Wachtel, "The Guts of *Mrs. Blood*," *Books in Canada*, Nov. 1979, p. 5. Further references to this work appear in the text.

[9] Phil Surguy, "Initiation Writes," *Books in Canada*, April 1978, p. 8.

[10] Rev. of *Intertidal Life*, in *Canadian Book Review Annual: 1984*, ed. Dean Tudor and Ann Tudor (Toronto: Simon and Pierre, 1985), p. 203.

# Dave Godfrey (1938–  )

## MICHAEL LARSEN

DAVE GODFREY was born in Winnipeg in 1938; he grew up in Manitoba and Ontario. Godfrey's family moved quite often, perhaps instilling the restlessness, openness to the unfamiliar, and sense of cultural relativism that are important undercurrents in his career. After he finished high school, Godfrey sampled the academic life at Harvard and the University of Toronto, taking writing courses and working very hard on his own fiction. Then, in 1958, he enrolled in the University of Iowa, home of the well-known Writers' Workshop. Godfrey received his B.A. from the University of Iowa in 1960 and his M.A. from Stanford University in 1963. He also studied at the University of Chicago and received M.F.A. and Ph.D. degrees from the University of Iowa. In 1963 Godfrey married Ellen Swartz. They had three children: Jonathan Kofi, Rebecca, and Samuel; their eldest son died in 1981. Ellen Godfrey is also a novelist and publisher.

From 1963 to 1965 Godfrey was in Africa with CUSO (Canadian University Service Overseas). He taught English in Ghana and toured parts of West Africa in a jazz and high-life band, absorbing local history and culture. His impression of Ghana and Mali are recorded in a "Letter from Africa, to an American Negro," published in *The Tamarack Review* in 1966. In this letter Godfrey emphasizes the vast cultural divide between Africans and North Americans, even Black Americans, and he warns against the assumption that Western solutions should be applied to African problems. Clearly, the CUSO experience was formative for Godfrey, supplying raw material for a good deal of his fiction and underscoring the influence of culture on individual perception and behaviour. Godfrey returned to North America in 1965.

While he was gathering valuable experience abroad, Godfrey was achieving recognition at home for his fiction, which had been appearing in Canadian periodicals since 1961; some was even reappearing in major short-story anthologies. His reputation as an important young writer was growing, and in 1965 he was awarded a University of Western Ontario President's Medal for his short story "Gossip: The Birds That Flew, the Birds That Fell." These medals are awarded annually for the best general article, scholarly article, short story, and single poem published in the previous year by a Canadian or in a Canadian periodical. In 1967 Godfrey won for best story ("The Hard-Headed Collector") and for best article ("Letter from Africa, to an American Negro").

Godfrey spend the summer of 1965 at the University of Chicago and 1965–66 at the University of Iowa. In the spring of 1966, he completed his general Ph.D. work at the University of Iowa and accepted an appointment as an assistant professor of English at Trinity College, University of Toronto. (Final approval of his Ph.D. dissertation took place in 1967.) He taught at Trinity and at other colleges of the University of Toronto until 1976. In 1967 he cofounded House of Anansi Press, one of three nationalistic presses he would establish over the years. House of Anansi published Godfrey's first collection of short stories — *Death Goes Better with Coca-Cola* — in 1967. In 1968 Godfrey and Bill McWhinney edited *Man Deserves Man: CUSO in Developing Countries,* in which the CUSO story is narrated by some of the volunteers who lived it in Africa, Asia, the Caribbean, South America, and India. Also in

1968 Godfrey, David Lewis Stein, and Clark Blaise edited *New Canadian Writing, 1968*, a selection of their stories.

Since his return from Africa, Godfrey had been publishing selections from a novel-in-progress. In 1969 he and his family went to France, where he completed this novel, *The New Ancestors*. He returned to Canada in the summer of 1969, left House of Anansi, and cofounded new press, which published his novel the next year. *The New Ancestors* met with critical acclaim and won the Governor General's Award for Fiction in English (1971). Also in 1970 Godfrey and Mel Watkins edited *Gordon to Watkins to You*. This book, subtitled *Documentary: The Battle for Control of Our Economy*, is a mosaic of reports, debates, and commentary portraying the political, social, and cultural costs of the vast American influence on the Canadian economy. Godfrey's nationalistic instincts were again evident in 1972 when he joined with Robert Fulford and Abraham Rotstein to edit *Read Canadian: A Book about Canadian Books*. In *Read Canadian* more than two dozen experts in the humanities and social sciences survey the best Canadian literature in their fields, and the editors suggest ways of strengthening the Canadian book industry. Always a man of energy and variety, Godfrey at this time was also writing literary reviews for *The Canadian Forum* and playing trumpet with a group of African rock musicians/ composers.

Godfrey founded Press Porcépic, his third publishing house, in 1973. That year it reprinted a slightly revised and beautifully designed edition of *Death Goes Better with Coca-Cola*; book design was by Tim Inkster. Godfrey left new press in 1974. From 1973 to 1975 he was writer-in-residence at the University of Toronto, Erindale, and in 1976 he published *I Ching Kanada*, his transformation into a Canadian context of the ancient Chinese text. During 1976–77 he taught at York University, and in 1977 he was appointed associate professor and chairman of the Creative Writing Department at the University of Victoria. He was chairman from 1977–78 until 1981–82; he was made a full professor in 1981. His latest collection of stories, *Dark Must Yield*, appeared in 1978. In the 1980s he also published a sequence of very experimental fictions, mainly in *Rampike*.

Since the publication of *Dark Must Yield*, Godfrey's interest in science and technology, so evident in his fiction, has led him to edit and author a number of books dealing with development in communications and computer technology. In 1979 he and Douglas Parkhill coedited *Gutenberg Two: The New Electronics and Social Change*; in 1981 he and Ernest Chang coedited *The Telidon Book*; in 1982 he and Sharon Sterling coauthored *The Elements of* CAL, a book on computer-aided learning; another text on computer-aided learning followed in 1984; and in 1985 he edited the selected proceedings of the Canadian Conference on Electronic Publishing, of which he had been chairman. In 1985 and 1986 he brought his cycle of technology and communication books to a close with a revised (4th) edition of *Gutenberg Two*, containing his important essay on the "crofter" mentality in Canada, and a new edition of Harold Innis' seminal *Empire and Communications*, to which he added a preface and afterword.

There are a number of important strands in Godfrey's life that should be separated out. The first is his academic orientation. He prepared himself for an academic career, and since 1963 he has been actively engaged in teaching literature and creative writing. He is, then, one of a new breed of writer-academics, and like many of them he brings to his work an extensive knowledge of literary tradition, an innovative spirit, and sharply honed critical skills and judgements. Even the early short stories show a competence and a professionalism that derive from a strong academic background.

Second, a great deal of his time and energy over the years has been devoted to establishing and operating small presses to provide the outlets and stimulate the markets for a broad range of Canadian writing. And if, as Archibald MacMechan claimed, ". . . a country comes into being only as it is written about . . . ," then Godfrey by his publishing endeavours has contributed more than most to the development of a distinctly Canadian sensibility and identity. Besides founding and directing three presses, he has been coordinator of the Literary Press Group, was a founding director of the Association of Canadian Publishers, has served on the editorial board of *The Canadian Forum*, *Waves*, and the *Journal of Canadian Fiction*.

Finally, although Godfrey is intensely nationalistic, he has travelled widely, written often of other countries and cultures, and freely used or adapted exotic literary forms and techniques, including Chinese hexagrams, the French *nouveau roman*, the tall tales of the American West, Indian fables, and African proverbs. To some extent we can see this wide-ranging experimentation as evidence of a restless and innovative spirit. It also illustrates a sensibility attuned to the complexity and variety of contemporary life. Moreover, we can see here Godfrey's determination to be an important writer, to extend his appeal beyond his own time and country. And in books like *The New Ancestors*, *I Ching Kanada*, and *Dark Must Yield*, he clearly establishes a claim to international stature and significance.

# Jack Hodgins (1938– )

## DAVID JEFFREY

ON VANCOUVER ISLAND along the Island Highway past Courtenay towards Campbell River, one of the smaller patches of housefronts and corner store that suddenly appear out of the bush and as suddenly vanish again, is a place called Merville. Its very existence is hardly noticed, much less the quaint irony of its name, by passing cars and camper-loads of tourists. Pronounced by its native residents almost as a person from West Ireland would pronounce *marvel*, its road-front lies well back from the sea, doubly confusing the literal French of the person who named it. Tiny, rural, ironically christened, Merville, British Columbia, might seem unlikely to offer up to the world any story much worth the telling. In fact, the hamlet illustrates in an off-handed way one of Jack Hodgins' central convictions — that reality is often much more than what it seems — for Merville has granted us many of the fine achievements in recent Canadian fiction.

As it happens, the centre of Hodgins' fictional world is, quite literally, the centre of his actual world: Merville is not only the site of his own upbringing but that of his parents as well. His mother, Rita Blakely, was born in Alberta but moved to a farm in the Comox Valley as a child. His father, Stanley Hodgins, was born in Metchosin, British Columbia; he also came as a child to Merville, where, in the mid-1930s, he was hired on to work for Rita Blakely's father. Like other hired men for the Blakely family, he ended up by marrying (in 1937) one of the farmer's daughters. Jack was their firstborn, on 3 October 1938, and he was followed by a younger brother and sister. All were educated down the highway at the small Tsolum school from first to twelfth grade, but his parents' stump ranch — forest-bounded, rough-cut meadows with white-faced cattle grazing around great blackened stumps, and a simple house long without electricity or indoor toilet facilities — is the principal focus for his childhood memories.

Framing this centre we should imagine a strongly developed interlaced border of immediate relationships in the rural community, a kinship with which Hodgins still identifies:

> My mother was one of six, my Dad was one of thirteen. So every second person in the community was a relative. If he wasn't a relative, he was a friend. So that kind of an extended family is just part of the way I see the world.[1]

Perhaps as a consequence, interlocking relationships have proven to be an integrating force in most of Hodgins' published work, not merely within individual novels or collections of stories, but across and between them, as though each of his books had centred itself in a common family experience. It is amusing, but not at all insignificant, that the earliest fictional mirror for Hodgins' childhood world was the cartoons of Al Capp and that he should claim the Dogpatch world of *L'il Abner* to be the closest analogy to his own early experience. It is consistent with such a context that he should have become, on the one hand, "no respecter of persons," but, on the other, an admirer of distinct character.

As a small child, Jack was a voracious reader, and when one day he complained of having exhausted the volumes available to him, his mother is reported by him to have said, "Well, then you'll just have to write one of your own."[2] He did and, as a nine-year-old, was able to persuade his babysitter to type up his first story, a murder mystery. When she had finished, he took the pages and sewed them into a book. Other projects followed, and by the time he was ready to leave the Island to study English literature and do a Secondary Education Certificate at the University of British Columbia, the determination to pursue his interest in writing was well fixed in his mind. Shortly after arriving on the University of British Columbia campus in 1957, he enrolled in his first creative-writing course, with the poet and Chaucerian Earle Birney. At that time there was no separate department or program of creative writing at the University of British Columbia, and the course was still considered by the university to be a luxury. The class, including six other students and Birney, met "every Thursday evening and ripped each other's work to shreds."[3] Birney was a good influence, Hodgins reflects, especially in reinforcing his determination to write:

> He somehow gave me the confidence that it wasn't a wasted dream. I'd gone through my childhood believing this was a fantasy that couldn't possibly come true. I hadn't seen it come true for anyone else. He treated our work with respect, even though now I can see some of it was very bad.[4]

During his years as a student at the University of British Columbia, he also established a friendship with William H. New (then editor of *Canadian Literature*). New's collegial interest over the intervening years has been important to Hodgins, not primarily for their formal collaborations (in 1981 they edited an anthology, *Voice and Vision*), but for New's encouragement of Hodgins' own writing. Although he is reserved, almost to the point of shyness, Hodgins is congenial and generous, and he has attempted to establish numerous friendly relationships with colleagues, fellow writers, and editors wherever he has worked. Among these, Ray Smith, Robert Kroetsch, and Roy MacGregor figure importantly at various periods of his life.

However, the most significant friendship Hodgins developed in those years has endured to become the most influential: he met his wife, Diane, while they were studying together at the University of British Columbia, and they were married in 1960. A thoughtful, cheerful person, her deep and evident religious convictions (the family are conscientious adherents to Christian Science) are manifestly an anchor to family life as well as a source of additional influence on the character of Hodgins' own thoughtfulness and, perhaps, especially, his general optimism about human experience and community. Herself from the city of Vancouver, Diane adapted admirably to life on the Island, where Jack took his first teaching assignment (senior secondary English and creative writing) at Nanaimo in 1961. Three children soon followed (Shannon, Gavin, and Tyler). Belying his slight build and sometimes quiet bookishness, Hodgins then drew on his early practical experience as a logger, first to clear part of a four-acre lot in Lantzville, then to build an attractive and spacious house so completely surrounded by the remaining trees that they impede entirely the view the family might otherwise have had of Georgia Strait. For many happy family years this was their version of life "up-island," Diane teaching English as a second language, Jack teaching English literature and composition. Well before the time he discontinued his eighteen-year relationship with the Nanaimo District High School in 1979, Jack and Diane had become to their area what Jack's parents were still in Merville — quiet, widely respected and trusted members of their rural community.

Despite his preoccupations as a beginning teacher, Hodgins wrote steadily following his graduation from the University of British Columbia. Yet for eight discouraging years he received little more than rejection slips for his efforts. In 1967 he sent some work to an American journal, "just to see what would happen."[5] Suddenly, he had sold his first story. "Every Day of His Life" appeared in the *Northwest Review* for February 1968. This initiation was soon confirmed by a series of acceptances from several magazines, including *The North American Review*, *Descant*, *Viva*, and the *University of Houston Forum*. Encouraged, he took his pen more firmly in hand (he claims to despise typewriters and will only resort to them for later drafts), devoting more and more of his nonteaching time to writing. Later, he tried again to break into the Canadian market, and stories soon appeared in *Wascana Review*, *The Antigonish Review*, *The Capilano Review*, *The Canadian Forum*, *Canadian Fiction Magazine*, and the *Journal of Canadian Fiction*, several of which he then collected into his first volume, *Spit Delaney's Island* (1976).

Possessed of some new ideas and with a desire to experience something of his roots, Hodgins gathered up his family and went to Ireland for several months in 1975. Having immersed himself in Irish literature as a "preparation" for his visit, he spent his time there "listening," trying to catch the rhythms of Irish speech and hoping that he would come to understand the background of some of his own transplanted literary characters.[6] While there, he wrote more stories and redrafted sections of his first novel, *The Invention of the World* (1977), part of which was to be set in Ireland. Of his wanting to go there himself, Hodgins has said simply: ". . . the island of Ireland to me always had a kind of romantic aura. The islandness of it itself attracted me."[7] Some other of the analogies he found were not to appear until later, in his second volume of stories.

After his return, the publication of *Spit Delaney's Island* by Macmillan confirmed a publishing relationship begun when Hodgins edited two literary anthologies, *The Frontier Experience* (1975) and *The West Coast Experience* (1976) — in both of which he demonstrated his affinity and sense of literary community with writers of the West Coast — and charted the course for a mutually happy relationship with Macmillan's fiction editor, Doug Gibson.

About the time Macmillan's Laurentian Library was bringing out *Spit Delaney's Island* in paperback, Hodgins accepted an invitation from Simon Fraser University to become a writer-in-residence (1977). This was an eventful year, for it also saw the publication of *The Invention of the World*, and receipt of Eaton's British Columbia Book Award for his volume of short stories. *The Invention of the World* was an instant success. Widely heralded by critics on both sides of the border, it became a Macmillan paperback almost immediately and was introduced in the United States by Harcourt Brace Jovanovich in 1978. More awards have followed: Gibson's Literary Award for First Novels (1978), the Author's Award from the Association of Periodical Distributors (1979), the Governor General's Award for Fiction in English (1980), and the Canada-Australia Literary Prize (1986).

When a chance to do a term as writer-in-residence at the University of Ottawa materialized for 1979, Hodgins was prompted to consider severing ties with his teaching position in Nanaimo. The initial decision came, as usual, after long hours of family deliberation, involving his wife's need to obtain a leave from her position as an ESL teacher for the Nanaimo District; yet all the evidence suggests that it was an enthusiastic family undertaking. After a season in Ottawa and with the final decision to leave high-school teaching, Hodgins' career as a writer became a full-time vocation. In the same year, sponsored by the Department of External Affairs, he made a highly successful trip to Japan, making speeches to the Japan-Canada Conference as well as to academic and literary groups in Tokyo. Once again, as in the case of his trip to Ireland, the new cultural experiences quickly began to be reflected back on the character of his island fiction: soon he was well into the first draft of his story "Sumo Revisions," which appears in *The Barclay Family Theatre* (1981).

The term in Ottawa was a quiet success for the Hodgins. Living in a rented house in Vanier, they met the rigours of their first eastern winter with determined cheer. Though his writing schedule had him at work from early morning without a break until late afternoon, Jack still managed to find time to explore the area, including parts of the Ottawa Valley where some of his ancestors had settled (Shawville, Quebec). He travelled *en famille* to Boston and New York and visited in literary and academic circles in Toronto, partly in connection with the release of his second novel, *The Resurrection of Joseph Bourne; or, A Word or Two on Those Port Annie Miracles* (1979). At the time he was working on another group of Vancouver Island stories and a play. But he was experimenting also with the possibility of writing something set in Ottawa or in the Ottawa Valley. He went out into the streets, to the By-Ward Market, and along the Rideau Canal, listening to conversations and accents, observing and enjoying a world so different from his native Vancouver Island that he felt it could be a different country. He tells of one occasion when he was stopped in the By-Ward Market by a valley-accented Christmas-tree salesman: "You look familiar. You're from around Shawville someplace, aren't you? Let's see now, by that face you'd be a Hodgins."[8] This uncanny lesson in genetics, he says, left hair prickling on the back of his neck.

He also saw a very different side of life in the national capital, attending various soirées, and was a fascinated guest at the annual reception in honour of the Revolution at the Soviet embassy. In the spring of 1980, the Canada Council awarded him a year-long Senior Arts Award, which left him free to work on his collection of stories, at that time provisionally titled "Allied Invasions," which included a story inspired in part by his experience at the Soviet embassy.

Travelling to the West Coast again, he concluded his collection, now titled *The Barclay Family Theatre*, and considered an invitation to return to Ottawa as a permanent writer-in-residence and creative-writing teacher, an arrangement that would leave him free to work half-time on his university responsibilities, half-time on his writing. On the other hand, he would have to face the cold and snow, which even on bright sunny days he claimed to find so depressing as to make him long heartily for the foggy rains of January on the Island. The decision was not arrived at quickly, but the interim choice was once again to turn east. For the next two years, the Hodgins made their home in Ottawa. In 1982 Jack made a film, "Jack Hodgins' Island" (NFB; produced by Don Hopkins, directed by Robert Duncan), in which he talks about his work and his "world" of Vancouver Island. In Ottawa, he set to work on two significant projects. The first was a children's book, undertaken with his youngest son, Tyler, a budding cartoon artist. This book was published as *Left Behind in Squabble Bay* (1988), illustrated by VictoR GAD (sic); Tyler is now a professional artist. In 1982, with the draft of *Left Behind* completed, Hodgins turned his full attention to a major, three-part novel, "Lost Villages," on which he was still working when he decided in 1983 to return to Vancouver Island. The return was inevitable but, in the circumstances, not without complications, including a major career decision. A tension between the two places, the urban national capital and rural Vancouver Island, to be manifested in his new novel, was finally resolved with a decision to go to Victoria. Hodgins spoke of it as "a compromise." He was nonetheless excited at the prospect of his return to the familiar coast, even while bracing himself for the impact of full-time duties in the Department of Creative Writing at the University of Victoria, where he began teaching in September 1983. In this new milieu, the "Lost Villages" manuscript presented unexpected difficulties; it was soon replaced by a short story which, in many redraftings, became a novella and finally a novel, *The Honorary Patron* (1987). Hodgins' latest novel, *Innocent Cities*, was published in 1990. A book about his travels in Australia is due for publication in 1992 in both Canada and Australia. Hodgins is currently working on new fiction going back to "Spit Delaney country," but it is not yet clear whether this new work will take the form of a novel, short stories, or a trilogy.

## NOTES

1 Alan Twigg, "Jack Hodgins: Western Horizon," interview, in his *For Openers: Conversations with 24 Canadian Writers* (Madeira Park, B.C.: Harbour, 1981), p. 187.

2 David Jeffrey, personal interview with Jack Hodgins, Feb. 1981.

3 Geoff Hancock, "An Interview with Jack Hodgins," *Canadian Fiction Magazine*, Nos. 32–33 (1979–80), p. 37.

4 Hancock, p. 37.

5 David Jeffrey, personal interview with Jack Hodgins, Feb. 1981.

6 Peter O'Brien, "An Interview with Jack Hodgins," *Rubicon*, No. 1 (Spring 1983), p. 49.

7 O'Brien, p. 49.

8 David Jeffrey, personal interview with Jack Hodgins, Dec. 1979.

# John Metcalf (1938–  )

## DOUGLAS ROLLINS

JOHN WESLEY METCALF was born in the northern English city of Carlisle on 12 November 1938, son of a former schoolteacher and a Methodist minister. His father's profession required frequent relocations, and Metcalf spent his childhood in Yorkshire, the resort city of Bournemouth, and the London dormitory suburb of Beckenham. He spent part of the war and many subsequent holidays on his uncle's farm in County Cumberland. During his academic career, Metcalf was in the shadow of his older brother Michael, now a distinguished mediaeval scholar and lecturer at both Cambridge and Oxford, where he is a Keeper at the Ashmolean Museum. Rejected by Cambridge, Metcalf was awarded a scholarship to the University of Bristol in 1957. He read English and theology under such scholars as L.C. Knights and Basil Cottle but was more interested in "friendships, sex, drink, rock-climbing, travel in Europe, and being generally disreputable."[1]

Always a voracious reader, Metcalf expanded his knowledge of modern literature, which was not taught at the university. His passion for the writing of Ernest Hemingway led him to an interest in bullfighting and, on two occasions, to Pamplona for the fiesta, where he had a chance meeting with Hemingway himself. Metcalf's taste for travel had been whetted in his early teens when he had accompanied his brother on a research trip to Yugoslavia and Greece. During university vacations, he either travelled (scruffy and penniless; he once had to be repatriated from Calais at British government expense) or worked, once in a Leicester bakery, once as an agricultural worker on the island of Jersey, more often in restaurants. Awarded a B.A. in 1960 and a Certificate in Education in 1961, Metcalf taught at a secondary modern school in Bristol and later in a boys' reformatory. Before being fired from his Borstal school position, Metcalf became friendly with James Gaite, now an eminent educational psychologist and university administrator, who persuaded Metcalf to join him in his application to the Protestant School Board of Greater Montreal. The pair arrived in Canada in the summer of 1962, and Metcalf soon found himself at Rosemount High School teaching English and, to his dismay, Canadian history.

Metcalf first began writing for publication after a student showed him an advertisement for a CBC short-story competition. His first effort, "Early Morning Rabbits," won a 1963 prize of $100 and was broadcast on the CBC. Initial success was followed by disappointing rejections; however, in 1964 Earle Birney, then editor of the quarterly *Prism International*, recognized Metcalf's potential and made the unusual decision to publish eight of his stories over two issues.[2] That year Metcalf returned to England briefly for his father's funeral. Partly to save money to finance full-time writing and partly to escape a troubled love affair, Metcalf took a teaching position at the remote and aptly named RCAF base of Cold Lake, Alberta. His enthusiasm for classic blues and traditional jazz led him from Montreal to Alberta via New Orleans. Metcalf found the military atmosphere at Cold Lake extremely uncongenial, and his time there was lonely and difficult. Encouraged by the publication of one of his stories in *The Canadian Forum*, he worked on a novel (later scrapped) and produced more stories, all of which were rejected. However, he could state confidently, "I'm quite pleased with the writing. . . . I think its [sic] getting better even if the whole publishing continent of North America declares otherwise."[3] That Easter holiday he returned to Montreal and the relationship he had hoped to end. In August 1965 he married Gale Courey, a student he had met at Rosemount; they left for England the day after their wedding.

Metcalf's plan was to spend at least a year exclusively at writing, but his savings were soon exhausted, and he took a job at a Catholic comprehensive school. His intention to settle permanently in England was also revised; his second decision to live in Canada was much more considered than his first. "England irritates me all the time," he has written. "Its class attitudes, after the easiness of Canada, seemed more rigid than ever. It was inefficient and parochial in its attitudes and made me feel very cramped."[4]

Shortly after Metcalf's return to Montreal in 1966, his work appeared in book form for the first time when two of the *Prism* stories were included in the Ryerson anthology *Modern Canadian Stories* (1966). Ryerson Press's fiction editor, Earle Toppings, became a valuable source of advice and encouragement. Metcalf lasted two years with the Montreal school board; he then worked part time in a private school and marked essays to finance his writing. Publication in Canadian literary magazines increased, and Metcalf received a Canada Council arts grant in 1968 and was awarded the President's Medal of the University of Western Ontario for "The Estuary," judged the best short story published in Canada in 1968. The Metcalfs' daughter Elizabeth was born in 1969, and five of his stories appeared in *New Canadian Writing, 1969: Stories by John Metcalf, D.O. Spettigue and C.J. Newman.* His first book, *The Lady Who Sold Furniture*, containing a novella and five stories, appeared in 1970. He taught part time at McGill University and at Loyola College, which is now part of Concordia University. With the aim of creating a wider audience and promoting Canadian writing, Metcalf initiated the formation of the Montreal Storytellers Fiction Performance Group[5] and, with fellow members Hugh Hood, Ray Smith, Clark Blaise, and Ray Fraser, read to high school, college, and university audiences in Quebec and the Maritimes. By 1971 Metcalf had won a third Canada Council grant and was completing his first published novel, *Going Down Slow*, when his marriage suddenly and unexpectedly broke up. In the academic year 1972–73, he took up his first writer-in-residence appointment at the University of New Brunswick in Fredericton. Although his literary output was relatively small, he was already recognized as an important writer and as an editor of taste and intelligence.

Metcalf taught at Loyola during 1973–74 and then at Vanier College in Montreal. He was awarded his first Senior Arts Award from the Canada Council in 1974. A collection of stories, *The Teeth of My Father*, appeared in 1975. The next academic year was divided into stints as writer-in-residence at the University of Ottawa, and Loyola. Metcalf married Myrna Teitelbaum in 1975, received a second Senior Arts Award from the Canada Council in 1976, and moved with his wife and stepson to an old fieldstone house outside the village of Delta, Ontario. He supported himself writing, editing, and doing literary assignments for various publishers and government arts councils, and with a Senior Arts Award in 1978, a short-term award in 1980, and awards in 1983 and 1986. He published two novellas under the collective title *Girl in Gingham* in 1978 and his second novel, *General Ludd*, in 1980. He taught creative writing and served as writer-in-residence at Concordia University during 1980–81 and was writer-in-residence at the University of Bologna in 1985. In June 1981 the Metcalfs moved to Ottawa, where they still live.

Metcalf's determination to promote modern Canadian literature in schools has resulted in his editing of poetry texts and anthologies of Canadian short stories, the most innovative of which, *Sixteen by Twelve* (1970), *The Narrative Voice* (1972), *Stories Plus* (1979), and *Making It New* (1982), allow contemporary Canadian writers to comment on their own work. His concern for promoting deserving lesser-known and younger writers is particularly demonstrated in his initiating and editing a series of anthologies (*First Impressions* [1980] and *Second Impressions* [1981]) designed to introduce them to a wider audience. He coedited the series of annual anthologies *Best Canadian Stories* during 1976–82 and, with Clark Blaise, the anthology *Here and Now* (1977). With Leon Rooke, Metcalf coedited *The Macmillan Anthology 1* in 1988 and the second volume of the anthology in 1989; he edited the third volume in 1990 with Kent Thompson. *The New Story Writers*, a collection Metcalf edited for Quarry Press, is scheduled to appear in 1992. A book of essays, *Kicking Against the Pricks*, appeared in 1982, as did Metcalf's *Selected Stories*. In 1986 he published another book of stories, *Adult Entertainment*.

Metcalf writes extensively on Canadian intellectual life and cultural policy; on this topic he has published *The Bumper Book* (1986), *Carry On Bumping* (1988), *What Is a Canadian Literature?* (1988), *Writers in Aspic* (1988), and (with Sam Solecki and W.J. Keith) *Volleys* (1990). Since 1988 he has been most actively involved in a debate over the status and function of the Canada Council.[6] Metcalf's latest writing project is a collection of stories, *How Stories Mean*, published with The Porcupine's Quill. He also works with The Porcupine's Quill as an acquisitions editor.

In 1988, Metcalf's contributions to Canadian literature were honoured at a three-day conference at the University of Guelph on the short story, hosted by Tim Struthers. Hugh Hood, Alice Munro, Leon Rooke, and Keath Fraser, among others, paid tribute to John Metcalf.

## NOTES

[1] John Metcalf, quoted by Kent Thompson in "John Metcalf: A Profile," *The Fiddlehead*, No. 114 (Summer 1977), p. 59. This valuable essay appeared as part of the "Special John Metcalf Section."

[2] *Prism International*, 4, No. 1 (Summer 1964), 6–30; and 4, No. 2 (Autumn 1964), 28–43. Eight stories published under the general title "The Geography of Time: A Sequence of Stories by John Metcalf" included "Early Morning Rabbits," which won the CBC Radio's Young Writer's Contest Prize for 1963 and was broadcast on CBC Radio's *Anthology*.

[3] Letter received from John Metcalf [3 April 1965].

[4] Thompson, p. 59.

[5] See Douglas Rollins, "The Montreal Storytellers," *Journal of Canadian Fiction*, 1, No. 2 (Spring 1972), 5–6.

[6] See for example, John Metcalf, "Trial by Jury: Millions for Subsidy, but Not Much Sense of Excellence," *Books in Canada*, Oct. 1991, pp. 22–24.

# Margaret Atwood (1939– )

## ILDIKÓ DE PAPP CARRINGTON

THE EARLY, formative years of Margaret Eleanor Atwood, who was born in Ottawa on 18 November 1939, were shaped by her father's profession and by her reading. The daughter of a forest entomologist, Atwood "grew up in and out of the bush, in and out of Ottawa, Sault Ste. Marie and Toronto" and "did not attend a full year of school until . . . grade eight."[1] The fall and spring "transitions" between the bush and the city were made "dramatic" by the way her family changed appearances — "especially her mother, who put on nylons and dresses and hats and gloves and make-up when they came south. They had one identity for the city and one for the bush." This "rhythm of going back and forth made" Atwood "double-natured."[2] So did her reading of American comic books, Grimms' *Fairy Tales*, and Canadian animal stories.[3] In the comic books, she found "fantasy escape" (*Survival*, p. 29); in the fairy tales, fantastic "transformations" (Oates, p. 43). But in the Canadian animal stories, ". . . the world of dangers was *the same* as the real world . . . ." She learned that "in this world, no Superman would come swooping out of the sky at the last minute to rescue you . . . ; no rider would arrive . . . with a pardon from the king" (*Survival*, p. 30).

At seven, she began writing, "suddenly the only thing [she] wanted to do." Her parents, "great readers," expected her to utilize her "intelligence and abilities and . . . did not pressure" her into marriage (Oates, p. 43). At Victoria College, University of Toronto, where her teachers were Jay Macpherson, Northrop Frye, Kathleen Coburn, and Millar MacLure, the exciting discovery that Canadians were writing and publishing made her feel that she could, too. She read the poetry of P.K. Page, Margaret Avison, James Reaney, D.G. Jones, and Douglas LePan. In 1961, with a B.A. from Victoria College, the E.J. Pratt Medal for her first book of poems, *Double Persephone*, and a Woodrow Wilson Fellowship, she left for Harvard graduate school.

The Harvard experience, from 1961 to 1963 and from 1965 to 1967, had far-reaching effects on her self-image as a Canadian. Cambridge was where she "started thinking seriously about Canada as having a shape and a culture of its own." Canadians "had never been taught much about [their] own history or culture," but if Americans could study Puritan literature, "not notable for its purely literary value," then why couldn't Canadians also study their own? Americans at Harvard found Canadians "boring": "The beginning of Canadian cultural nationalism was not 'Am I really that oppressed?' but 'Am I really that boring?' "[4] So it seems only natural that her writing eventually developed into a search for a visible identity on several levels.

After receiving an M.A. from Harvard in 1962, Atwood began a ten-year period in which she held several academic and non-academic positions, published fiction and poetry, and continued postgraduate work. From 1963 to 1965, she worked for a market-research company and wrote an unpublished first novel.[5] While teaching at the University of British Columbia in 1965, she wrote her second novel, *The Edible Woman*, published in 1969. Returning to Harvard, she married a fellow postgraduate student, James Polk, when she was twenty-seven, but in 1973 they separated. After leaving Harvard for the second time, she taught at Sir George

Williams University in Montreal (1967–68), the University of Alberta (1969–70), and at York University in Toronto (1971–72). During this time, she published five volumes of poetry: *The Circle Game* (1966), *The Animals in That Country* (1968), *Procedures for Underground* (1970), *The Journals of Susanna Moodie* (1970), and *Power Politics* (1971). *The Circle Game* won the Governor General's Award for Poetry in English in 1966. *The Animals in That Country* won first prize in the Centennial Commission Poetry Competition in 1967. Five poems from *Procedures for Underground* were awarded the Union Poetry Prize by *Poetry* [Chicago] in 1969.

In 1972, while an editor with House of Anansi Press in Toronto, she published *Surfacing* and *Survival: A Thematic Guide to Canadian Literature*. Although not original in its method and frequently criticized for the narrowness of its sampling, the selectivity of its noninductive approach, and the subjectivity of its emphasis upon victimization and survival as the central themes of Canadian literature, *Survival* had a great impact on the development of Canadian cultural nationalism, an impact deriving its power from Atwood's analysis of victimization as "a structural feature of Canadian life."[6] Atwood also furthered the cause of Canadian literature by working to organize the Writers Union of Canada, which she chaired in 1981.

With the consolidation of her reputation, many books and honours followed. She published eight more volumes of poetry, *You Are Happy* (1974), *Selected Poems* (1976), *Two-Headed Poems* (1978), *True Stories* (1981), *Interlunar* (1984), *Selected Poems II: Poems Selected and New 1976–1986* (1986), *Selected Poems 1966–1984* (1990), and *Margaret Atwood Poems 1965–1975* (1991); five more novels, *Lady Oracle* (1976), *Life before Man* (1979), *Bodily Harm* (1981), *The Handmaid's Tale* (1985), and *Cat's Eye* (1988); and four collections of short stories, *Dancing Girls* (1977), *Murder in the Dark: Short Fictions and Prose Poems* (1983), *Bluebeard's Egg* (1983), and *Wilderness Tips* (1991). A new collection of stories, *Good Bones*, was published in 1992. Atwood published three children's books, *Up in the Tree* (1978), *Anna's Pet* (1980), and *For the Birds* (1990). She also published *Second Words: Selected Critical Prose* (1982), which collected book reviews and essays published earlier and also included many of Atwood's lectures and speeches. She coedited, with Shannon Ravenel, *The Best American Short Stories 1989*. *The Handmaid's Tale* was made into a major Hollywood motion picture in 1990.

She was writer-in-residence at the University of Toronto (1972–73) and was awarded honorary doctorates by Trent University (1973), Queen's University (1974), Concordia University (1980), Smith College (1982), the University of Toronto (1983), the University of Waterloo (1985), the University of Guelph (1985), Mount Holyoke College (1985), Victoria College (1987), and the Université de Montréal (1991). *You Are Happy* received both the City of Toronto Book Award (1976) and the Canadian Booksellers Association Award (1977). In 1977 Atwood received the St. Lawrence Award for Fiction (for *Dancing Girls*) and the award of the Periodical Distributors of Canada for Short Fiction. She was hailed by *The Malahat Review* as "the presiding genius of Canadian letters."[7] In 1980 she received a Graduate Society Medal from Radcliffe College. In 1982 she won the Welsh Arts Council International Writer's Prize. In the last decade Atwood has received honours and awards too numerous to list, including the Ida Nudel Humanitarian Award (1986), the Toronto Arts Award (1986), the Governor General's Award for Fiction in English (1986, for *The Handmaid's Tale*), the *Los Angeles Times* Fiction Award (1986), *Ms.* magazine's Woman of the Year Award (1986), a spot on the Booker Prize short list (1987, for *The Handmaid's Tale*), the Regional Prize of the Commonwealth Literary Prize (1987), the Arthur C. Clarke Award for science fiction (1987), the National Magazine Award for Environmental Journalism (1988), and the Centennial Medal from Harvard University (1990). Margaret Atwood was made a Fellow of the Royal Society of Canada in 1987 and received the Order of Ontario in 1990. Her latest book, *Wilderness Tips*, was nominated for the Governor General's Award for Fiction in English in 1991.

Her personal life has changed along with her career. After her divorce from James Polk in 1973, she moved to a farm near Alliston, Ontario, with Graeme Gibson, the novelist. Their daughter, Eleanor Jess Atwood Gibson, was born in 1976; a fictionalized account of her birth is included in *Dancing Girls*. In 1980 Atwood moved to Toronto, where she now lives with Gibson and their daughter. They lived in Berlin for four months in 1984, while

Atwood finished *The Handmaid's Tale*. The family spent several months in 1991–92 in Provence, where Atwood researched her next work of fiction, which will probably be based on her Huguenot ancestors.

Atwood is now a major public figure, not only delivering lectures at universities in Canada and abroad, but also addressing the Empire Club of Canada, the Modern Language Association of America, the Harvard Consortium on Inter-American Relations, and the world meeting of Amnesty International. She gave the Clarendon lectures at Oxford in the spring of 1991. The University of Tampa in Florida has a Margaret Atwood Society, affiliated with the Modern Languages Association since 1991. With her work published in fifteen countries, she has achieved an international reputation.

## NOTES

[1] Joyce Carol Oates, "Margaret Atwood: Poems and Poet," interview, *The New York Times Book Review*, 21 May 1978, p. 15. Further references to this work appear in the text.

[2] Valerie Miner, "Atwood in Metamorphosis: An Authentic Canadian Fairy Tale," interview, in *Her Own Woman: Profiles of Ten Canadian Women*, ed. Myrna Kostash (Toronto: Macmillan, 1975), p. 179.

[3] Margaret Atwood, *Survival: A Thematic Guide to Canadian Literature* (Toronto: House of Anansi, 1972), p. 29; Linda Sandler, "Interview with Margaret Atwood," *The Malahat Review* [Margaret Atwood: A Symposium], No. 41 (Jan. 1977), p. 14. Further references to *Survival* appear in the text.

[4] Joyce Carol Oates, "A Conversation with Margaret Atwood," *The Ontario Review*, No. 9 (Fall–Winter 1978–79), pp. 9, 10.

[5] Sherrill Grace, *Violent Duality: A Study of Margaret Atwood*, ed. Ken Norris (Montreal: Véhicule, 1980), p. xi.

[6] Eli Mandel, "Criticism as Ghost Story," in his *Another Time*, Three Solitudes: Contemporary Literary Criticism in Canada, No. 3 (Erin, Ont.: Porcépic, 1977), p. 149.

[7] Linda Sadler, Preface, *The Malahat Review* [Margaret Atwood: A Symposium], No. 41 (Jan. 1977), p. 5.

# Clark Blaise (1940–  )

BARRY CAMERON

"I'M A KIND of tropical tree with an awful lot of shallow roots and I can easily be blown over. On the other hand, I can survive a lot of changes. I adapt very easily to just about anything around me,"[1] Clark Blaise says speaking of the double-edged legacy bequeathed to him by his wandering parents: a sense of ultimate rootlessness coupled with a positive ability to adapt, a sense of vulnerability coupled with an instinct to survive. Blaise was born on 10 April 1940, in Fargo, North Dakota (from where he moved six months after birth), to Canadian parents — his mother, English-Canadian from Manitoba, and his father, French-Canadian from Quebec — who had come to the United States in search of the American ideal of success.[2] Because his father's career as an itinerant furniture salesman took him there, Blaise spent part of his childhood in the Deep South of Alabama and Georgia, but most of it in central Florida.[3] According to the dust-jacket of *A North American Edu-*

*cation: A Book of Short Fiction* (1973), Blaise's first book, he
"attended twenty-five schools" during this period of time. That
fact alone, if one were seeking direct autobiographical influences
on Blaise's work, might account for the predominance of alienation
and dislocation as psychological and metaphoric motifs in his
fiction.

Blaise's childhood, particularly in Florida, gave him his first
apprehension of "a continuity between the moral and the physical,"[4] a perception he would experience again and deepen when he
moved to Montreal. Landscape and cityscape are, as John Metcalf
has said, moral landscapes in Blaise's fiction (p. 77). Setting in a
Blaise story, down to the minutest detail, is consistently metaphoric, often synecdochic, correlative in a variety of ways to the
human "action" of the story. For Blaise, as for many other writers,
the South as a region and Montreal as a city "are places where
setting is not merely an excuse, but where setting is in fact the
mystery and the manner" (Metcalf, p. 78). In an interview with
Geoff Hancock, Blaise speaks revealingly of the formative quality
of his Florida experience:

. . . Florida was physically, morally and historically an apt
place for me: I exploited it ruthlessly and it exploited me in
turn. It was a location (thinking back now to the still-rural,
Deep South Florida of the mid- and late-40s) that was made
for the hounding out of some central worm-like creature in
myself.

Florida was foreign to everything in my nature. It was a
brutal confrontation, but it was physically so interesting and
physically so unforgettable that it linked up forever a notion
of nature, of water, of solitariness, and a kind of harshness
that I lost myself in for hours every day. . . . In Florida . . . you
literally passed through a wall at seven in the morning and
came back at dusk and were out in it all day walking through
jungle and water and you never felt as though you were in
particular danger. Yet you were always seeing things that were
dead or dying, or crawling up from the mud or down from the
trees. You saw putrefaction, you saw the tropical world in
which all the processes are speeded up and [in] which the chain
of exploitation is just so much more vivid than it is up here.

So I was the beneficiary of that and later on . . . I came to
see the social and historical and economic analogues to that
kind of nature. The myth was laid down for me pretty early,
and it was a matter of feeding into the myth with plots and
psychologies and characters.[5] (p. 48)

After spending 1950 and 1951 in Winnipeg, where he had moved
from Florida, Blaise moved to the American Midwest, living for
some time in Springfield, Missouri, and Cincinnati, Ohio, and then
in 1953 settling in Pittsburgh, Pennsylvania, where he attended
high school.[6] In 1957 he went to Denison University in Granville,
Ohio, where he first majored in geology and then, after eight
months out of university, switched his major to English. It was
during this period that Blaise first began to write intensely and to
read "serious" fiction:

In the eight months I was out of school I read never less than
a book a day, and often two or three. Nothing heavy; I was
still courting facts, and the only writers I really valued were
those who described experiences, appearances, or states of
mind that I knew to be true. Theodore Dreiser, Sinclair Lewis,
and Thomas Wolfe were obvious early favourites; they reaf-
firmed the helplessness I felt; the venality of my petty-bour-
geois surroundings, and the noble calling of "writer." At the
close of that period I discovered the French: Flaubert (not of
*Madame Bovary*, but of *The Sentimental Education*), Alain-
Fournier's *Le Grand Meaulnes*, Zola, Céline and Stendhal. I
even liked Camus, something I would now avoid. . . . Lawrence and especially Faulkner became even more important
. . . "influential" . . . since I had begun to write by then, out
of the same desire to capture moments of myth acting through
nature, as Lawrence had, and to capture as intensely as
Faulkner did the palpability of time-passing in a geographical
and historical milieu that I too knew very well. Thomas Mann
had been with me from the beginning.[7]

After graduation from Denison with a B.A. in 1961, Blaise went
to Harvard, where he attended Bernard Malamud's class in creative
writing.[8] In February 1962 he moved to the University of Iowa

Writers' Workshop. At Iowa, he met in 1962 and married in 1963 (during their lunch hour on the first day of the academic year) Bharati Mukherjee, the talented Bengali-Canadian novelist of *The Tiger's Daughter* (1972) and *Wife* (1975). The Iowa experience was important for Blaise, for, like others who attended the Workshop in the 1960s,[9] Blaise learned "a sense of obligation to craft and community and standards and articulateness about aims" (Metcalf, p. 77).

After graduation from Iowa in 1964 with an M.F.A. — his thesis was a story collection entitled "Thibidault et fils" — Blaise taught at the University of Wisconsin in Milwaukee; but, because he had "dreamed restless dreams of Canada, especially of Montreal,"[10] he immigrated to Montreal in 1966 and became a Canadian citizen in 1973. Except for sabbaticals in India during 1973–74 and 1976–77, Blaise remained in Montreal for twelve years, teaching modern fiction and creative writing at Sir George Williams University (subsequently Concordia University). In 1978 he moved to York University to become a Professor of Humanities; in 1980 he left Toronto to share a teaching position with his wife at Skidmore College in Saratoga Springs, New York. In 1983 he moved on again to join his wife and two sons — with interruptions for short stints of teaching and reading tours — in Iowa City. Blaise has kept moving: in 1985 he was writer-in-residence at Emory University in Atlanta; that summer he was the co-director (with Bharati Mukherjee) of the Emory Summer Festival of Writing. He directed the Emory Summer Festival again in 1986 and 1987. In 1986 Blaise taught at the Columbia University Graduate School of the Arts, and in 1986–87 he was writer-in-residence at Concordia University in Montreal. In 1987 he taught at Columbia's School of the Arts and General Studies, and from January to May 1988 was again writer-in-residence at Emory. Since June 1990 Blaise has directed the International Writing Program at the University of Iowa, renewing his old ties to that school.

Blaise has been involved in a variety of projects: writing, teaching, lecturing. In 1986 he published a novel, *Resident Alien* and, in 1990, a work of comparative American-Canadian fiction with Russell Brown, *Border as Fiction*. His latest writing projects are two film scripts, *Days and Nights in Calcutta*, for Sunrise Films, Toronto, and *Orbiting* (with Bharati Mukherjee), for Twentieth-

Century Fox; as well as a book of stories, *Man and His World* (published in 1992), and his autobiography, *I Had a Father* (1993). In 1991 Blaise was a special lecturer in Estonia and Finland with the Arts America Program, and in 1992, as part of an American government program, he will give writing workshops in Poland and Lithuania. In 1991 he was the Chair of the National Endowment for the Arts (NEA) prose panel; in 1992 he will chair the NEA's committee for grants to artistic organizations.

## NOTES

[1] Geoff Hancock, "An Interview with Clark Blaise," *Canadian Fiction Magazine*, Nos. 34–35 (1980), pp. 46, 48. Further references to this work appear in the text.

[2] Blaise's parents divorced some twenty years later, and his mother returned to Winnipeg. In 1978 his father, who had remained in the United States, died in Florida, while Blaise was writing his novel *Lunar Attractions*. According to Blaise, that novel is indirectly dedicated to his father.

[3] Leesburg, Florida, where Blaise lived for a time, is the fictional Hartley of several of his stories.

[4] John Metcalf, "Interview: Clark Blaise," *Journal of Canadian Fiction*, 2, No. 4 (Fall 1973), 77. Further references to this work appear in the text.

[5] In another interview with Hancock, Blaise says, "The Florida I knew as a child was very wild and untamed, full of nature, poverty, illness, violence, and terror for me" ("Interview," *Books in Canada*, March 1979, p. 30).

[6] Pittsburgh is the fictional Palestra of *Lunar Attractions*.

[7] Sandra Martin, "The Book That Changed My Life," *Saturday Night*, May 1976, pp. 34–35.

[8] Bernard Malamud's *The Assistant* affected Blaise as offering "a fresh way of telling a story" (Martin, p. 35), and *Lunar Attractions* is dedicated to Malamud and his wife.

[9] Among other Canadian writers who have attended the Iowa Writers' Workshop are Dave Godfrey, W.D. Valgardson, Rudy Wiebe, and Kent Thompson.

[10] Bharati Mukherjee, "An Invisible Woman," *Saturday Night*, March 1981, p. 36.

# Matt Cohen (1942-  )

## GEORGE WOODCOCK

MATT COHEN was born at Kingston, Ontario, on 30 December 1942. In early childhood, he moved with his family to Ottawa, and there he attended grade school and high school, from which he graduated in 1960. His parents were Jewish, but, as he has remarked, he was not brought up very religiously. After graduating from high school, he went on to the University of Toronto, where he graduated with a B.A. (honours) in 1964. His postgraduate degree was an M.A. in political theory, gained from the University of Toronto in 1965; the subject of his thesis was the French novelist and political maverick Albert Camus. In 1967 Cohen began his brief academic career as a lecturer in the Department of Religion at McMaster University; he has always been careful to explain that he was not teaching theology, but the sociology of religion. His academic preoccupations have found their places in his writing, for political theory provides the central thematic cord in his futurist novel *The Colours of War*, and religion, observed as a force in society, plays a high role in *Flowers of Darkness*.

In 1968 Cohen abandoned his teaching career to take up full-time writing, though on several occasions since that time he has loosely remade his academic links; he was writer-in-residence at the University of Alberta between 1975 and 1976, visiting professor of Creative Writing at the University of Victoria between 1979 and 1980, writer-in-residence at the University of Western Ontario in 1981, and visiting professor at the University of Bologna in 1984.

After leaving McMaster, Cohen lived briefly in Toronto and in 1970 retired to write on a farm near Godfrey, in the country north of Kingston. Later he returned for a while to live in Toronto, though rural Ontario has always drawn him back. He was fiction editor at The Coach House Press for a period and prepared the second volume of Coach House's anthology *The Story so Far*, which appeared in 1973. He has lived briefly in the Queen Charlotte Islands off the coast of British Columbia; a Canada Council grant in 1977 took him to England, and, among his other travels, after his assignment at the University of Victoria came to an end, he spent a period in Spain in 1980, collecting material for the novel that eventually became *The Spanish Doctor*. He spent time in Paris in 1985, funded by a second Canada Council grant, researching *Emotional Arithmetic* (1990), the story of three survivors of Drancy, a Nazi prison camp near Paris, who are reunited in rural Ontario.

Cohen has worked in a variety of genres. He has written a radio play and two television plays; he has done sporadic book reviewing; there is the ironic poetry of *Peach Melba* (1974); and there are the children's fantasies *Too Bad Galahad* (1972) and *The Leaves of Louise* (1978). But, principally, he is known as a writer of fiction, and this has been his real literary vocation.

His first novel, *Korsoniloff*, appeared in 1969, and this story of a schizophrenic teacher of philosophy derived a great deal from the author's experience of university life. But Cohen's later works show him as a mainly inventive writer, rather than one who derives his material from direct experience. They began with the fantasy novella *Johnny Crackle Sings*, which appeared in 1971. Then, after writing an unsuccessful novel with a linear chronology, which he abandoned unpublished, Cohen went on to the series of substantial novels — less overtly experimental than his first books yet based largely on the manipulation of time flows — that began with the publication of *The Disinherited* in 1974, and carried on at surprisingly regular intervals through *Wooden Hunters* (1975), *The Colours of War* (1977), *The Sweet Second Summer of Kitty Malone* (1979), *Flowers of Darkness* (1981), *The Spanish Doctor* (1984), *Nadine* (1986), and *Emotional Arithmetic* (1990).

All these novels — except for *Wooden Hunters*, which is set in the Queen Charlotte Islands, and *The Spanish Doctor*, which is set in fifteenth-century Europe — take place in the country north of Kingston where Cohen has spent so much of his time in recent years. It was on his farm there that he wrote the first of his country stories — "Country Music" — and in a letter he told the author of the present essay that ". . . it and especially material that was rejected from it became the basis for *The Disinherited* and *The Sweet Second Summer of Kitty Malone*."[1] Several of his stories and novels are centred around an imaginary town named Salem. "*Flowers of Darkness* is the fourth of the Salem novels," Cohen remarked in the same letter, "and I like to think it will be the last."

Cohen's short stories have been published widely in Canadian magazines and have been collected in five volumes: *Columbus and the Fat Lady and Other Stories* (1972), *Night Flights: Stories New and Selected* (1978), *The Expatriate: Collected Short Stories* (1982), *Café le Dog* (1983), and *Living on Water* (1988).

Matt Cohen lives as much as he can on his 170 acres of rocky farmland near Verona, north of Kingston, with intervals in Toronto.

"For some people the right thing to do is to leave home and go somewhere else," Cohen said in a 1981 interview with Alan Twigg. "It's almost inevitable for them. For other people it's almost inevitable to go away and come back. I think I understand those people who come back better than those who go away."[2]

In the same interview, he also said, ". . . I think I could quit writing quite soon."[3] In the more than ten years since that declaration, however, Cohen has shown no signs of slowing down. Besides his writing, he has served as chairperson of the Writers Union of Canada in 1985–86. At present he is working on three projects: an anthology of selected Quebec writers, a new novel, and ". . . a book of connected short stories introducing Roberto Freud, Sigmund's fictional Italian brother."[4]

## NOTES

[1] Matt Cohen, letter to George Woodcock (1983).

[2] Alan Twigg, "Matt Cohen: Eastern Horizon," in his *For Openers: Conversations with Twenty-Four Canadian Writers* (Madeira Park, B.C.: Harbour, 1981), p. 181.

[3] Twigg, p. 184.

[4] Marke Andrews, "Author Dispels Despair," *The Vancouver Sun*, 27 Oct. 1990, p. H9.